TKL/UNYS
5/7/09
1 COPY IN CATALOG

Metacognition
and
Reading Comprehension

COGNITION AND LITERACY
Series Editor: Judith Orasanu
U.S. Army Research Institute

Metacognition and Reading Comprehension, Ruth Garner

In preparation

Becoming Literate in English as a Second Language, Susan Goldman and Henry Trueba (eds.)

Literacy Development: Comparative Studies in the Acquisition and Practice of Literacy, Stephen Reder and Karen Reid Green

METACOGNITION
AND
READING COMPREHENSION

Ruth Garner
University of Maryland

ABLEX PUBLISHING CORPORATION
NORWOOD, NEW JERSEY

Printed in the United States of America

Library of Congress Cataloging in Publication Data

Garner, Ruth.
    Metacognition and reading comprehension.

    (Cognition and literacy)
    Bibliography: p.
    Includes indexes.
    1. Educational psychology. 2. Metacognition. 3. Reading comprehension. I. Title. II. Series.
LB1051.G225   1987   370.15   86-22261
ISBN 0-89391-398-7

Ablex Publishing Corporation
355 Chestnut Street
Norwood, New Jersey 07648

Contents

Series Preface   *vii*

Preface   *ix*

Chapter 1   **Reading Comprehension**   *1*
An Interactive Model of Reading Comprehension   *2*
Schema Theory: Reader Expectations for Text Input   *3*
Reader Expectations for Technical Prose   *10*

Chapter 2   **Metacognition and Executive Control**   *15*
Metacognitive Knowledge, Metacognitive Experiences, and
    Strategy Use   *16*
Executive Control   *21*
Boundaries Between Metacognition and Executive
    Control   *23*
Unresolved Conceptual Issues   *26*
Metacognition, Executive Control, and Reading
    Comprehension   *28*

Chapter 3   **Metacognitive Development**   *31*
Differences in Metacognitive Knowledge Among
    Learners   *31*
Differences in Metacognitive Experiences Among
    Learners   *39*
Differences in Strategy Use Among Learners   *49*

Chapter 4   **Methodological Concerns: Metacognitive Interviews**   *61*
General Concerns About Interview Data   *62*
Specific Concerns About Interview Data from Young
    Children   *66*

Suggestions for Collecting and Interpreting Interview
        Data   67
The Think-Aloud Method as an Alternative to
        Interviews   69
Other Methodological Alternatives to Interviews   78

Chapter 5   Methodological Concerns: Error-Detection Research   85
Explicit Directions to Locate Errors   86
Inclusion of Blatant Errors   89
Use of Relatively Naturalistic Research Settings   92
Use of Nonverbal Measures of Detection   94
Provision of Standards for the Error-Detection Task   97
The Future of Error-Detection Research   100

Chapter 6   Training Students to Use Strategies   105
Strategy Training Research: What Do We Need
        to Know?   107
Specific Strategy Interventions   109
Strategic Responsibility Shifts   122
Final Notes on Strategy Training   125

**Chapter 7   Applications of Metacognitive Research to Classroom
        Instruction   127**
Candidate Strategies   128
Guideline #1: Process Instruction   131
Guideline #2: Task Analyses   133
Guideline #3: Generalizing Strategy Application   134
Guideline #4: An Entire Year's Instruction   135
Guideline #5: Guided Practice   136
Guideline #6: Children Teaching Children About
        Strategies   137
A Final Note on Classroom Strategy Instruction   138

References   139
Author Index   159
Subject Index   164

Series Preface

Judith Orasanu

Great strides have been made in the past decade toward understanding the nature of many complex human cognitive processes, including learning, reasoning, problem solving, and communicating. Literacy research has been especially fruitful, yielding new insights into the nature of text comprehension, visual processing, discourse genres, and writing.

Transmitting literacy skills to those who do not have them—be they children in schools or adults in work or school environments—requires more than just understanding the nature of the cognitive processes involved in literacy. Two additional ingredients are needed. One is understanding the practice of literacy in social context. This includes how people use literacy in their daily lives, the functions literacy accomplishes in a society, and the values and attitudes surrounding literacy.

The second additional ingredient is understanding how literacy skills are acquired and how instruction can help them develop. Merely understanding how competent adults perform literacy tasks provides slim guidance for practitioners, other than establishing one picture of proficiency. Obviously, the acquisition process reflects the social and instructional environment in which it takes place, and must be thus contextualized.

The books in the series Cognition and Literacy integrate all three aspects of literacy research—cognitive processes, social context, and instruction—with varying emphases. The theme of literacy and cognition emphasizes research on the cognitive processes involved in literacy practices. But these research findings cannot be properly understood without considering the literacy practices and the meanings of literacy for members of a society. Cognitive skills do not develop in a vacuum.

Similarly, effective instruction is grounded in understanding the nature of literacy skills and how they are acquired. Too many education or training efforts based on incomplete understanding of the skills to be taught have met with sad failure, despite the best intentions of those promoting them. Frequently these failures have been dominated by concern for method, in the absence of understanding.

The ultimate goal of this series is to present research that may improve literacy acquisition by both children and adults. That means bringing to the reader recent research findings about literacy processes and practices, along with instructional implications. The research findings support theory-building on the premise that sound theory is a necessary foundation for improved instruction. Instructional research has lagged behind current theories of comprehension, however, so some of the instructional implications will be more in the nature of hypotheses than verified practice. Particular emphasis will be given to research that was done in diverse cultural settings, with participants representing diverse language backgrounds and literacy practices. The aim is to understand the contribution of culture to cognitive processes, the diversity of acquisition paths, and the variety of learning and teaching strategies.

Ruth Garner's volume focuses on the role of metacognition in reading. She pulls together the burgeoning literature on readers' awareness of their own comprehension abilities and controlled efforts to understand what they read. Basic research findings are examined from both methodological and developmental perspectives, and classroom teaching strategies are suggested.

Subsequent volumes will emphasize the interactions between language learning, literacy acquisition, and functional aspects of literacy, specifically with learners whose home languages are not English.

The target audience for this series is professionals who are concerned with the scientific bases for educational improvement. This includes educational psychologists, educators, developmental psychologists, adult literacy specialists, and those with responsibility for curriculum and in-service training in the schools. A broader audience of special educators, reading teachers, educational researchers, and cross-cultural researchers may find it useful, as well. I hope these volumes will spawn educational improvements that open the door to literacy for both children and adults.

Preface

The intended audience for this book is anyone who conducts or consumes research in the broad area of cognitive processes. Psychologists and educators interested in problems of text processing should find the volume particularly useful. It is intended to provide a synthesis of the literatures that converge on the areas of metacognition and reading comprehension. It is also intended to present a discussion of important methodological dilemmas in these research literatures. The book should be useful in cognitive, developmental, and educational psychology courses at the graduate level.

The book begins with definitional chapters on reading comprehension (chapter 1) and metacognition (chapter 2). Chapter 3 presents a number of research studies that document metacognitive performance differences along the dimensions of age and reading proficiency. The next two chapters present methodological concerns for interview studies (chapter 4) and for error-detection studies (chapter 5). Chapter 6 presents a series of research studies that provide successful training of cognitive and metacognitive strategies. In the final chapter (chapter 7), extension of this training work to classroom settings is discussed.

I am grateful to Patricia Alexander, Linda Baker, and Victoria Chou Hare, all of whom read and offered comments on drafts of the book. The series editor, Judith Orasanu, raised many perceptive questions about content and structure of the volume. Funds to support the preparation of the book were provided by the General Research Board of the University of Maryland, College Park; these funds and a sabbatical from the University of Maryland allowed me to work in the congenial environment of the Department of Psychology at Stanford University, where I was a Visiting Scholar for the 1984–1985 academic year. I am very grateful to John Flavell, who arranged for my visit to Stanford, who made the considerable body of theoretical and empirical work in cognitive development for which he is responsible readily available for my scrutiny, and whose probing questions about my ideas changed my view of children's cognitions about their own cognitions on more than one occasion. Finally, I appreciate the good academic advice and consistent support of Mark Gillingham.

Chapter 1

Reading Comprehension

Reading comprehension has always been important to psychologists and educators interested in learning from text, in school and out. Though descriptions of reader-text interactions have changed in nontrivial ways over the years, those interactions have always occupied a great deal of theoretical, research, and instructional energy. "Metacognition" is a relatively new label for a body of theory and research that addresses learners' knowledge and use of their own cognitive resources. In just the past few years, educational researchers have appreciated that this body of work has enormous explanatory power for descriptions of the reading process. For instance, the theory and research can help explain performance differences in readers of various ages and language proficiency levels, and can offer a theoretical framework for devising instructional interventions to promote greater strategy use among readers.

In this chapter, I will present current views of reading comprehension: first, a representative interactive model for text processing; next, schema-theoretic approaches to reading; and, finally, models of processing technical prose, the sort of text most often encountered in school.

Certain assumptions have been made about reading instruction, reading research, and readers. For example, I assume that the only serious competitor to psychology in the shaping of teachers' views of teaching and learning from text is common sense (Floden, 1981). I assume that "mentalistic" explanations of human behavior and introspection about unobservable mental activity, such activity as human intuition, mental processes, and tacit knowledge (Beaugrande, 1982) are once more acceptable, as we have shifted from primarily behavioristic to primarily cognitive views of the world. I assume that the mind is a rule-governed information-processing system. I assume that readers are potentially active, constructive, motivated learners (Wittrock, 1979), "active agents" (R.C. Anderson, 1970, p. 349) in their own learning. These assumptions are consistent with the views of reading comprehension presented in this chapter and with the "metacognition" literature to be presented in chapter 2.

An Interactive Model of Reading Comprehension

Until recently, information processing in general and reading in particular were often described as a series of discrete stages, proceeding from incoming visual data to higher-level encodings (Stanovich, 1980). These earlier conceptualizations have come to be called "bottom-up" models of processing, a borrowing of computer-use jargon. These models are now seen as inadequate, for they fail to explain important empirical findings. Two of those findings are that (a) when word recognition errors are made, the substituted word tends to be the same part of speech as the word appearing in text; that is, syntactic processing affects word perception (Kolers, 1970); and (b) prior presentation of a sentence context lowers the threshold for recognition of a word; that is, semantic processing affects word perception (Tulving & Gold, 1963). In general, the serial-stage models run into difficulty because they contain no mechanism "whereby higher-level processes can affect lower levels" (Stanovich, 1980, p. 34).

Reading has also been modeled in an essentially "top-down" fashion, with higher-level processes directing the flow of information through lower levels. Goodman (1970) and Smith (1982), in particular, have maintained that fluent readers sample text information only to test conceptually driven hypotheses. As Smith puts it, "The twin foundations of reading are to be able to ask specific questions (make predictions) in the first place, and to know how and where to look at print so that there is at least a chance of getting these questions answered" (Smith, 1982, p. 166), and "Prediction through meaningfulness is the basis of language comprehension. By prediction I do not mean reckless guessing but rather the elimination of unlikely alternatives on the basis of prior knowledge" (Smith, 1977, p. 388). Pure top-down processing in reading is, of course, "psychologically absurd" (van Dijk & Kintsch, 1983, p. 25). Such activity would have to be labeled "thinking," not "reading."

Top-down models are now seen as inadequate for much the same reason as the bottom-up models are: they fail to explain existing data. For example, Samuels, Dahl, and Archwamety (1974) have noted that the speed for hypothesis generating must be higher than the speed for bottom-up word recognition for the models to be tenable; yet this is not the case for fluent readers reading meaningful material. In addition, these models are often attacked for vagueness of conceptualization (see Stanovich, 1980).

An interactive model differs from either a bottom-up or a top-down model of reading in that it does not define information flow as unidirectional. Sensory, syntactic, semantic, and pragmatic information is used, and these various sources provide information simultaneously, rather than serially (Samuels & Kamil, 1984). Rumelhart's (1977) description of reading as simultaneous joint application of multiple knowledge sources is probably the best articulation of a current interactive model.

Rumelhart (1977) proposes that graphemic input produces information from which important features are extracted. Simultaneous to this extraction, syntactic, semantic, lexical, and orthographic information is being used. Information from all of these sources converges upon the "pattern synthesizer." The "pattern synthesizer" uses all the information to produce a "most probable interpretation" of the input. Each of the knowledge sources may use the information provided by other sources; the sources "interact" with each other.

Stanovich (1980) has pointed out that once the idea that initiation of a higher-level process must await completion of all lower ones is dispensed with (once bottom-up models are rejected, in other words), we are free to assume that a process at any level can compensate for deficiencies at any other level. This is a critical point. A reader who has weak decoding skills but some prior knowledge of topic X may be able to apply top-down processing strengths in reading successfully about X. A reader who is skillful in decoding but unfamiliar with topic X may be better off relying on mostly bottom-up processes. Highly proficient readers tend to be better than less proficient peers both at decoding in a rapid, accurate, relatively attention-free manner and at guessing at meaning by exploiting prior knowledge and linguistic context (Lesgold & Perfetti, 1978; Perfetti & Lesgold, 1977; van Dijk & Kintsch, 1983).

These between-reader processing distinctions are important. There are also important differences between text types. For simple stories, for which substantial prior knowledge and predictable text structure are the norm, reliance on top-down processing is usually appropriate. For technical prose, on the other hand, in which expectations and structural constraints are less pronounced, reliance on more bottom-up processing is usually appropriate. This latter case does not exclude active hypothesis-formation and strategic sampling of text; it simply "tips the balance" toward greater attention to on-the-page data. In fact, changing processing to meet text demands, to the extent that it is a conscious shift, is a highly adaptive response from a reader (Gibson & Levin, 1975).

Schema Theory: Reader Expectations for Text Input

A schema is an abstract knowledge structure derived from repeated experiences with objects and events. It is knowledge stored in memory that plays an important role in the interpretation of new information

(McNeil, 1984). A schema is a set of expectations. When incoming information fits those expectations, the information can be encoded into memory so that the "slots" in the schema are "instantiated." Information that does not fit expectations may not be encoded or may be distorted. The expectations that guide encoding of information also guide its retrieval (R. C. Anderson, 1984).

R. C. Anderson and Pearson (1984) provide the example of a SHIP CHRISTENING schema. Anyone who has seen or read something about a ship christening has a set of expectations about the information to be encountered in a particular description of such an event. One expects a celebrity to be mentioned, a new ship to be involved, a bottle containing champagne to be broken on the ship's bow, and so on. These various "slots" are "instantiated" with particular information in the following passage from Anderson and Pearson (1984, p. 260):

> Queen Elizabeth participated in a long-delayed ceremony in Clydebank, Scotland, yesterday. While there is still bitterness here following the protracted strike, on this occasion a crowd of shipyard workers numbering in the hundreds joined dignitaries in cheering as the HMS *Pinafore* slipped into the water.

Anderson and Pearson note that the fit of this new information to old information in the SHIP CHRISTENING schema is generally good. Queen Elizabeth fits the celebrity slot, and the *Pinafore* fits the new ship slot. No mention is made of champagne being broken on the ship's bow, but a "default" inference that this occurred is easily made, particularly as this is an especially salient element of the schema. Such inferences can occur at points of encoding and retrieval.

Without a set of expectations, that is, without a schema for topic X, reading or hearing about X can be uncertain going. Bransford (1979) designed a series of now classic experiments to demonstrate the existence of "cognitive prerequisites for comprehension" (p. 129). To show that prior knowledge must be activated in order to enhance one's abilities to understand and learn, Bransford and Johnson (1973) read the following to adult subjects without providing a topic:

> The procedure is actually quite simple. First you arrange items into different groups. Of course, one pile may be sufficient depending on how much there is to do. If you have to go somewhere else due to lack of facilities that is the next step; otherwise, you are pretty well set. It is important not to overdo things. That is, it is better to do too few things at once than too many. In the short run this may not seem important but complications can easily arise. A mistake can be expensive as well. At first, the whole procedure will seem complicated. Soon, however, it will become just another

facet of life. It is difficult to foresee any end to the necessity for this task in the immediate future, but then, one never can tell. After the procedure is completed one arranges the materials into different groups again. Then they can be put into their appropriate places. Eventually they will be used once more and the whole cycle will then have to be repeated. However, that is part of life. (p. 400)

Most subjects in this condition rated the passage as incomprehensible and exhibited low levels of recall. Subjects given a topic after hearing the passage, but before rating and recalling, fared no better. Those subjects who were told before reading that the topic of the passage was "Washing Clothes" achieved much higher comprehension and recall scores. They were able to use their prior knowledge of laundry operations in processing the text. The thematic title in this condition activated appropriate cognitive structures (Schwarz & Flammer, 1981).

R. C. Anderson (1984) notes that a more likely situation than having no schema for a topic is having a partially articulated one. R. C. Anderson, Spiro, and Anderson (1978) prepared two passages, one about dining at a fancy restaurant and the other about shopping at a supermarket. Both passages described the same items of food and drink being selected by the same characters. Anderson et al. hypothesized that some information such as order of food consumption (e.g., appetizers, entrées, desserts) and match of a person selecting a food item to that particular item would matter in a fine-restaurant schema, but not in a supermarket one. That is, we expect to read or hear that people eat entrées before dessert at fine restaurants, but we are not particularly mindful of whether a beef roast or an apple pie should reach a shopping cart first. Furthermore, we expect that the person who orders veal at a restaurant should be allowed to consume it, but we are not shocked to read or hear that either of two people shopping together in the market tossed a food item into the cart.

R. C. Anderson et al. (1978) asked adult subjects to read one of the two passages and to recall it. In accord with their predictions, they found that food and drink items were recalled better by subjects reading the more structured restaurant-schema passage, that foods were more accurately ascribed to characters in the restaurant passage, and that order of recall of food and drink items corresponded more closely to the order of mention in the restaurant passage than in the supermarket one. Also as expected, subjects assigned the different passages did not differ in recall of propositions judged to be equally important to either schema.

R. C. Anderson et al. (1978) submit that since the same target information appeared in both narratives, superior recall for the restaurant passage cannot be attributed to differential learnability or memorability of the information itself. Instead, they attribute contrasting levels of recall to differences in constraints in the schemata evoked by the passages. They note that "the schemata a person already possesses are a principle determiner of what will be learned from a text" (R. C. Anderson et al., 1978, p. 439).

One way of investigating schematic influences on learning from text is to present passages expected to evoke differentially articulated schemata, as Anderson et al. did. Another research strategy is to locate subjects who have different levels of knowledge in a particular domain but who are equivalent in verbal ability, and to ask them to read or listen to and recall texts from that domain. Voss and his colleagues (see Voss, 1984) used this contrastive method in a series of studies with adults who differed in their knowledge of baseball.

In one study (Spilich, Vesonder, Chiesi, & Voss, 1979), a text describing a half-inning account of a fictitious baseball game was presented to subjects who listened to the text, recalled text content, and answered questions about the content. High-knowledge subjects recalled more information than did low-knowledge subjects. Of greater interest, however, was the pattern of recall. High-knowledge subjects recalled more information directly related to the goal structure of the game. Low-knowledge subjects, on the other hand, tended to recall the teams, weather, and other less tactically significant information.

Other interesting differences emerged as well. For instance, high-knowledge subjects occasionally elaborated on key events (e.g., a text statement about a left-handed pitcher who typically struck out many batters became a "big, fastballing lefthander"). High-knowledge subjects were much more likely than low-knowledge subjects to report more information for a given event (e.g., rather than reporting "the batter got a double," reporting "the batter lined a double down the left-field line"). Finally, low-knowledge subjects often presented information in an inappropriate sequence, whereas high-knowledge subjects seldom did. It seems that knowledgeable listeners' recall of information included both more (elaborations on text) and less (deletions of tactically insignificant information) than the original text presented.

The notion that organized old information affects the processing of new information is not a new one. Bartlett (1932) described the constructive nature of memory for text in his study of recall of the folktale "The War of the Ghosts." He found that subjects' knowledge and interests affected both textual information recalled and reader intrusions in protocols. He summarized his results with the statement, "The description of memories as 'fixed and lifeless' is merely an unpleasant fiction" (Bartlett, 1932, p. 311), adding that memory is schematic, rather than detailed, in that it is driven by general impressions that assist in "efforts after meaning."

Ausubel's work on meaningful learning (see Ausubel, 1963) is another important antecedent of current formulations of schema theory. Ausubel proposed that old information in memory can "anchor" or provide general "ideational scaffolding" for new information in text. In instances in which activation of relevant knowledge is unlikely to occur, writers or instructors may provide "advance organizers" (i.e., pretext statements intended to bridge old and new information) for readers. These organizers explicitly draw upon and mobilize relevant subsuming concepts already in learners' cognitive structures (Ausubel, 1980).

Much of the recent work on vocabulary knowledge is also related to schema theory. R. C. Anderson and Freebody (1979) suggest that one reason vocabulary knowledge is such a strong correlate of linguistic ability is that vocabulary tests tap schematic knowledge so essential to comprehension processes. Word meanings are "the exposed tip of the conceptual iceberg" (R. C. Anderson & Freebody, 1979, p. 5).

Though important antecedents exist, much of the work conducted to explore schema effects on understanding and learning from text has been recent. Much of it has emanated from the Center for the Study of Reading (CSR) at the University of Illinois, Urbana, particularly in the middle to late 1970s. With Rumelhart (1980), most CSR researchers have treated schemata as "the building blocks of cognition" (p. 33), the elements upon which information processing depends. They have discovered, among other things, that (a) adult subjects will introduce disambiguations and intrusions for an ambiguous passage according to their backgrounds and life situations (R. C. Anderson, Reynolds, Schallert, & Goetz, 1977); (b) adults will choose "important information" from an ambiguous passage based upon an induced perspective (Pichert & R. C. Anderson, 1977) and will recall different information following a shift in perspective (R. C. Anderson & Pichert, 1978); (c) adults from different cultures will show different patterns of intrusions, inferences, and distortions in text recall, depending on the match between their cultural background and the text content (Steffensen, Joag-dev, & R. C. Anderson, 1979); and (d) some young readers and stimulus-bound adults will at least partially accept the fallacy that "meaning is in the text" and will underutilize schematic information while reading (Spiro, 1979; Spiro & Tirre, 1980). It appears that readers' experiences, perspectives, and views of reading determine to a substantial degree how attention is allocated at the encoding stage and how memory is searched at the retrieval stage (R. C. Anderson, 1977).

Most of the CSR work has employed highly contrived, often ambiguous texts that are vulnerable to the criticism of being "somewhat deficient in ecological validity" (Neisser, 1982). In addition, much of the work has been done with adult subjects. A passage used by R. C. Anderson et al.

(1977) to demonstrate that adult subjects will introduce disambiguations and intrusions for an ambiguous passage according to their backgrounds is a good example:

> Rocky slowly got up from the mat, planning his escape. He hesitated a moment and thought. Things were not going well. What bothered him most was being held, especially since the charge against him had been weak. He considered his present situation. The lock that held him was strong but he thought he could break it. He knew, however, that his timing would have to be perfect. Rocky was aware that it was because of his early roughness that he had been penalized so severely—much too severely from his point of view. The situation was becoming frustrating; the pressure had been grinding on him for too long. He was being ridden unmercifully. Rocky was getting angry now. He felt he was ready to make his move. He knew his success or failure would depend on what he did in the next few seconds. (p. 372)

This passage can be interpreted either as a description of a convict planning his escape from prison or as a description of a wrestler trying to break the hold of an opponent. In the Anderson et al. (1977) study, both disambiguations (i.e., paraphrases of propositions that indicate a subject's interpretation) and theme-revealing intrusions (i.e., phrases or sentences appearing in the recall protocol that do not appear in the passage) were related to subjects' backgrounds. For instance, more physical education students than music students revealed a wrestling interpretation of the Rocky passage.

For the purpose of demonstrating generality of schematic processing, it is important to know that expectations affect text processing for less contrived texts and for children as well. Two studies that employed naturally occurring texts with children can be mentioned. Pearson, Hansen, and Gordon (1979) pretested second-grade students for knowledge of spiders and divided them into high-knowledge and low-knowledge groups. Children in the two groups did not differ in either measured IQ or reading ability. A week later, the investigators asked the second graders to read a basal reader selection on the topic of spiders and to answer 12 questions about the content. The high-knowledge group performed significantly better than the low-knowledge group.

Taylor (1979) used a different design to test for knowledge effects on comprehension of text. She presented good and poor readers in grade 5 and good readers in grade 3 with passages on a familiar topic (bird nest building) and an unfamiliar topic (bee dancing). Passages were quite similar, except for their topical familiarity to children. Subjects read and recalled the content of both passages. All subjects recalled less information from the unfamiliar-topic text than from the familiar. Good and poor fifth-grade readers' recall scores did not differ for the familiar topic. Taylor notes that poor readers, like good readers, employ schema-based processing strategies.

Most of the work to which I have referred has examined readers' existing knowledge of objects and events, what have been called "content schemata" (R. C. Anderson, Pichert, & Shirey, 1979). Readers also have knowledge of discourse conventions or "textual schemata" that assist in text processing. That is, they have expectations about what they will encounter when they read stories, personal letters, research reports, or telegrams. For simple stories, in particular, a rich literature on adults' and children's expectations for internal structure (i.e., particular narrative components in a particular sequence) has developed.

"Story grammars" assume that stories have several unique parts that are conceptually separable, though rarely explicitly partitioned. These parts are usually identified inferentially by a reader. Thorndyke (1977) has demonstrated that adult ratings of passage comprehensibility decline as structure in the material diminishes. He suggests that both structure and content play a role in memory for connected discourse. A grammar seems to provide the basis for retrieval of information from a story. The longer the delay between encoding and recalling, the more recall will approximate an ideal story schema rather than the actual story heard or read (Mandler & Johnson, 1977).

We know from "story grammar" research that adult listeners impose the expected sequence on stories that deviate from this temporal order (Stein & Nezworski, 1978). We know, additionally, that child listeners will recall certain story components (e.g., major settings, initiating events, direct consequence statements) consistently better than others, regardless of narrative content (Stein & Glenn, 1979). It seems that, with text structure knowledge as well as with nontext knowledge of the world, our knowledge is organized; it is "not a 'basket of facts' " (R. C. Anderson, 1984).

That point seems beyond dispute now. When text comprehension "works," it does so because knowledge packaged into units (i.e., schemata) is activated to assist in processing new information represented in text. As Rumelhart (1980) notes, the process may fail in any of three ways: (a) the reader may not have the appropriate schemata (for instance, of baseball or of spiders); (b) the reader may have the appropriate schemata, but textual clues provided by the author may be insufficient to activate them; or (c) the reader may find a consistent interpretation of the text but may not find the one intended by the author.

When the fit between old in-head information and new on-the-page information is good but not perfect, learning from text can occur, and new schemata can be developed. We can add pieces of information to an old schema (e.g., "a high ERA for a pitcher is not good" can be added to a set of information about baseball pitchers); or we can modify an existing schema (e.g., noting that a "sacrifice" is not really just an "out"; the batter successfully executing one was congratulated by the coach who called the play); or we can structure whole new schemata (e.g., distinguishing "singles," "doubles," and "triples" from the global category of "hits"). Rumelhart (1980) labels these three learning mechanisms "accretion," "tuning," and "restructuring," respectively. The specific mechanisms involved in acquisition and modification of schemata are not well established in the current research literature.

Reader Expectations for Technical Prose

Kieras (1985) notes that the comprehension of technical expository prose is at once extremely important in school and little assisted by the sort of content-schematic knowledge we have been discussing. It is important because textbooks presenting densely packed, complex information likely to be novel to most students serve as core curriculum items, as "vehicles for knowledge acquisition" (Kintsch, 1982, p. 87) in school. This sort of comprehension is little assisted by content-schematic knowledge, in that the very novelty of the material ensures that readers will be unable to fit much of the new information to their old in-head information. Rather, they will need to deal with a great deal of the passage content at the level of individual propositions that convey new information.

The theoretical system that best explains current data on processing of technical prose is undoubtedly that proposed by Kintsch and van Dijk (1978; van Dijk & Kintsch, 1983). They suggest that comprehension of technical prose involves extracting the microstructure (specific content carried by individual propositions) from the text and then deriving a passage macrostructure (gist or important content) through the application of three macrorules—deletion, generalization, and construction. Macrostructure propositions might be expressed in a summary or an abstract (Kintsch, 1979). "Comprehension" of technical prose, then, is really a superordinate term for separate psychological processes that operate at different levels: a microprocessing level and a macroprocessing level (see also Meyer & Rice, 1984).

Macrostructure propositions are stored in memory, and are expanded, upon recall, to produce a paraphrase, often with intrusions, inferences, and distortions, of the original text. In the most recent formulation of the theory (van Dijk & Kintsch, 1983), it is noted that a reader need not wait until the end of a passage to infer what it is about, globally speaking. A reader will make guesses based on many different kinds of information (e.g., titles, thematic first sentences). Writers and speakers often provide macropropositions for language users, usually at the beginning of a single paragraph or at the start of an entire discourse. However, van Dijk and Kintsch argue persuasively that data support that macrostructures are generated during reading, whether or not they appear explicitly in text and whether or not subjects are asked to generate them.

It seems that both a particular reader's goals for reading a particular text and within-culture "textual schemata" for highly conventionalized text types help us predict what readers will consider to be relevant for the macrostructure. Van Dijk (1979) considers both in labeling the assignment of relevance value on the basis of reader interest, attention, or knowledge as "contextual relevance" and the assignment of relevance on the basis of purely text structure grounds as "textual relevance." A problem for prediction of macrostructure propositions arises when people read loosely structured texts with no clear goals in mind, a relatively common phenomenon (Kintsch & Yarbrough, 1982). Kintsch and Young (1984) note that essays and descriptive texts only minimally constrain macrostructure production, and Kieras (1978) suggests that much educational material is only loosely structured.

Kieras (1985) proposes that the macrostructure-building process uses the propositional content of the passage, but is guided by the passage surface structure. Readers attend, Kieras suggests, to both *what* is said in a passage and *how* it is said. Kieras has conducted research in which he has asked adult subjects to read a passage and generate a single main idea statement. Williams (1984) compares this task to the categorization task in which one refers to a group of objects by means of a summary (category) label. Content of these responses, reading times for individual sentences in a passage, and during-reading importance ratings for sentences all yield important information about processing of technical prose.

In a series of experiments, Kieras (1982) presented "good" and "bad" technical expository prose passages to adult subjects, one sentence at a time in a self-paced procedure implemented on the computer. "Good" versions presented a generalization explicitly stated in the first sentence, followed by several examples. In the "bad" versions, the first statements were deleted, and paragraphs began with sentence two.

Across passage topics, "good-version" first sentences were recognized (and often reproduced) as main ideas, were read for a relatively long time, and were rated very high in importance. "Bad-version" passages, not surprisingly, yielded many revisions of the main idea. Kieras (1982) suggests that a "subsuming" strategy is operating. That is to say, readers test the first sentence to see if it expresses a reasonable main idea. General concept reference seems to be part of this test. If the first sentence is tentatively accepted, the reader then attempts to fit or subsume each succeed-

ing sentence into the provisional main idea. If this attempt fails, revisions
in the main idea are considered. For the "good" version, revisions are unnecessary, but in the "bad" version several revisions are likely to take
place. When the passage does not obey the "initial mention convention"
(Kieras, 1980), that is, when the main idea is not explicitly stated in the
first sentence, readers change their minds about gist quite frequently during the macrostructure-building process.

Though adults accord special status to first-sentence main idea statements, elementary school children utilize topic-sentence information less
effectively, probably because of less experience with expository text
(Williams, Taylor, & Ganger, 1981). Gaps in awareness of text structure
are not found only among the very young, however. Though Danner
(1976) documented that such gaps exist among young children, Taylor
and Samuels (1983) found deficiencies among fifth- and sixth-grade children, Meyer, Brandt, and Bluth (1980) found structural knowledge deficiencies for ninth graders, and Hiebert, Englert, and Brennan (1983) even
identified gaps in structural knowledge among some adults. Slater, Graves, and Piché (1985) found that ninth-grade students who were given
information about the organization of an expository text before reading
and an outline grid to be filled in during reading far outrecalled peers assigned to alternate conditions. Given that the "structural organizer" effects held for high-, middle-, and low-ability students for a variety of text
types, it might well be argued that most ninth-grade students either do
not possess or fail to use knowledge of an author's organization to aid recall in the absence of such structural assistance.

Rothkopf (1982) raises two concerns about the body of work we have
just examined. One is that instructional expository text has no "true"
specifiable content for which all readers will demonstrate degrees of understanding or recall across instructional contexts. Rather, he suggests,
the successful use of such text is better evaluated with reference to a criterion outside the text. A second concern is that structure, according to
Rothkopf, is determined "by the psychology of writers, by changeable
custom, by aesthetics, and by current methods for the manufacture of
text" (Rothkopf, 1982, p. 111). He suggests that structural features will
surely change with new rapidly evolving electronic media.

I think there is merit to Rothkopf's first argument, but confusion in his
second. In his second argument I believe Rothkopf confuses format
(which surely will change with the evolution of electronic media for text
presentation) with structure. The latter, the relationships among ideas in
text (most especially superordination and cohesion), is relatively unaffected by aesthetics or print convention if it has, as I suggest it does, psychological reality for language users within a culture. Were there not such
reality, it would be difficult indeed to explain how it is that readers come

to unfamiliar texts and rate the importance of ideas with extremely high reliability (Johnson, 1970) in ways that predict recall across a variety of text types (Omanson, 1982; Piché & Slater, 1983).

It is clear, in this chapter's discussion of texts and of readers, that reading comprehension is considered to be an interaction of reader expectations with textual information (R. C. Anderson, 1984). What is understood and remembered from text is both more and less than the original input, for the reader draws inferences, embellishes ideas, and ignores details that are perceived to be of little textual or contextual importance. It is this active, constructive reader who will interest us in chapter 2 as well, as we turn our attention to cognitive and metacognitive resources available to readers.

Chapter 2

Metacognition and Executive Control

Because current conceptions of reading comprehension discussed in chapter 1 portray readers as active learners who direct their own cognitive resources to learn from text, bodies of research investigating learners' knowledge and use of cognitive resources have been very appealing to reading researchers. Two bodies of research have been particularly useful: the work done by developmental psychologists with children in the area of "metacognition," and the work done by information-processing cognitive psychologists with adults in the area of "executive control." As we shall see, these areas of research are not precisely bounded.

This work has been very important in prompting researchers of reading to examine readers' knowledge of the reading process, monitoring of their reading comprehension, and use of a variety of reading strategies. In addition, reading researchers have attempted to teach learners to use strategies to make and monitor cognitive progress while reading, in cases where spontaneous strategy use does not occur. Most of this work, which will be discussed extensively in future chapters, has evolved from basic research presented in the metacognitive and executive control literatures.

Unfortunately, "metacognition" is an abused concept in some educational circles. The appending to studies of "metacognitive interviews" that may be as brief as two questions and may require learners to reflect on matters far broader than their own cognitions is one example of conceptual abuse. Another is designating metacognition as a curriculum priority for a school district. The very popularity of the concept, it seems, has created difficulty. Given distorted and vague renderings of the concept, Flavell's description of metacognition as a "fuzzy concept" (Flavell, 1981, p. 37) seems particularly apt.

One purpose of this chapter is to reduce the "fuzziness" of this important concept. I will restrict the meaning of metacognition by relying on

Flavell, who first coined the term "metamemory" (that is, knowledge about one's own memory) in the early 1970s (Flavell, 1971). A second purpose of the chapter is to note overlap and uniquenesses in the metacognitive and executive control research questions, methods, and results. A third purpose is to present unresolved conceptual issues.

Metacognitive Knowledge, Metacognitive Experiences, and Strategy Use

About various "metas," Flavell and his colleagues have had the following to say:

> Metacognition refers to one's knowledge concerning one's own cognitive processes and products or anything related to them, e.g., the learning-relevant properties of information or data. (Flavell, 1976, p. 232)

> Some situations call for planful memory-related exertions and some do not. A person no doubt comes to know this fact . . . . Performance in a memory situation or task is influenced by a number of factors, the nature of which a person must know. We see three main classes of such factors: (1) memory-relevant characteristics of the person himself; (2) memory-relevant characteristics of the task; and (3) potential employable strategies. (Flavell & Wellman, 1977, p. 5)

> Metacognitive knowledge consists primarily of knowledge or beliefs about what factors or variables act and interact in what ways to affect the course and outcome of cognitive enterprises. (Flavell, 1979, p. 907)

> Metacognition can be differentiated into metacognitive knowledge and metacognitive experience, and one can distinguish between metacognitive and cognitive strategies. (Flavell, 1981, p. 38)

The first three statements emphasize that metacognition is essentially cognition about cognition. If cognition involves perceiving, understanding, remembering, and so forth, then metacognition involves thinking about one's own perceiving, understanding, and the rest. These various cognitions about cognition can be labeled "metaperception," "metacomprehension," and "metamemory," with "metacognition" remaining the superordinate term.

The last statement from Flavell is important in that it distinguishes among metacognitive knowledge, metacognitive experiences, and strategy use. That distinction is important. Sorting out what is metacognitive from what is cognitive (Brown, Bransford, Ferrara, & Campione, 1983) and differentiating the contents of a relatively stable knowledge base from what is situation-specific executive processing have proven to be difficult tasks. Some of the "fuzziness" of the concept of metacognition undoubtedly arises from the fact that researchers have used the term in very diverse ways. Some have restricted usage to what is known, excluding ways in which that knowledge is used (see Cavanaugh & Perlmutter, 1982); others, as Brown, Bransford, Ferrara, and Campione (1983) note, have dubbed nearly all strategic actions as "metacognitive."

I will adhere rather closely to Flavell's (1981) construction of what counts and what does not count as metacognition. First, I will describe how metacognitive knowledge can serve as a base for metacognitive experiences that in turn trigger strategy use. Then, I will address other possible interrelationships among knowledge, experiences, and strategies.

Metacognitive Knowledge

Metacognitive knowledge is relatively stable, usually statable information about cognition (Baker & Brown, 1984b). This knowledge is about *ourselves*, the *tasks* we face, and the *strategies* we employ. About ourselves we may know such things as these: We are generally more successful at providing fill-in answers than multiple-choice responses; we are not as proficient as our peers at completing analogical reasoning tasks; material that is read to be remembered must be read more carefully than material read strictly for enjoyment. Flavell (1981) would label these three pieces of information as data about intraindividual differences, interindividual differences, and universals, respectively.

About tasks, many of the things we know have something to do with their relative difficulty. Examples in the area of reading include the following: Familiar-topic material is easier to understand than unfamiliar; conventionally ordered stories are easier to recall than scrambled narratives; explicit topic sentences assist us in tasks that require reduction of texts to their gists.

About strategies we know such things as the following: Verbal rehearsal and elaboration of material assist in retrieval; reinspection of text for material once read, but not now remembered, aids in answering questions; prediction of article content based on titles improves comprehension. Consumers of the reading and general cognitive psychology literatures know this information to be empirically supportable. Children probably acquire the same information, if they do acquire it, through abstraction of regularities in their cognitive processing over time (Flavell & Wellman, 1977).

Obviously, these three classes of variables (i.e., person, task, and strategy) are hardly independent of one another. On the contrary, metacognitive knowledge is highly interactive (see Flavell, 1985; Wellman, 1978; Wellman, Collins, & Glieberman, 1981). It is not a collection of facts about cognition, but rather "an intricately interwoven system of knowledge" (Wellman, 1983, p. 32). If I know, for instance, that inventing a topic sentence where one is not provided by the author assists me in completing a summarization task, I have task × strategy information. If I know that I tend to read with a global processing approach and if I expect that the criterion task for understanding a text chapter will be a detail-oriented test, I might well decide that a note-taking or underlining strategy (emphasizing details) is in order to prepare for the test. This latter case demonstrates person × task × strategy information.

An interesting point made recently by Flavell (1985) is that there is no good reason to think that metacognitive knowledge is qualitatively different from other kinds of knowledge, about classical music or computer programs or elephants, for example. He points out that some metacognitive knowledge, like other knowledge, is declarative, and some is procedural. As with other knowledge acquisition, metacognitive knowledge grows in a slow and gradual fashion through years of experiences in the "domain" of cognitive activity. Like other stored knowledge, it can be activated quite automatically. Finally, metacognitive knowledge bases can be flawed, just as other knowledge bases can be. For all these reasons, Flavell acknowledges the importance of metacognitive knowledge, the abiding interest learners have in it (it is about them in a way that knowledge about tennis or computer programs or elephants may never be), but says it is not as mysterious or alien to our other systems of knowledge as it sometimes seems to be.

Metacognitive Experiences

Following the sequence we have begun with metacognitive knowledge, let us assume that a learner is involved in the complex cognitive activity of reading and studying a textbook chapter on the topic of the westward expansion of the United States. Metacognitive experiences are likely to occur before, during, and after the reading (Flavell, 1979, 1981). The experiences will most likely have to do with progress toward the goal of completing the study activity successfully. Assuming that this particular learner has some of the metacognitive knowledge of person, task, and strategy variables that we have already discussed, metacognitive experiences might occur along these lines. Before beginning the reading, the learner might experience relief that the next day's class will bring a fill-in format quiz on the material, a format with which he or she is relatively comfortable. While reading, the learner might realize that verbally rehearsing dates, perhaps noting interval patterns in a string of dates, might assist in retrieval for the quiz (the learner might come to this realization after noting that many dates are mentioned, and that most are confused in the learner's mind). After reading the chapter, the learner might become aware of the boldface topic sentences which will make further prequiz studying fairly easy.

The before-reading knowledge tapped relates to a personal strength, the during-reading information is strategy knowledge, and the after-reading knowledge utilized is task information. In all three cases, meta-cognitive knowledge has served as a base for metacognitive experiences that are perhaps best described as awarenesses, realizations, "ahas," or—as T. H. Anderson (1980) describes them—"clicks and clunks" of actual or anticipated cognitive success and failure.

A prevalent everyday phenomenon discussed by Flavell and Wellman (1977) is an example of a metacognitive experience in memory monitoring. It is the "tip-of-the-tongue experience," where someone fails to recall information, but knows that he or she knows it. In this instance, the metacognitive experience is one of the person's monitoring the item even in its absence from working memory.

Metacognitive experiences often occur when cognitions fail. Either a brief or fairly lengthy feeling of confusion about the cognitive enterprise is then the immediate outcome of the failure. It is important to note, as Markman (1981) does, that an explicit question "Do I understand? or "Am I doing this correctly?" need not be posed for metacognitive experiences to occur. In the very process of attempting to think through a task, some information about how well the processing is going will be obtained. What the learner makes of a feeling of confusion and what he or she decides to do about it are guided to varying degrees by the metacognitive knowledge base (see Flavell, 1979).

A less satisfactory state of affairs than detected cognitive failure is undetected cognitive failure, that is, cognitive failure compounded by metacognitive failure. Markman (1981) gives a nice example of such a situation. She describes a reading setting in which her mind begins to wander. As she becomes increasingly engrossed in her daydream, she understands less and less of what is read. She continues to read, persisting in the profitless venture because she is unaware that she is not understanding. A large literature on comprehension monitoring documents the pervasiveness of learners' failure to detect comprehension failure of this sort (see Baker & Brown, 1984a, 1984b; Brown, Armbruster, & Baker, 1986; Wagoner, 1983, for reviews).

Strategy Use

The last step in the sequence being outlined is the deployment of cognitive and metacognitive resources to remedy or further assess perceived cognitive failure. Following our learner reading about westward expansion, let us imagine that the learner has an "aha" that dates will be tested, and a subsequent realization of the need to rehearse them while reading and studying.

The learner employs the cognitive strategy of verbal rehearsal, and might well also employ a metacognitive strategy, a strategy invoked to assess progress toward goals (for example, jotting down all the critical dates that might be tested, checking off the ones the learner thinks he or she knows, and referring back to the textbook to assess the accuracy of predictions and the need for further rehearsal before the recall test). According to Flavell (1979), cognitive strategies are invoked to make cognitive progress, metacognitive strategies to monitor it.

It is fairly clear that motivation plays an important role in cognitive and metacognitive strategy use. Paris, Lipson, and Wixson (1983) address this point by talking about strategies having components of "both skill and will" (p. 304). In this regard, strategies are, as Rothkopf (in press) notes, like manners or dietary information, areas of endeavor where translating knowledge into action in appropriate fashion is surely as important as the knowledge itself. Unless a learner wants to accomplish a particular goal, it is unlikely that he or she will expend the time and energy it takes to engage in cognitive and metacognitive strategies. In some cases, external incentives (such as grades or financial rewards) prompt extra efforts, but it is not at all clear that strategic inclinations continue when these rewards are removed. A good deal more will be said in future chapters about motivational and other conditions that determine whether or not strategies are implemented.

Relations Among Metacognitive Elements

I said some time ago that a straightforward sequence would be described, one in which metacognitive knowledge is a basis for metacognitive experiences that in turn prompt the use of cognitive and metacognitive strategies. That has been done. However, other interrelationships also exist. Metacognitive experiences can prompt revision of metacognitive knowledge. For example, the realization that dates are easily confused prompts inclusion of this information in the knowledge base: Dates require extra studying effort. Metacognitive experiences can prompt additional metacognitive experiences. For example, realizing that boldface sentences highlight information leads to the "aha" that really critical dates often appear in these sentences. Metacognitive strategy use can induce both cognitive strategy use (e.g., self-testing leads to more rehearsal of dates) and revision of metacognitive knowledge (e.g., dates require extra studying effort; verbal rehearsal helps). Cognitive strategy use can produce metacognitive experiences, for example, "Aha, this rehearsal works; I'm getting the dates now!"

All of this is to say that each component of metacognition can prompt each of the others. The sequence established earlier of knowledge prompting experiences prompting strategy use may be the modal one, but it is by no means the only possible one. Flavell (1981, p. 40) provides us with a model of these interrelationships, reproduced here in slightly modified form in Figure 2.1.

Executive Control

Developmental psychologists well grounded in orthodox Piagetian theory traditionally ask questions about a child's developing cognitive structures and rely primarily on clinical interview methods in their research. Information-processing cognitive psychologists ask questions about processing demands and rely on simulation combined with experimental intervention methods to test processing hypotheses. Both groups of psychologists are very interested in learner strategies, but the emphasis is different. As we have seen, developmental psychologists talk about strategies as part of the metacognitive picture. Many information-processing theorists place strategic processing (or "executive control") at the heart of cognitive activity. To see what executive control is, a bit of background on current information-processing approaches may be useful. Sources for much of the highly abbreviated material that follows are Floden (1981), Mayer (1983), Miller (1983), and Simon (1979, 1980, 1981).

Information-processing approaches have in common an emphasis on input into and output from the human (typically adult) cognitive system. Between input and output, cognitive processes are involved in taking in information, performing mental operations on it, and storing it. The similarity in descriptions of operations between the adult and a computer is not accidental; computer programs that simulate human cognitive processing of complex tasks have been written as theories of mind. Basic to most such theories is a postulated increase in problem-solving capacity

Figure 2.1. Flavell's model of metacognitive components

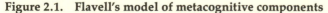

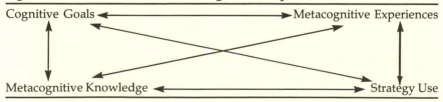

Cognitive Goals ⟷ Metacognitive Experiences

Metacognitive Knowledge ⟷ Strategy Use

with the use of automatic processing for the more routine elements of an activity, and the releasing of control resources for the more novel elements (Frederiksen, 1984).

Domains that have been investigated fairly extensively in the information-processing laboratory are chess, medical diagnosis, and college-level physics. In most instances, the adequacy of computer simulations has been tested by comparing the computer's performance with that of human subjects on problems varying in critical aspects, such as structure or difficulty. Human cognitive processes are inferred by asking subjects to "think aloud" during problem solving or by recording their eye movements during processing (Larkin, McDermott, Simon, & Simon, 1980).

A critical set of processes called "control processes" make for efficient use of the limited-capacity processing system. This set of processes directs the activities at each processing stage and makes certain that the system functions as a whole through the many processing steps. Brown (1977) stresses that part of development is a gradual increase in control of cognitive processing. Acquisition of the strategies and routines is usually explained as an outcome of practice with feedback (Calfee, 1981). Just how central executive control is to processing is reflected in Brown's comment that "in the domain of deliberate learning and problem-solving situations, conscious executive control of the routines available to the system is the essence of intelligent activity" (Brown, 1977, p. 4).

The executive is usually given credit for slowing down and allocating extra processing capacity to cognitive problem areas, that is, "debugging" the problem, which requires turning off the "automatic pilot" that characterizes skilled performance. Brown (1980) provides an example: A skilled reader proceeds merrily through a relatively easy reading task with rapid construction of meaning until a comprehension failure occurs and is detected. An unconfirmed expectation, an unfamiliar concept, or an important information gap could cause the failure. This situation can be characterized as cognitive failure, metacognitive success. At this point, the skilled reader slows down his or her processing and deploys resources (remedial strategies) to overcome the difficulty. The reader may decide to continue reading in a more analytical style, hoping that the confusion is resolved, may opt to reread earlier material, or may choose to consult an external source. In each case, the purpose of strategic action is resolution of the comprehension dilemma.

Wagner and Sternberg (1983) have attempted to isolate and quantify executive processes and assess their importance to adult reading comprehension. They have found that skilled readers monitor their ongoing performance, revise their strategies, and perform at high levels. It seems that able readers are more likely than less able readers to determine what to read and how to read it more strategically. For instance, the skilled readers allocated more time to reading passages for which they would be tested in greater detail and less time to reading passages for which less detailed tests would be administered.

Elsewhere, Sternberg (1984) provides a list of executive processes that might be used in planning, monitoring, and evaluating one's information-processing skills. They are as follows: (a) deciding on the nature of the problem; (b) deciding on performance components relevant for solving tasks; (c) deciding on how strategically to combine performance components; (d) selecting a mental representation for information; (e) allocating resources for problem solution; (f) monitoring solution processes; and (g) being sensitive to external feedback. Sternberg argues that these processes, along with performance components and knowledge-acquisition components, are critical to individual differences in intelligence.

An important feature of executive routines is that they can be taught. A current emphasis is psychology and education (to be treated in detail in chapter 6) is what Brown, Campione, and Day (1981) label devising instructional routines "to help students learn to learn" (p. 14), particularly slow-learning students for whom repeated exposure to academic tasks is an insufficient impetus to strategy acquisition. Brown et al. discuss blind training studies (students are induced to use a strategy without an understanding of the significance of the activity), informed training studies (students are induced to use a strategy and are given some information about the significance of the activity), and self-control training studies (students are instructed in the use of a strategy, and are also explicitly instructed in how to employ, monitor, check, and evaluate the strategy).

Recent research shows superior benefits (efficacy, durability, generalizability) for self-control training. Brown and Campione (1978) describe the properties that cognitive activities to be trained should have: (a) transsituational applicability; (b) the sense from children that these are reasonable activities that work; (c) a counterpart in real-life experiences; and (d) an understanding of component processes so that effective training techniques can be devised.

Boundaries Between Metacognition and Executive Control

In trying to understand the distinctions between metacognition and executive control, it is important to note that the two lines of research have different ancestries, make different assumptions about human development and learning, and employ different research methods. For all of these reasons, the language used in the two areas varies. Concerning ancestry: metacognition grew out of orthodox Piagetian developmental theory; executive control has its roots in information-processing research, grounded in the computer metaphor for mind. Concerning research methods: metacognition research employs adult-child clinical interviews; executive control studies rely on task analysis, computer simulation, and intervention research with (typically adult) human subjects. The language associated with each line of work is quite distinct. Metacognitive researchers talk about development of knowledge and awareness and conscious access. Executive control investigators talk about instruction for symbol manipulation, storage, input-output, and information flow. The latter lexicon is decidedly more task-focused and mechanistic in tone.

There is substantial lexical and conceptual overlap, however. Both areas of work, for instance, emphasize metacognitive knowledge of or detailed, sequential analysis of tasks. Both stress strategies used by learners (metacognitive and cognitive or detailed, trainable routines). Cognitive monitoring of movement toward goals is important to both areas. Also, both areas have converged on examination of productions, production systems, and what Flavell (1970) has called "production deficiencies" (that is, children's failure to use strategies spontaneously when appropriate, but ability to use them effectively when explicitly directed to do so). The emphasis in the explanations of these deficiencies does vary, however: self-knowledge gaps (Flavell & Wellman, 1977) versus control mechanism failures (Wagner & Sternberg, 1983).

Actually, what distinguishes the two areas of inquiry is relative emphasis. Whereas researchers in metacognition emphasize the *knowledge* learners bring or fail to bring to learning situations, researchers of executive control emphasize the *control* learners bring or do not bring, the success or failure at "orchestrating" (Cavanaugh & Perlmutter, 1982) knowledge. People interested in applications of these bodies of inquiry (for example, reading educators) tend to talk about both knowledge and control, showing less concern for ancestry and methodology and greater concern for implications for areas of interest, including instruction.

Reading educators have particularly emphasized the right half of Flavell's model (1981; see Figure 2.1) that coincides with executive control emphases: that is, monitoring of cognitive success and failure and the use of strategies to remedy perceived failures. This half of the model can be tested in most instances with relatively straightforward performance measures (one of which, error detection, has received a great deal of attention, and will be discussed in detail in chapter 5). It might also be argued that this half of the model is easier to "fix" in deficit instances. One might claim it is easier to change strategic repertoires than to alter meager knowledge bases. A theorist who subscribes wholly to the cognitive/metacognitive system specified in Flavell's model might respond that strategy changes are implemented more readily, but that it is knowledge base changes that, over time, make for real differences in cognitive functioning.

Two things can be said with some certainty about metacognitive and executive control views of cognitive processing. One is that there is important consensus. Perhaps most important is that both views emphasize active organisms at the center of cognitive processing. When learners ask questions, reread difficult material, or select learning activities appropriate to a given task, they are, to a considerable degree, "in charge" of their cognitive resources (Garner, Macready, & Wagoner, 1984). This active-learner focus places both areas of inquiry in the center of cognitive approaches that imply that learning "is scientifically more productively studied as an internally, cognitively mediated process than as a direct product of the environment, people, or factors external to the learner" (Wittrock, 1979, p. 5).

The second, related point to be made about metacognition and executive control is that, given all of the overlap mentioned so far, it seems unwise to cast the two lines of inquiry as inconsistent or incompatible, one of which can be confirmed empirically as more correct than the other. Something like this position has been taken recently by Fischer and Mandl (1982, 1984).

Fischer and Mandl differentiate Flavell's views from Brown's, saying that Flavell emphasizes a conscious, deliberately acting thinker, whereas Brown focuses upon the doing itself, regulated by an autopilot executive mechanism. Fischer and Mandl label Flavell as Hegelian "in that manipulation of practice is to take place by means of manipulation of consciousness" (1984, p. 219). They describe Flavell's theory of cognitive processing as difficult to apply in academic settings, and pronounce his various models (including the one presented here) as too fluid, tentative, and interdependent in their components to be testable. Fischer and Mandl label Brown's thinking as more materialistic in that differences between efficient and less efficient learners are seen mainly as differences in executive functioning that can be taught. (They note, as I have, the knowledge versus control-of-knowledge emphases.)

Representative quotes are interesting: "Brown does not search for the cognitive map in the head of the learner, as does Flavell" (Fischer & Mandl, 1984, p. 227). "According to Brown's notion, one has to foster skills, but not the knowledge" (p. 228). "Flavell tries to foster learning efficiency by enriching the cognitive map of the learner via informing him about cognitive functioning. Brown, on the other hand, seems to say: 'Don't tell the learner what he has to do (or why), but rather tell him how he might proceed (and give him feedback about his efficiency after he has done it)' " (p. 228).

This construction of diametrically opposed views is not supported by the literature, some of which has been cited in this chapter. For one thing, Flavell (1981) does write about cognitive and metacognitive actions to make and monitor cognitive progress; he specifically prescribes training in introspection plus fostering metacognitive experiences that stimulate compensatory action in school settings. For another, Brown and her colleagues (1981) make much of "self-control training," which prescribes just the opposite of rote learning of routines in the absence of a sense of purpose.

Unresolved Conceptual Issues

I have suggested that one important task for theorists and researchers working on problems of metacognition and executive control is restricting meaning so that the overlap and uniqueness of the two concepts are clear, so that all cognitive events are not dubbed "metacognitive," and so that some activities of learners are excluded from sets of either cognitive events or metacognitive ones. Concepts that are overly inclusive lose precision, and ultimately all meaning.

There are important issues to be addressed as well. One particularly knotty one is the description of the relationship between metacognitive knowledge and performance. As we shall see in future chapters, research findings show that relationship to be complex. Intuitively, we might predict that improved metamemory or metacomprehension will be accompanied by improved memory or comprehension performance; that is not necessarily true.

At least three possible explanations can be offered for the weak to moderate correlations between knowledge and performance: (a) meager sampling of both knowledge and cognitive performance (see Cavanaugh & Borkowski, 1980), that is, we may not be asking enough of the right questions or observing enough of the right behaviors to discern connections that are truly there (see Flavell, Friedrichs, & Hoyt, 1970; Gelman, 1979; Young & Schumacher, 1983); (b) verbal-report dilemmas (see Chi, 1985; Ericsson, 1984; Ericsson & Simon, 1980; and future chapters in this volume), that is, children may be handicapped in demonstrating knowledge they have; or (c) glib verbalizing (see Nisbett & Wilson, 1977) in the absence of either a firm knowledge base or performance strengths.

In the second case, the verbal product is less than the process it reflects; in the third case, the verbal product exceeds the process it seeks to describe (Garner, Wagoner, & Smith, 1983). In both cases, verbalized knowledge poorly reflects actual cognitive processing. There is, in both cases, a discrepancy between what one says one does and what one really does. Some rather ingenious methodological solutions have been utilized to reduce this discrepancy. They will be presented in chapter 4.

Another issue that remains troublesome is the relation between metacognitive knowledge and content knowledge brought to all cognitive enterprises, deliberate and involuntary (see Chi & Glaser, 1980). This is the relation between what Brown (1975) has labeled "knowing" and "knowing about knowing."

It is clear, as Brown points out, that both world knowledge and metacognitive knowledge undergo qualitative changes in the course of human development. It is not clear whether improvement in one of these categories is accompanied automatically by improvement in the other. It is not clear whether or not knowledge of one sort can compensate for knowledge deficiencies of the other sort. It is also not clear whether certain prerequisite levels of one are required before improvement in the other takes place. Finally, it is not clear, from an applied perspective, toward which category one should turn for high-benefit intervention purposes. However, studies that have fostered both domain-specific knowledge and metacognitive knowledge have generally found improved performance. Some of these studies will be discussed in chapter 6.

Still another issue is the area of ill-structured problems, for which there are no absolutely correct and knowable solutions. This is the area of knowledge limits. Kitchener (1983) establishes a "meta-meta level of cognitive monitoring" which has to do with epistemic cognition. She contrasts this level with cognition and with metacognition. Epistemic cognition, according to Kitchener, includes the individual's knowledge that some things can be known and others cannot, that some things can only be known probabilistically, and that criteria (e.g., scientific verification) do exist for whether one knows or does not know. She mentions jurisprudence, public policy, philosophy, scientific inquiry, and artistic interpretation as areas where epistemic cognition is exercised.

It would seem that the highly sophisticated judgment of whether or not a problem is even solvable under the best of conditions (that is, given maximum knowledge of self, task, and strategies and expert monitoring, plus cognitive/metacognitive strategic repertoires) is clearly a "meta" judgment. Perhaps the sophistication of it, far from the unthinking application of instructed routines, necessitates a "meta-meta" label. The danger, of course, lies in the potential proliferation of "meta" levels. The issue of what is knowable and what is solvable is particularly important for theorists and researchers of adolescent and adult cognition, the investigators who will surely prove to be most interested in the developmental level where such judgments would be refined.

A last unresolved issue that must be mentioned is the relative lack of success with which we have explained how metacognitive knowledge and skills and strategies develop. Much evidence supports that "knowing" and "knowing about knowing" and "knowing how to know" all improve with age and experience, but the specific mechanisms that move novices to experts are not at all well established. DeLoache, Cassidy, and Brown (1985), for instance, report rudimentary mnemonic strategies among very young children, particularly in unfamiliar settings, and suggest that either microgenetic or longitudinal research is needed to trace the evolution of these activities into mature mnemonic activities. Flavell (1984) has suggested that both the child's developing sense of self as an active cognitive agent and an increase in planfulness could facilitate metacognitive progress. He also ascribes an important role to practice of metacognitive activities.

Some of this practice occurs in school, in academic settings that demand goal-driven, planful, self-assessing, strategic behaviors. Some of the practice occurs in the home, between parent and child. Flavell (1984), Cavanaugh and Perlmutter (1982), and Baker and Brown (1984b) urge consideration of Vygotsky's notion that capacity for independent strategic functioning evolves from social interaction of an expert (the parent) and novice (the child). From this perspective, "interior intellectual work is almost always a continuation of a dialogue" (Bruner, 1979, p. viii). In this view, expanded by Wertsch (1979; Wertsch & Stone, 1979), the child is "coached" or led through a task that is slightly too difficult to be solved independently, one that lies in the child's "zone of proximal development" (Vygotsky, 1978, p. 86). This work will be presented in some detail in chapter 6.

Metacognition, Executive Control, and Reading Comprehension

Reading, as we have seen, is a complex cognitive task of immense importance in school settings. It is, as Resnick (1981) notes, the instructional domain "to which psychologists have attended for the longest time and in the greatest numbers" (p. 661). Our recent insights about its interactive, constructive nature (see chapter 1) place a great deal of emphasis on an active learner who directs cognitive resources to complete the task. It is not surprising, therefore, that many of the richest applications of metacognitive and executive control theory and research have been to reading, for the active learner optimizing his or her own learning sits, as we have seen, at the very center of these views of the cognitive enterprise.

Perhaps the two most replicated results from the research of recent years tying metacognition to reading are that (a) "younger and poorer readers have little awareness that they must attempt to make sense of text; they focus on reading as a decoding process, rather than as a meaning-getting process" (Baker & Brown, 1984b, p. 358); and (b) "younger children and poorer readers are unlikely to demonstrate that they notice major blocks to text understanding. They seem not to realize when they do not understand" (Garner & Reis, 1981, p. 571). A large number of interview studies and error detection experiments have yielded these robust findings. (This research will be presented in detail in the next chapter.)

More recently, strategic repertoire differences among readers have been studied from a metacognitive perspective. Because of the modal sequence of metacognitive experiences ("Oops, I don't think I found three main crops of the western states, and the text heading indicated that there were three") prompting action that is cognitive ("I think I'll reread the last two paragraphs") and metacognitive ("I'm going to quiz myself on all three after rereading"), it is not surprising that younger and poorer readers who differ from older, more successful readers in comprehension monitoring are also likely to differ in employment of compensatory strategies. Such strategies that have received recent research attention include using text reinspection to remedy memory failure (Garner, Macready, & Wagoner, 1984; Garner, et al., 1983); studying text segments previously found difficult more extensively than easy segments (Brown & Campione, 1977); or summarizing succinctly just the important information from an expository text (Winograd, 1984). As Ryan, Ledger, Short, and Weed (1982) note, "Comprehension problems among unsuccessful readers with reasonably adequate decoding skills are often related to their failure to participate actively and strategically while engaged in the reading process" (p. 54).

Therefore, we have descriptive information about individual differences among readers of different abilities and ages in metacognitive knowledge, metacognitive experiences, and strategy use (or executive control). Some interventions with less effective readers have been attempted. Most interventions have been with adults who "apply strategies which are intuitively compelling yet incorrect" (Case, 1978, p. 458) or with children who need general remedial assistance in reading. (Representative training efforts will be presented in chapter 6.)

We do not have any greater clarity for reading than we have for other cognitive activities about the relationship between knowledge and performance (the same readers are seldom assessed for both in current research); about the relationship between "knowing" and "knowing about knowing"; or about development, in school and out, of metacognition in the area of reading.

Reading educators and other practitioners are being treated to exciting concepts embedded in theories that have some gaping holes. One of the challenges to theorists and researchers interested in metacognitive and executive control problems is to lend clarity and precision, through careful thinking and diligent empirical work (a "plodding enterprise"; see Gage, 1978, p. 41), before "fuzzy" concepts become still fuzzier amidst unbridled application of these currently popular ideas.

Chapter 3

Metacognitive Development

Though we do not have a theory of the developmental mechanisms that move relatively unknowledgeable, nonmonitoring, strategically naive individuals to a more metacognitively sophisticated state, we do have a rich research base documenting that the movement occurs. Thus, we have reduced our collective ignorance of metacognitive phenomena at a descriptive level, if not at an explanatory one.

This chapter will present a sampling of the recent research literature that describes differences in metacognitive knowledge and skill along the dimensions of age and reading achievement. In discussing differences in reading achievement among learners, I will follow Carr's (1981) lead in referring to "good" and "poor" readers, intending to indicate a contrast between two points located on a continuum of reading proficiency. I will follow the scheme established in the previous chapter, presenting the research as it applies first to metacognitive knowledge, then to metacognitive experiences, and finally to strategy use.

Differences in Metacognitive Knowledge Among Learners

Most researchers interested in metacognitive knowledge differences would agree with Baker and Brown (1984b) who have said, "One simple way of assessing what children know is to ask them" (p. 358). The interview—whether highly standardized (i.e., the same questions are asked in the same way of all respondents), nonstandardized (i.e., no structured schedule of questions is used, and responses determine successive questions), or something in between—has been the most frequently used method in this area of research. This is true for examining differences related to both age and reading achievement.

Age-Related Differences in Metacognitive Knowledge

The prototypic study is one conducted by Kreutzer, Leonard, and Flavell in 1975. The study was exploratory, an initial effort to get an estimate of elementary school children's knowlege of memory phenomena sampled from person, task, and strategy categories. Children from four grades (kindergarten, 1, 3, and 5), were interviewed individually for about 30 minutes in what are described as relaxed and informal sessions. The sessions were audiotaped and transcribed later.

The older children (grades 3 and 5) differed from the younger children (kindergarten and grade 1) in a number of important ways; five specific differences will be highlighted here. One was conceptualizing memory ability as something that varies with occasion and with individuals. One older child, for instance, stated, "Sometimes I remember better than them and sometimes they remember better than I—I've got one older friend and that's all—he'd probably remember more than me" (Kreutzer et al., 1975, p. 6). A second difference was the older children's understanding that information in short-term memory is susceptible to rapid forgetting. Children who were aware of rapid information loss verbalized a need to use a just-heard phone number before forgetting it. A third difference between older and younger children was that the older children recommended using category structure (e.g., body parts, food, and clothing) to memorize a set of pictures.

A fourth difference was that older students provided more means of assisting recall than younger students. The task involved preparing to take an object somewhere, and the planful memory activity required. The interviewer posed the following problem: "Suppose you were going ice skating with your friend after school tomorrow and you wanted to be sure to bring your skates. How could you be really certain that you didn't forget to bring your skates along to school in the morning? Can you think of anything else? How many ways can you think of?" Older students mentioned four strategies for aiding recall: manipulating the skates themselves; using external cues other than the skates (e.g., writing a reminder, tying a string around a finger); getting assistance from others; and using internal efforts to stimulate recall (e.g., thinking about the skates the night before or anticipating skating with great eagerness). It is for this interview item that some truly impressive displays of knowledge were elicited. One third-grade girl, for instance, responded, "I could put them in my book bag, or set them on the table. Or I could always write myself a note, and put it up on my bulletin board. Or I could tell my mom to remind me. Or I could take them to school the day before and just leave them there" (Kreutzer et al., 1975, p. 29).

A fifth difference between the older and younger children was the older children's awareness of the difference in difficulty between gist and verbatim recall tasks. A fifth-grade child, for instance, said that if a girl needed to listen carefully to a record and then to recount the story either word for word or in her own words, the latter option would be preferable because "You could like explain. But if you have to learn it word for word, you might forget some of the words, and that would ruin the whole story. But if you do it in your own words, you just try to get the main ideas, and then if you kind of get stuck, you could just fill it in" (Kreutzer et al., 1975, p. 49).

Clearly, the major finding of this important investigation was that younger children know substantially less than older children about the variables affecting their own memory performance. This does not mean, however, that the younger children were without any metamemory strengths. Even the kindergarten and first-grade children knew common mnemonic expressions such as "remember" and "forget." They verbalized some awareness that things once learned and later forgotten are more easily relearned than wholly new things. They seemed to have some knowledge of the value of study time and of the difficulty of learning large numbers of items. These young children displayed some prowess, though not nearly so much as the older children, at generating lists of appropriate actions to prepare for future retrieval. They were quite ready, they reported, to use inanimate external resources and other people as storage and retrieval devices.

Nonetheless, at grade 3 and beyond, children "seemed to know the same things better and a number of other things in addition" (Kreutzer et al., 1975, p. 52). At grade 3 and beyond, planfulness for retrieval problems was a predictable component in the children's responses. It is at this stage that the verbalized strategic repertoires for memory situations were dramatically expanded. Finally, among the older children, knowledge of the interactive nature of memory variables (see chapter 2) surfaced more frequently.

The Kreutzer et al. (1975) study generated a great deal of interest in the research community. While it has spawned a number of similar studies, it has also generated some methodological criticism.

For instance, Brown (1984) acknowledges that young children are less informed than older children about stable characteristics of cognition. She suggests that a possible explanation for this relative ignorance is lack of experience in deliberate learning situations that occur regularly in school. Young children have not had many opportunities to decontextualize cognitive activity and to make it an object of study. She worries, however, about the use of imaginary or yet-to-be experienced situations, into which the child must project himself or herself as a participant. Additionally, she notes that a number of the processes examined in the Kreutzer et al. (1975) interview were quite general. Asking subjects to report on general internal events that are not available in short-term memory is generally considered unwise (see Ericsson & Simon, 1980; and chapter 4, this volume). Process-report disparities are likely to result, Ericsson and Simon suggest, under these conditions.

The criticisms of hypothetical scenarios and probing of general processes are only two of the criticisms leveled at interview research in general, and at metacognitive knowledge interview research in particular. Additional concerns will be mentioned as other studies are discussed, and the whole matter will be treated extensively in chapter 4.

Myers and Paris (1978) modeled their investigation after the Kreutzer et al. (1975) study, but focused on metacognitive knowledge about reading processes. Children in second grade and in sixth grade were selected without regard for reading achievement level. Again an adult interviewed individual children for just under 30 minutes. Again sessions were audiotaped and transcribed later. Again person, task, and strategy variable knowledge was assessed.

In a number of important ways, the younger children showed a lack of knowledge about critical reading parameters. Compared to the sixth-grade readers, they mostly did not know the following: (a) readers have special skills; (b) motivation is linked to reading performance; (c) reading silently is faster than reading aloud; (d) the first and last sentences of a paragraph are particularly important ones; (e) retelling a story is more efficiently done at gist level, rather than at verbatim level (replicating a Kreutzer et al., 1975, finding); (f) skimming is reading the words that yield the most information; and (g) rereading of text is an important strategy for resolving comprehension failures.

The younger children focused quite consistently on the decoding, rather than on the comprehension, aspects of the reading process. The grade 2 students were generally unable to report different strategies for tasks requiring exact recall versus meaning recall. They frequently mentioned "sounding out" words that are not understood. A full 30% of the second-grade students could not report any strategy to employ when an entire sentence is not understood. Myers and Paris (1978) suggest that direct instruction may be needed to alter young children's "limited understanding of reading as a cognitive activity" (p. 690).

Still another study examining cognitive phenomena with an interview method is the Miller and Bigi (1979) investigation of children's knowledge of attentional processes used at home and at school. Again person information, task information, and strategy information were tapped. The first part of the study was an interview, quite similar in form to those used by Kreutzer et al. (1975) and by Myers and Paris (1978). The second part of the study was designed to minimize verbalization, given the concern that verbal-response tasks can lead to a systematic underestimation of young children's knowledge (see Cavanaugh & Perlmutter, 1982). For part 2 of the study, children were given several answers for each item from which they might choose. The choices for the second part were the answers the children generated in part 1. An interval of 2 to 3 weeks separated sessions; the delay was intended to prevent contamination of second-part responses by first-part work.

Specific procedures were quite similar to those described for the earlier investigations. Children in grades 1, 3, and 5 were interviewed individually. Sessions lasted about 30 minutes (with an additional 15 minutes for the delayed forced-choice session) and were audiotaped.

The results were similar in general form to those of the foregoing studies. Miller and Bigi (1979) report a number of intriguing knowledge differences favoring the older children, some of which were (a) greater knowledge that television, radio, and outdoor distractions tempt one to ignore work and disrupt concentration; (b) greater awareness that an individual absorbed in reading a book might not hear a mother calling; (c) greater understanding that listening carefully to a teacher involves motivation; and (d) greater awareness of the strategy of moving away from a disruptive conversation in the library in order to resume quiet reading. First-grade children tended to know that they sometimes have trouble attending, that some children attend better than others, and that both age and situational variables affect attention. One of the most interesting developmental differences was the use of surrounding noise as an explanation for attentional problems among first-grade children, whereas older children mentioned interest, concentration, removal of temptation (all psychological factors) as the relevant variables.

A methodological point, which applies to the first part of the Miller and Bigi (1979) study and to most other metacognitive knowledge interview studies, has been raised by Meichenbaum, Burland, Gruson, and Cameron (1979). This point relates to scoring of data. In the case of open-ended questions, an investigator must reduce total verbal response to "distinct metacognitive themes" (Meichenbaum et al., 1979, p. 24). This reduction usually sets the stage for quantitative analysis of number of strategies reported, or some similar measure, across age or achievement level groups. The data reduction process is highly subjective, and agreement among theme-detectors (i.e., raters) must be assessed (Frick & Semmel, 1978). Inter-rater agreement assessment was made in each of the three interview studies discussed so far.

Before we turn our attention to a set of studies investigating reader-group knowledge differences, let me summarize what we know so far about age differences in metacognitive knowledge. Younger children (particularly those in kindergarten or in grades 1 or 2) know substantially less than older children (particularly those in grades 5 and 6) about themselves, the tasks they face, and the strategies they employ in the areas of memory, reading, and attention. None of the studies reviewed so far actually measured cognitive performance. That is, we do not know whether the children who differed in verbalizations of memory, reading, and attention *knowledge* actually differed in memory, comprehension, and attention *performance* as well. This is the old problem of the relation between metacognitive knowledge and performance. We will return to the problem in chapter 4.

Reading Achievement–Related Differences in Metacognitive Knowledge

Forrest and Waller (1980), like Myers and Paris (1978) before them, focused their attention on the relation between children's age and their metacognitive knowledge about reading. However, the relation between children's metacognitive knowledge and their global reading achievement level was also tested. Forrest and Waller subdivided metacognitive knowledge into knowledge about decoding, knowledge about comprehension, and knowledge about reading for a purpose (e.g., studying).

Subjects in the study were children at three reading levels in each of grades 3 and 6. Each child was presented 13 standardized questions in an individual interview. Two raters scored responses independently, awarding scores of 0 (a wrong response or no response), 1 (some appropriate information), or 2 (a complete and appropriate response). Interrater agreement was high.

This interview study showed an increase in metacognitive knowledge about decoding, comprehension, and reading for a purpose with both higher grade and reading achievement level. Items that differentiated most dramatically among children along these two dimensions were the following: (a) knowing that what a word "says" is not equivalent to what a word "means"; (b) knowing that self-test strategies are helpful in getting ready for a test; and (c) knowing that a repertoire of strategic behaviors is important for "study" reading, if not for "fun" reading. The findings of a decoding emphasis and meager strategic repertoires for complex reading situations among younger readers and older, poorer readers are reminiscent of some of Myers and Paris's (1978) results. It appears that reading novices, of whatever age, have some metacognitive deficiencies in common. These deficiencies appear in both declarative and procedural knowledge categories.

Still more evidence of meager strategy knowledge among less successful readers comes from part of an investigation conducted by Paris and Myers (1981). In this study, groups of good and poor fourth-grade readers were formed. Twenty reading strategies that could affect memory for narrative texts were generated.

The set was composed equally of strategies labeled "positive, internal" (e.g., asking oneself questions about the ideas in the story); "negative, internal" (e.g., thinking about something else while reading); "positive, external" (e.g., looking up words one doesn't know in the dictionary), and "negative, external" (e.g., watching TV while reading). Five neutral items were included as well. It is interesting to note that disruption of concentration and specific disruptive stimuli addressed by Miller and Bigi's (1979) study are also mentioned here in some of the negative strategies.

Individual sessions lasted about 25 minutes. Subjects read a narrative; were invited to use paper, pencil, and so on to study the story (strategic behaviors observed were noted); participated in free recall of the story; reported on their studying activities; and rated the utility of the 25 strategies on a 9-point graphic rating scale that ranged from "helps a lot" to "hurts a lot."

No differences between good and poor readers' rating of neutral items appeared. Both groups of readers rated external factors higher. Poor readers, however, were less aware of the detrimental influences on comprehension of negative factors. Poor readers also displayed more rating reversals, rating negative strategies as positive and vice versa. The number of reversed ratings was significantly negatively correlated with actual recall performance for the story.

The reader-group differences in strategy discrimination favoring good readers are not surprising, and corroborate Forrest and Waller's (1980) findings. The most important feature of Paris and Myers' (1981) work may be their attempt to assess knowledge and performance for the same group of children, a relatively rare occurrence in the metacognitive literature. This study provides evidence of a relation between faulty knowledge (reversed ratings) and poor recall performance. Thus, we have some support for a metacognitive knowledge–cognitive performance link.

Another study (Garner & Kraus, 1981–1982) also linked knowledge and performance. Again reading was the focus. In particular, differences between good readers and poor readers in decoding versus comprehension emphases were examined. Students in grade 7 at two reading levels were asked eight questions about reading in one session and were administered an error-detecton task in a second session 2 weeks later.

Responses to three questions of the eight on the interview were scored 0 (no mention of "meaning" or a synonymous term) or 1 (mention of meaning or a synonym) by independent raters. High agreement resulted, and significant good reader–poor reader differences were found.

A sample of responses illustrates the distinctly different emphases found in the two groups. To the question "What things does a person have to do to be a good reader?" good readers gave such responses as "understand what you're reading" or "get the ideas," whereas poor readers provided such answers as "pronounce the words right" or "know all of the words." To the question "If I gave you something to read right now, how would you know if you were reading it well?" good readers responded with "if I could understand it without reading it over and over again" or "if I didn't have trouble getting the point." Poor readers responded to the same question with "if I didn't pause much" or "if I read fluently out loud." Finally, to the question "What makes something difficult to read?" the good reader responses of "if you're not familiar with the important ideas" or "badly written stuff where the ideas are hard to get" can be contrasted with "small print," "a lot of big words," or simply "long words" mentioned by poor readers.

A bit more information was gleaned in this study. First, good reader–poor reader differences emerged in error detection as well as in interview responses. The same subjects who emphasized decoding at the expense of comprehension failed to detect investigator-inserted comprehension obstacles in text. This represents another knowledge-performance link. (Much more will be said about error detection as a research paradigm in the next section of this chapter and in chapter 5).

A second piece of additional information is the distinction in reader-group responses to the question "What do you do if you don't understand something you are reading?" Some strategies, such as asking someone, were mentioned frequently by readers in both groups. Other strategies were uniquely mentioned by good readers (e.g., "use context") or by poor readers ("skip it"). Good readers were far more likely than poor readers to suggest rereading of text.

It is important to ask why these good reader–poor reader differences exist, differences also found by Myers and Paris (1978), Forrest and Waller (1980), and Paris and Myers (1981). In contrast to Brown's (1984) suggestion that a lack of school experience accounts for missing information and misinformation, Garner and Kraus (1981–1982) suggest that some in-school experience may actually produce the knowledge problems. They point out that instruction strongly affects the students' perception of the reading process, and that primary-grade teachers and basal readers emphasize oral reading and decoding, occasionally at the expense of comprehension. They further suggest that good readers experience the "magic" of reading for meaning, and alter their perceptions of the ultimate goal of the process, but that poor readers, who have seldom experienced such "magic," who do not have a clear sense "of what their efforts are supposed to yield" (Scardamalia & Bereiter, 1983, p. 66), attend ever more zealously to classroom (i.e., decoding) emphases in an effort to improve their reading performance.

It may also be the case, as Allington (1983) suggests, that good and poor readers are treated differently in instruction, in ways that support development of appropriate reading concepts for the skilled readers and inhibit that development for the less skilled readers.

Allington notes that the well-documented off-task behavior among poor readers may be a result of distractibility in a word-focused oral reading–emphasis instructional setting with frequent teacher interruptions for feedback on oral rendering accuracy (see also Allington, 1980). Good readers, he notes, get more meaning-emphasis instruction and more silent reading practice. Because off-task behavior from uninvolved participants during oral reading produces "down time" in learning for an entire poor-reader group, and because oral readers of whatever proficiency level read fewer words per minute than do silent readers of the same level, good readers get more reading time in the classroom than their poor-reader peers whose needs for both direct instruction and guided practice are greater. A renewed interest in systematic examination of classroom practices in reading may eventually confirm or disconfirm these rather pessimistic views of confused readers and instructional inequity (see, for example, Borko, Shavelson, & Stern, 1981; Duffy, 1982; Durkin, 1978–1979, 1981; Hiebert, 1983; Mosenthal, 1983).

The evidence cited to this point in this chapter is quite convergent. Young children and poor readers have important knowledge gaps and misconceptions about critical cognitive activities. Methodological concerns about interviews notwithstanding, this information should raise the concern that metacognitive experiences, based as they are on the metacognitive knowledge one possesses, might be impaired for these learners as well. It is to the literature on differences in experiences, particularly in cognitive monitoring, that we turn next.

Differences in Metacognitive Experiences Among Learners

Recall for a moment the learner discussed in chapter 2 who was studying a textbook chapter on the westward expansion of the United States. I suggested that the learner might well have the following metacognitive experiences at various stages of the activity: He or she might experience relief about the format of the next day's quiz; might realize that dates are becoming confused in his or her mind and that a rehearsal strategy should be employed; and might have an "aha" that boldface topic sentences in the textbook highlight particularly important dates. Also noted was the fact that an explicit question such as "Do I understand?" need not be posed for such metacognitive experiences to occur and that many such experiences occur as a result of failed cognitions. Undetected cognitive failure, that is, cognitive failure compounded by metacognitive failure, is a fairly common phenomenon.

How do we know all this? Granted, we might devise careful observational studies where sighs of relief and overt strategy use and verbalized "ahas" could be noted, counted, and compared for groups of learners. But how could we possibly "observe" the acknowledgement of confusion about dates, a mental event?

The dominant paradigm for research that has evolved for tracking essentially unobservable cognitive events involves "rigging" the input to which learners are asked to react. For instance, we might provide games with incomplete instructions or exposition with inconsistent details, and ask children or adults to listen or to read the material and to edit or critique or act on the content. We note their detection of the problems. Either we ask them to report on aspects of the material that need "fixing" or we tally the number of seconds they spend on flawed versus unflawed portions of the material. We infer from this work with contrived materials that we have uncovered aspects of cognitive monitoring that occur in about the same way with about the same frequency in the uncontrived materials learners normally face, in school and out.

This "error-detection" paradigm (alternatively "contradiction" paradigm or "textual anomaly" method) has been used in a number of recent studies. It is not particularly surprising that the results of most of this research parallel the results of the work on metacognitive knowledge differences: Young children and poor readers perform detection tasks (and presumably monitor cognition of one sort of another in nonresearch settings) less well than older children and good readers.

The error-detection paradigm is not without its critics. Even researchers who use it caution against ignoring alternative explanations for results of nondetection. One reason for the caution is the much-replicated result of only moderate demonstration of detection, even among able adults (see, for instance, Baker & Anderson, 1982). Baker (1985a) describes this result as "considerable room for improvement 'at the top' " (p. 299). Some of the criticisms of the method will appear in this chapter in discussions of specific studies. The entire matter of appropriate methodologies for studying metacognitive experiences will be treated in some detail in chapter 5. Alternative methods to error detection will be presented in that chapter.

Listening and Cognitive Monitoring

Markman's work with error detection in listening situations is perhaps the best place to begin. Her 1977 investigation of "passive processing" and the "delusion of comprehension" has stimulated much of the research that has followed. The investigation was a preliminary study of developmental changes in comprehension monitoring. Children, who were asked to serve as editorial consultants, were presented with instructions on performing a task from which critical information had been deleted. The measure of whether the children noticed the incomprehensible nature of the instructions was whether or not they asked a question or requested additional information of the investigator.

Children in grades 1 through 3 served as consultants. Each child was seen individually and was given both game and magic-trick instructions to evaluate. Children were told explicitly that they should tell the investigator if she had failed to clarify something or had forgotten to give them information. Both sets of instructions were "rigged." For instance, for the game, the investigator said, "We each put our cards in a pile. We both turn over the top card in our pile. We look at cards to see who has the special card. Then we turn over the next card in our pile to see who has the special card this time. In the end the person with the most cards wins the game."

Alphabet cards had been distributed equally to both players (i.e., the adult investigator and the child). There was no mention, however, of what the "special card" might be. A series of 10 probes was begun. The eighth probe moved the child to actual playing of the game. Probes were terminated at the point that the child asked a question or made a comment that indicated awareness of missing information. Examples of relevant questions are: "How do you know who has the special card?" and "What is the special card?" A child's score matched the point at which probes were terminated.

First-grade children differed from third-grade children in the point at which they realized instructions were incomplete. It took an average of 9, 6, and 3 probes for grade 1, 2, and 3 subjects, respectively, to note the missing information. Of the 8 first-grade children who asked a clarification question, all but 1 had to attempt to play the game and fail before posing the question. Markman points out that these youngest children probably failed to execute the instructions mentally, and therefore did not notice the problems until they attempted to perform the task.

As part of this preliminary investigation of comprehension monitoring, a second study with children in grades 1 through 3 was conducted. In this study, children again evaluated the game and magic trick instructions, but they did so under one of two conditions: Either the investigator only told the children about the game and how to play it, or the investigator both told and showed something about the game and how to play it. Instructions, probing procedures, and scoring were exactly the same as in the first study.

In this study, detection scores for both first-grade children and second-grade children were significantly worse than those for third-grade children. For the game task, 13 of the 16 first-grade subjects who asked a relevant question did so only after being asked to execute the instructions, whereas only 4 of the 18 third-grade subjects who asked a question needed to enact the instructions. The demonstration condition, as might be expected, produced performance superior to the verbal condition.

The overall conclusion Markman draws from this initial investigation is that first-grade children do not demonstrate much awareness that their comprehension of instruction is faulty. She suggests that relatively superficial processing may be the reason.

Markman (1979) next turned her attention to detection of textual inconsistencies. In this investigation, children from grades 3, 5, and 6 were asked to be editorial consultants. The children were assigned to conditions of either explicit or implicit inconsistencies. A number of features were similar to the game/magic-trick procedure: multiple materials (three essays) to each child, a directive to inform the investigator of problems in the texts, a listening situation for the subjects, a series of probes, and scoring based on termination of probes when an appropriate question or comment arose.

The blatancy of the informational inconsistencies, confirmed by adults' high rate of detection, was as extreme as that of the informational gaps in the previous study. An example of an explicit-condition inconsistency on the topic of fish is as follows:

> Fish must have light in order to see. There is absolutely no light at the bottom of the ocean. It is pitch black down there. When it is that dark the fish cannot see anything. They cannot even see colors. Some fish that live at the bottom of the ocean can see the color of their food; that is how they know what to eat.

It is not surprising that the implicit condition was more difficult for children than the explicit. Somewhat surprising, however, is the low rate of inconsistency detection for the explicit condition in all grades; nearly half of the children missed all or all but one of the problems in the explicit condition. There were no grade differences.

Markman (1979) offers a number of possible explanations for the low inconsistency detection rates across age levels: memory failure, resolution of the contradiction through inferential "fix-ups," unwillingness to admit comprehension difficulty to an adult, or genuine lack of awareness of comprehension failure. (Note that, as mentioned earlier, a number of explanations in addition to comprehension monitoring failure exist.)

In further studies, Markman repeated the inconsistencies (with no effect) and warned the children that there was something tricky or confusing, something that didn't make sense in the essays (with an important effect). Sixth-grade subjects given this latter "nudge" to find an announced flaw in text were able to do so.

In evaluating all of this preliminary work, Markman (1979) raises an important point: Children may examine texts primarily for empirical truth or completeness, not for logical consistency. Each true statement, then, is accepted, and cross-sentence checks on informational consistency are simply not made.

Markman and Gorin (1981) devised a study to test this possibility. Children 8 and 10 years old listened to a series of short essays that contained a false statement in the final sentence, a final sentence that presented information that was incompatible with a preceding sentence, or no problems whatsoever. Children were assigned to one of three conditions: They received a general comment about problems in some of the essays, that comment plus a falsehood "set," or the comment plus an inconsistency "set." Children rated the essays as "okay" or "problem" and then described the nature of problems found.

Overall detection of problems was greater for the older children when they were given specific sets prior to listening to the essays. Furthermore, the type of set given affected the type of problem detected. Spurious questioning of truth value of essays occurred far more frequently than spurious questioning of consistency. Once again, the children, even the older ones given a set to find specific problems, performed far below ceiling level on the task.

Wagoner (1983) hypothesized a developmental sequence for text acceptability decisions that is quite consistent with Markman's data (1977; 1979; Markman & Gorin, 1981) and with data from other studies still to be presented. Wagoner suggests that initially a listener or reader supposes all comprehension problems reside with him or her, not with the text (see Robinson, 1981, for a summary of listener inadequacy versus message inadequacy views in young children). Once a listener or reader comes to understand that utterances and texts can be flawed, the listener or reader tests text content against reality for truth value. Finally, a listener or reader is able to test text against text for internal consistency. Many of the subjects in the studies being discussed have not reached the level at which they apply the internal consistency standard spontaneously, though Markman and Gorin's (1981) results indicate that they can be induced to do so.

Still another point to be made about young children is that they may well have evidence from everyday experience that some things they fail to understand are indeed comprehensible. Capelli (1982) argues that children might find directions or texts difficult to understand, but might still believe they are comprehensible by others and might rate them accordingly. In this case, the criterion variability between researcher and young subject is not internal logic versus external truth, but rather actual comprehensibility for self versus potential comprehensibility for others. This criterion of comprehensibility for others might have been applied in a number of the listening studies we have discussed.

Listening to text, of course, is not reading text. Though components of the two cognitive processes overlap, each poses unique cognitive demands (see Danks & End, in press). Think, for a moment, about evaluating the completeness and consistency of a text just read aloud to you versus one you have read and perhaps reread. There are advantages to the listening situation. Perhaps the person reading (if it is a person, not an audiotape) could not wholly remove reaction to a blatant gap or misstatement, and intonation, facial expression, or gesture could have conveyed part of that reaction. (This scenario is based on the assumption that the oral reader either is informed about the textual error or detects it.)

But those possibilities are balanced by the advantage of permanence that the written language option offers (see Garner & Reis, 1981; Kleiman, 1982; Rubin, 1980; Wilkinson, 1980). A reader can read part of an essay, read ahead, reread the first portion (perhaps checking for consistency of information), frame just two isolated sentences that appear incompatible for still further rereading—all of this typically at the reader's own discretion and rate. Though the remedy for detected incompleteness or inconsistency in nonresearch settings is probably superior in interactive listening situations (one can shout "Huh?" or in some other way indicate puzzlement, and presumably get clarification), the detection itself seems more likely to occur in a reading situation because of selective reinspection possibilities. The written test is continuously accessible as an external object for cognitive scrutiny (Bonitatibus & Flavell, 1985). We now turn our attention to studies of cognitive monitoring in reading. Other listening and cognitive monitoring studies that have included nonverbal behavioral indicants of monitoring will be mentioned in chapter 5.

Reading and Cognitive Monitoring

The eight error detection studies to be discussed in this section have a number of features in common. All of them presented readers with texts of varying lengths to be evaluated for acceptability. In nearly every case, the investigators considered in advance alternative explanations for potential low detection rates, and generally did two things: They (a) incorporated some controls in the designs of the studies, such as piloting with expert readers to assess blatancy of errors, pretesting readers to ensure decoding proficiency, providing clear directives to subjects to read material in an "editorial" and very analytical fashion, and using materials at a readability level lower than grade placement of poor readers; and (b) interpreted results cautiously, acknowledging a number of reasons in addition to faulty comprehension monitoring for failure to mention errors. The studies will be presented briefly. Highly convergent patterns in results should be evident.

Baker (1979) assessed error detection by undergraduate students, using three-paragraph passages, for which the middle paragraph in each contained inconsistent information, an unclear reference, or an inappropriate connective. After reading and recalling content, subjects were informed of the existence of these "confusions," and were asked to provide a retrospective account of their detection of the problems. All directions were written in a booklet, through which subjects moved at their own pace.

Only 38% of the problems were reported by subjects, even given an explicit directive to search for them after the reading and recall tasks had been completed. In analyzing recall protocols and retrospective reports, Baker (1979) suggests that there is evidence of two phenomena that depressed detection scores: (a) use of knowledge-based inferences and systematic deletion of information in an effort to form a plausible interpretation of the passages (i.e., some problems were noted and "fixed"); and (b) application of variable criteria for acceptability (i.e., some problems were noted and dismissed as trivial).

Garner (1980) worked individually with junior high school students selected at two levels of reading proficiency to discover whether or not good reader–poor reader differences in error detection exist. Subjects read two expository texts, each of which had been divided into four segments. Inconsistent information had been inserted into the second and fourth segments of one of the passages. Readers were asked to rate each segment of each passage as "very easy to understand," "okay," or "difficult to understand."

Good readers varied their ratings of consistent and inconsistent material, whereas poor readers made little distinction. It is of some interest that of 240 ratings given by all readers on all segments, only 4 "difficult to understand" ratings were given. Garner suggests that either unwillingness to admit serious comprehension problems to an adult in a school setting or use of an intrasentence acceptability criterion as the primary criterion for comprehensibility of text might account for this rating pattern.

A follow-up study (Garner, 1981) was designed to investigate this pattern further. Poor readers in grades 5 and 6 were given three short passages, one informationally consistent, one informationally inconsistent (conflicting pieces of information were given in the first and last sentences of the five-sentence text), and one containing two perfectly acceptable polysyllabic modifying words. The readers were asked to rate each passage on the same 3-point scale used in the 1980 study.

The hypothesis of "piecemeal processing" among poor readers, that is, poor readers' focusing on lexical items and on intrasentence consistency, rather than on intersentence consistency, received support. Readers did not differentiate ratings of the consistent and inconsistent texts, but they rated the texts containing such words as *expeditiously* and *multifarious* as significantly more difficult to understand, citing "tough words," "long words," and "words I don't know" as the sources of difficulty.

As Baker (1985b) states, an essential prerequisite for evaluating text on grounds of internal consistency is integration of separate text propositions. Readers who do not access appropriate memory representations, and then combine and compare propositions as they read could scarcely be expected to notice intersentence inconsistencies. Markman (1981) makes a similar point: "Each proposition could exist independent of the other and not in and of itself be seen as problematic" (p. 71). The children in the Garner (1981) study appear to have overused a word-understanding standard for comprehension, to the exclusion of an internal consistency standard. We have little information about whether or not children can keep several different standards in mind and use each of them. Baker (1984a) has recently conducted an investigation of use of multiple standards among children 5, 7, 9, and 11 years old, and found that they seemed to be able, with optimal information and feedback, to adjust their standards of message evaluation appropriately.

Still another study of detection of textual anomaly was conducted by P. L. Harris, Kruithof, Terwogt, and Visser (1981). These investigators, working with children in grades 3 and 6, separately assessed constructive processing and comprehension monitoring. Constructive processing was operationally defined as reading time for target-consistent or anomalous lines of text exposed line by line with a window card, and comprehension monitoring was defined as verbalization of an anomalous line's "not fitting" in the short narratives presented. Titles for the stories were manipulated, thus creating anomaly in one line or another.

P. L. Harris et al. (1981) found that both groups read the anomalous lines more slowly than consistent lines, but that age differences in monitoring, favoring older children, surfaced. It is not clear whether the need for somewhat equal-length lines of text for window-card exposure (a computer terminal presentation might have been preferable) or rough translation from the original Dutch report accounts for the somewhat stilted "stories" apparently used in this study. An example is as follows:

Title 1: At the hairdresser's
Title 2: At the dentist's

John is waiting.
There are two people before him.
After a while, it is his turn.
He sees his hair getting shorter (anomaly, title 2).
Luckily, there are no cavities this time (anomaly, title 1).
After a while he can get up.
John puts his coat on.
He can go home.

Baker and Anderson (1982), working with adults, did use a computer terminal to present texts for evaluation. As in the earlier Baker (1979) study, the middle paragraph contained the problem, this case in inconsistencies in either main idea or details. Both the amount of time spent on each sentence and the identification of inconsistencies (the P. L. Harris et al., 1981, outcome measures) were assessed.

Baker and Anderson (1982) found that more time was spent on text segments containing main-point inconsistencies than on segments containing either detail inconsistencies or no problems. In addition, main-point inconsistency material was reexposed more often by subjects. A final finding is by now somewhat predictable, even for adult subjects: A full third of the inconsistencies went "undetected" (i.e., they were truly undetected, they were detected and fixed, or they were detected and ignored).

A report of a study of reading and error detection that is much cited, more for the commentary on the method than for the substantive findings, is one from Winograd and Johnston (1982). At this point, we will deal with study specifics, returning to the important criticisms of error detection presented by Winograd and Johnston in chapter 5. These investigators asked good and poor sixth-grade readers to read short texts with anomalous sentences near the end. The readers were either given a prior knowledge preparation exercise (to activate world knowledge) or not. The children repeated the entire procedure in a second session. Probes were used to determine anomaly detection.

There was no preparation effect. Both groups did better on the second go-round. Good readers were superior to poor readers in detection. Once again, however, neither group performed at ceiling level. Winograd and Johnston (1982) raise the by-now familiar query: "Did the children fail to detect the errors or did they just fail to mention them?" (p. 69). They also note a problem other investigators have not addressed: probing. They suggest that subjects became impatient with the redundancy of the probes, and that there may be serious violations of assumptions of equal-interval probes, that is, that assistance distance between probe 1 and probe 2 may be either larger or smaller than distance between probe 7 and probe 8, and so forth. These assumptions are basic to analyses used in many of the error-detection studies.

When Glenberg, Wilkinson, and Epstein (1982) conducted an error-detection study, they labeled the phenomenon under study, that is, comprehension monitoring failure, as "the illusion of knowing." Glenberg and his colleagues asked undergraduate students to read short expository texts and to apply a rating scale for comprehensibility. In this study, contradictory material appeared in adjacent sentences. The paragraph containing the contradictions either appeared alone or was preceded by two introductory paragraphs. Furthermore, half of the contradictions were syntactically marked as new (e.g., preceded by an indefinite article such as *a*) and half were marked as given (e.g., preceded by a definite article such as *the*). An "illusion of knowing" was indicated by failure to detect contradictory material plus a high confidence rating for comprehension.

Overall, there was a high incidence of illusion, even among adults in a college sample. There were more illusions for new than for given material, and more for material with a lengthy introduction than for material with no introduction.

A final error-detection study to be mentioned is one conducted recently by August, Flavell, and Clift (1984). The uniqueness of this study is that the "error" occurred at the page, rather than the word or proposition, level. Each child (either a skilled or less skilled fifth-grade reader) read five 8-page stories. In three of the five stories, a portion of the story was intentionally omitted to render the overall narrative confusing. Stories were presented, page by page, on the computer terminal. On-line measures were time spent reading pages following problem areas (and comparable time spent with perfectly acceptable texts) and number of text lookbacks employed for acceptable and unacceptable texts. After reading, subjects were quizzed about error detection, location of the missing page, and remedy.

Good readers detected more errors, located the errors more frequently, and reported the correct repair strategy with higher frequency than poor readers. In addition, the good readers spent more time on inconsistent stories than poor readers. Very few readers from either skill group used text lookbacks. A great many readers in both groups generated inferential "fix-ups" to create an acceptable story from unacceptable input.

The point was made earlier that the results of the error-detection work in reading situations are highly convergent. Let me be more explicit about the nature of that convergence: First, anywhere from one third to almost two thirds of the intentionally inserted errors went unreported, even by adult subjects, even in situations where analytical processing was encouraged and reinspection of text was sanctioned; and second, more experienced and more proficient readers, though not performing at ceiling level, outdetected (or at least outreported) less experienced and less proficient readers on a variety of on-line and post-reading measures.

A final point about these results for metacognitive experiences, or rather the lack of them, is that the findings are particularly worrisome given what we know about flawed texts. Armbruster and T. H. Anderson (1981) have reminded us that school texts, which drive instruction to a large degree, are often "inconsiderate"; that is, they require readers to expend extra cognitive effort to compensate for authors' failures to provide adequately structured, coherent, unified, information-appropriate text. Examples of characteristics of "inconsiderate text" are: (a) a mismatch between structural signals such as headings or topic sentences and the content that follows; (b) short, choppy sentences that obscure relations among ideas; (c) insufficient information given the probable prior knowledge of readers; (d) irrelevant information which potentially distracts readers; and (e) an absence of definitions for difficult vocabulary words.

There is some support (Alvermann & Boothby, 1983; Kantor, T.H. Anderson, & Armbruster, 1983; Loman & Mayer, 1983) for a relation between existence of these characteristics and comprehension-learning difficulties. If readers do not notice blatant errors in research materials (assuming for now that at least a substantial portion of nonmentioning instances that have been discussed are also nondetection instances), they surely are not likely to notice and seek remedies for some of the problems found in "inconsiderate" school materials. We next turn our attention toward remedies for detected cognitive difficulties.

Differences in Strategy Use Among Learners

Just as the term "metacognition" has been applied to a large set of only loosely related phenomena, the label "strategy" has been used for a wide range of activities, some complex and some simple, some imposed on learners and some selected spontaneously by learners, some highly routinized techniques and some consciously applied means to ends. To attempt to discuss all of these activities would be folly, and one might well ask why some of the simpler, routinized procedures through which learners move quite passively and obediently belong in a volume on metacognition and related matters. Once again, then, I will attempt to restrict our focus a bit.

I begin by defining strategies in such a way (see Garner, in press-a, in press-b, for more extended discussions) that sequences of activities not single events (Kail & Bisanz, 1982), are considered; these, I would submit, are the interesting activities that make a difference in school learning situations. These are the activities for which learners need to acquire both the component processes and a routine for organizing the processes into integrated strategic wholes. I continue by emphasizing that, though subroutines may be learned to a point of automaticity, strategies are generally deliberate, planful activities undertaken by active learners, many times to remedy perceived cognitive failure. When entire strategic routines become automated, I agree with Paris (in press) that they are better labeled "skills." It should be added that strategies must be applied flexibly, that learners must know when and where as well as how to use them (Brown et al., 1986). Paris et al., (1983) accord this sort of "when" and "where" knowledge a special label, that of "conditional knowledge."

To focus still more, in this chapter only correlational data on the relation of strategy use to age and achievement level will be presented. Data on efficacy of experimental interventions, efforts to train, maintain, and extend strategic behaviors, will be presented in chapter 6. And finally, in this section, methods of observing strategy use, rather than of tapping strategy knowledge, will be considered. Three strategies, all extremely important in school settings, will be considered: allocation of study time, text reinspection, and text summarization. For thorough reviews of achievement level–related differences in other important strategic activities, the reader is referred to Carr (1981), Garner (1983), Golinkoff (1975–1976), and Ryan (1981).

Allocation of Study Time

Having the metacognitive knowledge that tasks are differentially difficult, that we are very good at some things and much less good at others, and that a wise strategy is to expend more time and energy on things that are generally difficult for us or that we have just experienced failure in (task × strategy information, as Brown and Campione, 1977, note) may be a prerequisite to use of the strategy of wise study time allocation. Monitoring our successes and failures may also be necessary, so that we know when and where to expend the effort. This strategy involves (a) evaluating whether or not something has been understood, remembered, perceived adequately, and so forth, and then (b) planfully regulating subsequent cognitive activity on the basis of this evaluation. It is surely a very useful strategy for a range of learning situations. It will perhaps come as no surprise that neither young children nor less successful learners are particularly effective at employing this strategy.

Masur, McIntyre, and Flavell (1973) investigated the management of resources for a memory task by subjects in grade 1, grade 3, and college. After obtaining an estimate of each subject's immediate memory span and after a warmup segment, an investigator described the task: memorizing a set of object drawings 50% longer than the subject's assessed memory span. Five trials, including study and recall periods, were given. After each of the first four recall periods, the subject was permitted to select for the next study period half of the total to-be-remembered set of objects. The measure of interest was the extent to which different learners would choose to keep for further study the items they had just failed to recall on the previous trial. (The investigator surreptitiously added a few new items to the set when a subject correctly recalled all the items.) Subjects were asked at the end of the last recall period how they had selected items for study and how they had studied.

The proportion of missed items selected for study to missed items that could have been selected by a particular subject was computed for trials 2, 3, and 4. Scores for first-grade students were significantly lower than those for the older subjects (grade 3, college) whose scores did not differ significantly. No first-grade subjects spoke of selecting missed items for further study, but the most frequent selection explanation for the third-grade and college subjects was selecting items they had just failed to recall.

Masur et al. (1973) conclude that the first-grade subjects failed to use an obvious and adaptive memory strategy that the older students employed with high frequency. They suggest that this rather obvious routine is probably acquired quite casually in the course of numerous school recall experiences.

A similar result in allocation of time and energy was found by Owings, Petersen, Bransford, Morris, and Stein (1980), who worked with "successful" and "less successful" fifth-grade students. Appropriate and inappropriate subject-predicate pairings (e.g., "The hungry boy ate a hamburger" and "The hungry boy took a nap," respectively) were embedded in simple stories. Measures of interest were detection of inappropriateness and regulation of study time for the stories in accordance with detection. Children read and studied two stories, one appropriate and one inappropriate, compared the two stories for ease of learning, and were then tested for knowledge of the two stories. A second series of two stories was then completed in the same fashion.

Differences favoring the more successful students over the less successful were found in difficulty ratings for stories and in justification for these ratings. The more successful students studied longer for the more difficult stories than for the easier stories, whereas less successful students studied the stories for approximately equal amounts of time.

Owings et al. (1980) conclude that despite the fact they seemed to be motivated to perform well, the less successful students did not adjust study time on the basis of the difficulty of the task. The researchers point out that lack of task familiarity is not a sound explanation for results, as all subjects had participated in a pilot study using the same procedure.

It seems, rather, that both the young children and the less successful learners "failed to regulate learning strategically and spontaneously" (Paris & Lindauer, 1982, p. 339). Poor cognitive monitoring, lack of declarative knowledge about tasks, or gaps in procedural (or "conditional") knowledge about strategies is most likely to blame. In any case, the first-grade memorizers and less successful fifth-grade story learners gave no indication of invoking a cognitive strategy of differential time allocation to make cognitive progress (i.e., to remember the objects or learn the content of the stories).

Text Reinspection

The text reinspection strategy is another obvious, adaptive strategy with particularly high benefits in school situations. The strategy involves (a) noting memory limitations (i.e., that information once read is not now remembered); and (b) intentional reaccessing of portions of text that provide the information. The strategy capitalizes on the permanence of print, an advantage written language offers over spoken language to learners who are aware of the distinction. It may well be that this strategy, and others like it that help overcome the capacity limitations of working memory, are among the most important routines learners acquire to assist them in studying practical problems in natural settings (Neisser, 1982), where many of the tasks have an "open-book, take-home exam" quality to them (Flavell, 1976, p. 233). Unfortunately, we have evidence that both children (Garner, Hare, Alexander, Haynes, & Winograd, 1984) and adults (Alexander, Hare, & Garner, 1984) often fail to distinguish between numerous reading and studying settings where text reinspection is "legal" and appropriate and those few test situations where it is "illegal" because in-head, not at-hand, information is being elicited.

"When" and "where" information (i.e., flexible application) is very important to successful employment of this strategy. As Garner et al. (1983) note, rereading an entire text in all instances where information is elusive is an inappropriate application of the strategy. Instead, learners should use reinspection (or, alternatively, "selective rereading" or "text look-backs") when information appears explicitly in the text and "in a style that begins with quick resampling that is followed by detailed rereading of just the appropriate text segment" (Garner et al., 1983, p. 446). They should direct their attention intentionally to only certain sets of textual information (DiVesta, Hayward, & Orlando, 1979; Goelman, 1982). Garner et al. (1983) point out that academic gains (for example, answering a

cussing this study, "the fact that good readers attempt to teach the lookback strategy to younger children indicates that they are well aware of the usefulness of this strategy for learning" (p. 63).

The tutoring paradigm was used again by Garner, Macready, and Wagoner (1984) in a study designed to investigate the order in which the components of the strategy are acquired. It was assumed that a strategy is indeed a sequence of activities and that learners at different levels of expertise may well have acquired some, but not all, of the sequence. The components investigated were (a) deciding that information already read is not remembered and that undifferentiated rereading, at the minimum, must be undertaken; (b) deciding that a portion of the text contains the information, and that the material must be scanned to locate this segment, typically using either rather vague topical or spatial memory for location of information in the passage (see Christie & Just, 1976) or key words in the question to assist in visual search; (c) deciding that, in certain instances, information needed is not in the text, and rereading is not indicated; and (d) deciding to manipulate the text (i.e., combine ideas across sentence boundaries) in searching for information. The components studied were the result of task analysis, involving both reexamination of data from earlier investigations and examination of "think-aloud" protocols of adults applying the strategy to natural text-processing tasks. Tutoring behaviors of fifth-grade students at two achievement levels as they worked with third-grade student-confederates were examined as overt manifestations of strategy components already acquired.

One linear hierarchy fit the data for both reader groups; that is, both successful and unsuccessful readers seemed to have acquired strategies in the following order: undifferentiated rereading skill, text sampling, differentiation of lookback and non-lookback situations, and text manipulation. However, substantial differences in proportions of subjects in the two groups having acquired particular components also emerged. Predictably, the pattern was one of less proficient readers displaying fewer component behaviors than their proficient-reader peers. Garner, Macready, and Wagoner (1984) suggest that the ordering provides empirical impetus to intervention research designed to teach the text reinspection strategy and perhaps, eventually to instructional practice.

All of this text reinspection work conducted by Garner and her colleagues shows a positive relation between successful use of the strategy and global reading performance level. One might argue that the poor readers' failure was not due to monitoring or strategy deficits, but rather to decoding and comprehension difficulties at the local level, a failure that would preclude the more sophisticated detecting and remedying behaviors from ever emerging. It is important to note that low levels of word recognition error and high levels of success in answering non-lookback questions were found in all three studies discussed. These results were taken as evidence of decodability and comprehensibility of materials for subjects in the studies. Thus it seems that the deficits were strategic, not code-breaking ones. Within the strategic deficiency category, problems may well lie in lack of knowledge of strategies, inability to choose an appropriate strategy for a particular occasion, ineffective monitoring of strategy effectiveness (Forrest-Pressley & Gillies, 1983) or some combination of these factors.

Text Summarization

The text summarization strategy differs somewhat from study time allocation and text reinspection in that the latter are both primarily cognitive strategies used when cognitions fail or are expected to fail (e.g., items are not recalled, as in Masur et al., 1973; or inappropriate segments in stories are detected, as in Owings et al., 1980; or information once read in text is not remembered, as in the work done by Garner and her colleagues). Text summarization, on the other hand, is as useful as a metacognitive strategy, a strategy to monitor cognitive progress, as it is as a cognitive strategy. As Palincsar and Brown (1983) note, if a reader cannot produce an adequate synopsis of what has been read, this is a clear sign that remedial action, perhaps rereading, is called for. As a cognitive strategy, of course, a self-generated summary every so often in a reading/studying task can be an excellent way of synthesizing information, perhaps from multiple sources, perhaps from diverse perspectives.

Because summarization is a tool for making cognitive progress and for monitoring it, and because summaries are common academic tasks in their own right, text summarization has great educational importance. Use of the strategy involves (a) judgment of which ideas in a text are important, and which are unimportant; (b) application of rules for condensing text; and (c) production of an abbreviated text in oral or written form. Brown and her colleagues are responsible for most of the recent work on differences in summarization strategy use among learners. The results of all of this work can be presented succinctly: The ability to provide an adequate summary of a lengthy text is a late-developing skill (Brown, 1981).

Brown and Smiley (1977) did the initial work probing age-related differences in judging importance of ideas. Subjects in grade 3, 5, and 7 and college read and listened to unfamiliar narratives. Narratives were presented with one previously identified pausal unit per line (college students not participating in the study had read the stories and placed vertical lines at all places where a reader might pause, a use of a procedure first proposed by Johnson, 1970). Subjects were told some of the less important units of the narratives could be eliminated. They were asked to cross out units that were least important, less important, and only somewhat important, in succession, using different colored pencils. The younger children's ratings of structural importance differed from those given by adults prior to the outset of the study. Below the seventh-grade level, there was little distinction provided by subjects among the four levels of judged importance. Even without apparent awareness of relative importance of units, however, the younger children followed the older subjects in favoring the important units in recall.

Brown and Day (1983) turned their attention to the application of rules for condensing text. They modified the three macrorules suggested by Kintsch and van Dijk (1978) to a set of six rules: (a) deletion of unnecessary material; (b) deletion of redundancy; (c) substitution of a superordinate term for a list of items; (d) use of a superordinate term for a list of actions; (e) selection of a topic sentence provided in text; and (f) invention of a topic sentence if none appears explicitly in text. Age differences in application of the six rules when paraphrasing expository text were then examined.

Subjects in grades 5, 7, and 10 and college were presented with two expository texts that had been constructed so that the six rules could be applied. Subjects were asked to read a text three times and then to write a good summary of the text. When this was done, they were asked to write a 60-word summary (without referring to the unconstrained summary). The procedure was repeated in a second session for the second text.

Both of the deletion rules were used effectively by all age groups. Age differences emerged for use of superordination and selection of a topic sentence. Application of the invention rule was least effective; very few fifth-grade or seventh-grade subjects used it, 10th-grade subjects used invention on about a third of appropriate occasions, and even college subjects used the rule in about only half of the instances where it would have been appropriate. College students produced better written texts than younger subjects, not surprisingly.

Brown and Day (1983) suggest that the rules differ in their ease of application because they demand different degrees of text manipulation from learners and because they differ in the extent to which they depart from an existing pattern used by younger learners, one Brown and Day label the "copy-delete" strategy. Deletion rules and even supordination map rather nicely onto this strategy of either eliminating or copying nearly verbatim the words in the text. Selection and invention rules do not. For selection, one must accord special status to topic sentences. For invention, one must add something of one's own, a synthesis of information in one's own words. Brown and Day point out that "copy-delete" is a partially adequate strategy, in that it produces something recognizable as an abbreviated, if not much altered, form of the original text. The fact that a primitive strategy that works to some degree must be replaced with a more sophisticated attack on the task of summarization can be an impediment to progress (Brown, Bransford, Ferrara, & Campione, 1983).

Brown, Day, and Jones (1983) investigated the text-summarization strategy further. Subjects in grades 5, 7, and 11 and college read and studied folk stories which had been divided into pausal units rated for structural importance. After learning the stories "perfectly" in their own words, subjects were asked to provide recall protocols for the narratives. Then, for a single story, subjects were told to pretend they were newspaper reporters and to write a summary of the story for their paper, a short version using the smallest number of words possible; the story was available to them at this time. Next, they were told an editor had cut their space, and the story needed to be rewritten in 40 words. In a final phase, a limit of 20 words was imposed.

Age effects were found for the unconstrained, the 40-word and the 20-word summaries. Most subjects included more of only the most important information when space pressure was exerted, but departure from the "copy-delete" pattern varied by age, with, for instance, 69% of grade 11 and college student subjects' productions being true paraphrases, while only 16% of the younger subjects' productions were so rated.

Still another study showing age-related differences in text-summarization proficiency was conducted recently (Garner, 1985) using a rather novel research paradigm, an adaptation of a method proposed for writing research by Bracewell (1983). Grade 9, grade 11, and college students were asked to generate optimal and nonoptimal summaries for a long expository text, based on their sense of what makes a short summary acceptable or unacceptable. Two alternative hypotheses were tested. If learners at various ages are not aware of what makes a summary acceptable, they would not be likely to differentiate optimal and nonoptimal products on measures of interest. On the other hand, if learners cannot produce adept summaries, they would be unlikely to achieve high scores on the same measures for the optimal product. The deficiencies (i.e., awareness gaps or production problems) are not mutually exclusive. The measures of interest in the study were (a) number of ideas judged important included, (b) number of words used, and (c) integration level for information judged important, a measure of text manipulation, of deviation from the "copy-delete" pattern.

All subjects demonstrated a substantial amount of awareness about including important ideas and very few subjects at any age demonstrated either awareness or production ability for integrating these ideas. Information integration, of course, represents a means, if it is exercised, to the end of producing summaries of important information in relatively few words. The youngest and the oldest subjects differed in production of important ideas and in production of succinct summaries.

In the area of text summarization facility, as in so many other metacognitive areas, there is also evidence of performance differences related to reading achievement level. Winograd (1984) asked good and poor eighth-grade readers and a group of adult readers to read expository passages and to write 60-word summaries. They also rated the importance of individual sentences to whole texts and selected the five most important sentences in each text. Prior to any work with the passages, subjects were interviewed about the text summarization strategy.

Winograd (1984) notes that the most central feature of a summary is that it contains the most important ideas in the original passage. Just as Garner (1985) found a substantial amount of awareness of this feature among ninth-grade subjects and up, Winograd found that most good and poor eighth-grade readers made an explicit reference to this feature in their interview responses. A second finding of the study was a higher correlation between good readers' judgments of importance and those of adults than between those of poor readers and adults. The relation between information judged important and that included in the summaries, however, was weak for poor readers, moderate for good readers, and strong for adults. This discrepancy between what is judged as important and what is included in summaries by poor readers parallels Brown and Smiley's (1977) finding of a low awareness of importance of ideas, but inclusion of the important ideas in recall protocols among younger children.

We conclude our discussion of differences in strategy use among learners much as we ended the discussion on knowledge and experience differences. The convergent findings from recent research can be summarized: Young children and poor readers are not nearly as adept as older children/adults and good readers, respectively, in engaging in planful activities either to make cognitive progress or to monitor it. Younger, less proficient learners are not nearly as "resourceful" in completing a variety of reading and studying tasks important in academic settings. The correlational data are quite clear. In chapter 6, we return to the young children and poor readers, who are clearly at a disadvantage in school because of deficiencies in strategic repertoires. In that chapter, some very successful intervention efforts designed to teach the flexible application of cognitive and metacognitive strategies will be reported.

Chapter 4

Methodological Concerns: Metacognitive Interviews

Young children and poor readers know less and have more misconceptions about important characteristics of cognition than do older children and good readers, respectively. We know this to be true from the results of a number of carefully crafted interview studies, such as those described in chapter 3.

A difficulty already mentioned in chapter 3 is that asking children, particularly young children, about their cognitive processing poses some special problems. Because of limited language skills, confusion about general processes being queried, or inability to speculate about hypothetical events, young children may be at a disadvantage in responding to interview probes. This means that metacognitive "deficiencies" may reflect not what the child respondents know or do not know, but rather what they can or cannot tell an interviewer. It may be the case, then, that we have systematically underestimated the stable knowledge, the knowledge available when needed, that young children have about person, task, and strategy aspects of a wide variety of cognitive processes.

Methodological problems are not restricted to interviews with children. Concerns about underestimating (and overestimating) knowledge of adult subjects have appeared in the literature for some time. General concerns applying to interviews with subjects of any age will be presented first in this chapter. Next, concerns about interviewing children will be offered. Then, a summary of suggestions for the collection and interpretation of verbal-report data from interviews will be provided. Finally, alternative methods will be considered.

General Concerns About Interview Data

Accessibility

The most basic concern expressed in the literature is that we may not be able to observe the workings of our own minds with any accuracy (see Nisbett & Wilson, 1977). That is, we may be mostly unaware of the operation of memory, attention, comprehension processes, and the like. Anecdotal evidence for this anti-introspection view is the common experience of our being unable to articulate how we have, for instance, remembered a name, attended to a visual detail, or comprehended a joke. In such instances, we often find ourselves stammering about how we "just did it," how the process "just worked." Indeed, these processes do seem to "work" rather automatically on many occasions.

Ericsson and Simon (1980) point out that there is a negative relationship between amount of practice of cognitive processes and awareness of intermediate stages of the processes. As parts of processes become automated, only the final products (the much-rehearsed name or joke, for instance) are left in memory, available for reporting to an interviewer. Automatic processes are, after all, "unconscious" in the sense that conscious attention is not necessary for their activation (Cavanaugh & Perlmutter, 1982).

How do subjects comply with interviewers' requests to provide them with details of processing when the details are no longer available in memory? A number of possibilities exist. Subjects may draw inferences about what probably has occurred in processing and report these events without any indication of their inferred status. Or subjects may draw upon prior information of what "ideal" thinkers know and do, perhaps what teachers have prescribed, and report this information as their own. Or, finally, subjects may provide incomplete, if veridical, reports that may be mistakenly interpreted as complete pictures of processing. The outcome in each of these cases is a process-report disparity, an undesirable state of affairs for researchers using interviews to uncover detailed knowledge about cognitions.

As both Nisbett and Wilson (1977) and Ericsson and Simon (1980) note, the accuracy of subjects' reports varies in predictable ways. Because we know that "processes that have been so often repeated as to have become automated are less often and less fully reported" (Ericsson & Simon, 1980, p. 242), we should avoid asking respondents about these processes. Introspection, it seems, is a valid tool for scientific observation or an invalid tool under different conditions (Kail & Bisanz, 1982; Kellogg, 1982).

Memory Failure

Accuracy of verbal reports of knowledge and actions varies, then, with amount of automaticity of processes being described. Accuracy of reports varies with the interval between processing and reporting as well. For instance, if an interviewer asks a respondent about the efficiency of oral reading versus silent reading, and the reader has not read aloud for years, the description of how the operations work for that reader is likely to be quite inaccurate or incomplete or both. Even with less extreme examples, perhaps asking children how to manage the situation of a disruptive conversation in the library when such an incident has not occurred recently or asking readers what makes something difficult to read when frustration-level materials have not been encountered for some time, a problem exists. Respondents must introspect about person, task, and strategy information at some distance. One account, then, of skimpy reporting in interviews remains a meager knowledge base, but an equally plausible one is failure by subjects to remember the cognitive objects and events targeted by the interview questions.

White (1980) sees memory failure as a particularly serious problem for verbal-report data. He points out that reports taken at a great distance from processes they are intended to tap may tell us nothing about consciousness at all. He urges reduction of the intervals between processing and reporting. Ericsson and Simon (1980), in prescribing the same action, mention that interference is an additional problem. They note that information that is confused with the events being probed in the interview may be retrieved by respondents in cases where inquiry substantially lags processing.

An experiment was designed (Garner, 1982) to test the effects of processing-reporting distance on completeness of reports of text summarization activity. Twenty college students participated in the study as summarizers, and 20 additional students participated as observers. Students were paired, roles were allocated, and summarizers were assigned to either a same-day writing and reporting condition or a delayed-reporting condition.

In both conditions, summarizers were told to read an expository text, to summarize the text succinctly with original material available, and to "pay attention to what you do and what you think while you complete the tasks." Observers were simply told to note all overt behaviors of summarizers, including utterances, and to record them in writing, with no exchange between summarizers and observers allowed. Same-day summarizers then wrote down everything they remembered doing and thinking. No cues to particular strategic behaviors were provided. Delayed-reporting summarizers performed the same task 2 days later.

Though summaries of students assigned to the two groups did not vary significantly, reports did. Same-day summarizers reported more cognitive events; had fewer "missed opportunities" (i.e., instances in which observers documented external indices of cognitive activity that summarizers failed to note); and included fewer trivial events than did delayed-report summarizers. These results support White's (1980) position. Accuracy, completeness, and amount of interference in the retrospective verbalizations all seem to have been affected by the interval between strategy use and strategy report in the study.

Knowledge Versus Use

Particularly in interviews designed to assess strategic knowledge, respondents can tell interviewers about strategies that are useful, about strategies they profess to use, when in fact they do not employ the strategies in "real-world" cognitive processing at all. Perhaps they have the ability to use an effective strategy, but not the habit of doing so. This dilemma led Phifer and Glover (1982) to caution, "Don't take students' word for what they do while reading" (p. 194). Students are particularly likely to mimic instructors' statements about the use of highly desirable strategies (Forrest-Pressley & Waller, 1984a, 1984b; Ryan, 1981).

Cavanaugh and Borkowski (1980) designed a study to examine the connections between memory knowledge and memory behavior. Children in kindergarten and grades 1, 3, and 5 were administered the entire Kreutzer et al. (1975) interview in one session. Then, approximately 2 weeks later, the children were given an opportunity to engage in strategic memory behavior for three tasks. The tasks were (a) free sorting and subsequent recalling of a 15-item list, with no constraints on study time; (b) sorting of a 30-item list into file boxes with category picture cues and subsequent recalling of the items; and (c) copying 20 letters of the alphabet and then recalling the letters and writing them down on a blank sheet of paper.

Interview results replicated the Kreutzer et al. (1975) findings. In general, older children were more aware of memory variables than were younger children, and substantial developmental differences were found between children in grades 1 and 3. Strong age-related differences were found for the three performance measures as well. Older children generally used more complex strategies, showed better recall, and demonstrated more clustering during recall. For the analysis of particular interest in the study, metamemory-memory connections, all memory measures except clustering for the alphabet task correlated significantly with at least seven metamemory subtests. No systematic developmental trends emerged in the metamemory-memory correlations.

Cavanaugh and Borkowski's (1980) inability to find "intuitively obvious or predictable patterns among the significant correlations" (p. 451) means that we are left confused about which specific aspects of memory knowledge and memory performance are strongly related. However, the moderate, broad-based correlations found across age groups are promising. It seems that we can argue that at least some of what we verbalize about cognition is related to how we in fact deploy cognitive resources.

We can also argue, however, that we can on occasion "tell more than we can know" (Nisbett & Wilson, 1977); that is, we can discuss processes that we neither wholly understand nor use, and we can know more than we use routinely in the everyday solution of cognitive problems. A task for theorists of cognition is the prediction of situations when telling what we know *and* use is most likely to occur. A requirement of researchers of cognition, until such predictions are broadly accepted, is the combination of verbal-report data with performance data. The latter can be used to validate or invalidate interview claims of broad strategy use.

Inadvertent Cuing

Respondents in interview situations can, knowingly or unknowingly, guess at what the investigator wants by way of a response and can respond accordingly (Meichenbaum et al., 1979). As Bower states quite unequivocally, "In normal conversation, even with a child, the answer you get to a question depends very much on what your listener assumes you want" (Bower, 1978, p. 350). Minimizing the number of probes used and constructing questions to be quite undirected (see Ericsson & Simon, 1980) are the standard solutions for this problem.

An example of undirected eliciting of information is Garner's (1982) instruction to same-day and delayed-reporting summarizers to write down everything they remembered doing and thinking. A more directed, if global, probe would have been the question "Did you use any strategies to help you summarize?" A still more specific directed probe would have been the question "Did you use the strategy of inventing a topic sentence when none appeared in the text?" As Ericsson and Simon (1980) suggest, the evidence of strategy use gleaned from the undirected probe is stronger than that elicited by the general directed probe, which in turn is stronger than that gotten from the specific directed probe. An increase in directedness brings an increase in hints to respondents about what the interviewer expects to hear.

Specific Concerns About Interview Data from Young Children

Verbal Facility

When an adult interviewer asks a young child a question about cognitive processing, the child can fail to provide a full response for a number of reasons other than lack of knowledge. One reason is limited language skills (Cavanaugh & Perlmutter, 1982). Even in instances in which cognitions are generally accessible and remembered, it is possible that they cannot be verbalized. (It should be noted that adults, too, vary in verbal skill and inclination. Miyake and Norman, 1979, remind us that considerable individual differences exist in the tendency to speak aloud.)

Another reason for meager interview responses is adult-child variation in use of language, so that a question intended to elicit one sort of response in fact brings something altogether different. Blank (1975) discusses research showing that questions such as "Why did you do X?" are intended to elicit a wealth of task-characteristic information, but instead often bring responses that make motivation for behavior explicit (e.g., "I'm smart," "I was tired," "I didn't try hard"). Such motivation-oriented responses are quite appropriate when "why" questions about action arise in nonresearch settings, but they do not provide the information the researcher seeks.

Techniques have been devised that reduce the need for verbal fluency in research settings. Yussen and Bird (1979), for instance, developed a nonverbal technique for evaluating memory, communication, and attention knowlege. To assess preschool and first-grade children's understanding that length of list, amount of interfering noise, amount of task completion time, and age all affect performance on cognitive problems, pairs of pictures were used. From an adult perspective, the child in one picture of each pair had an easier problem than the child in the other picture. Children were asked to select which picture depicted the harder job. The evidence that children's understanding of length, noise, time, and age effects on performance is similar across the three domains of memory, communication, and attention is important. Superior performance among 6-year-olds, compared to 4-year-olds, is also important. Given that lack of verbal fluency cannot account for the 4-year-old's performance, there appear to be genuine age differences in knowledge.

One problem in using pictorial stimuli is that ceiling effects are common. Yussen and Bird (1979) encountered this problem in presenting the noise picture pairs to 6-year-old subjects. Cavanaugh and Perlmutter (1982) suggest that the problem can be avoided by making differences between pictures less obvious and by tailoring the task to fit the ability level of the subjects.

Miller and Bigi's (1979) use of a recognition paradigm to study attention knowledge (see chapter 3) is another example of a methodological alternative to reduce heavy verbalization demands. In this instance, as in the Yussen and Bird (1979) pictorial study, children chose options from among those provided.

Hypothetical Situations, General Cognitive Events

Brown (1984) argues that the ability to construct possible worlds and to operate within them is a late-developing skill, which many younger respondents in interview studies probably have not acquired. Even given concrete props to assist in fantasy building, these younger subjects will be unlikely to fully understand what is being asked of them. Actually, Ericsson and Simon (1980) advise against asking even adults to perform the mental gyrations necessary to create hypothetical cognitive processing situations and then to imagine themselves as active participants in those situations.

Probing general cognitive events constitutes another problem in research with children, who seldom have general theories of cognition and are more at ease describing specific just-experienced events. Yussen, Mathews, and Hiebert (1982) have criticized a series of investigations of knowledge about reading for just this reason. When children are asked, "What is reading?" or, "If someone didn't know how to read, what would you tell him?" (note that the latter question is hypothetical as well as general), and respond with high frequency that they do not know, Yussen and his colleagues suggest children may have been uncertain about what aspect of reading they were expected to discuss. The high frequency of a second sort of response, reference to a specific classroom practice, further supports the point Yussen et al. make about children not being "formal definers" of things. They rely on specific events of importance to them for their interview responses.

Yussen et al. (1982) offer a research alternative to asking young children general questions about general events. Using reading as an example, they suggest providing vignettes about children reading, emphasizing a particular aspect of the process, and asking the child how salient this activity is to reading. Yussen et al. suggest that the method is sensitive to young children's cognitive and linguistic abilities.

Suggestions for Collecting and Interpreting Interview Data

From the preceding discussion of concerns about interviews, a list of prescriptions for researchers has emerged:

1. Avoid asking about processes that are engaged in automatically and which are therefore inaccessible upon reflection. Complex, difficult, and novel tasks should be better targets than much-practiced simple routines.
2. Reduce the interval between processing and reporting.
3. Use multiple methods that do not share the same sources of error (e.g., interview questions and performance measures) to assess knowledge and use of strategies. Data from performance measures can corroborate (or fail to corroborate) data from verbal reports.
4. Avoid experimenter bias effects by using undirected probes.
5. Consider using techniques that reduce the verbalization demands for respondents, particularly if respondents are young children.
6. Avoid hypothetical scenarios and very general questions, particularly in interviewing young children.

From the earlier discussion of the concern of Meichenbaum et al. (1979) about data reduction (see chapter 3), we will add a seventh prescription:

7. Assess inter-rater agreement in reducing total verbal responses to themes of interest.

A last prescription comes from Cavanaugh and Perlmutter (1982) who mention a concern far broader than metacognitive interview research. That concern is the general lack of reliability assessment for interviews. Cavanaugh and Perlmutter claim, rightly, that very few investigators have examined the stability of metacognitive interview responses over time. As a matter of fact, a search of the recent literature reveals only one published account of such reliability assessment (Kurtz, Reid, Borkowski, & Cavanaugh, 1982). The Kurtz et al. study yielded significant, but low, levels of reliability for metamemory subtest performance on two occasions. Administration of interview items on more than one occasion is an absolute necessity if we are to uncover the relatively stable information about cognition that we seek. The eighth prescription, then, is this:

8. Assess consistency of interview responses over time for a group of subjects.

The reason the concerns expressed in this chapter are so important, of course, is that when we uncover "metacognitive differences" among learners we have interviewed, we want those differences to reflect differences in knowledge, not differences in verbalizing skill. We want to know what respondents know or do not know, not what they can tell or cannot tell. As much as possible, we want to reduce the nontrivial measurement problems associated with the interview method. One solution researchers have adopted, though seldom with young children, is use of "think-aloud" procedures in preference to interviews. We turn our attention to this method next.

The Think-Aloud Method as an Alternative to Interviews

Description of the Method

In using the think-aloud method, researchers provide a task and ask subjects to say aloud "everything they think and everything that occurs to them while performing the task, no matter how trivial it may seem" (Hayes & Flower, 1980, p. 4). If subjects become so engrossed in task completion that they fall silent, they are nudged back to verbalizing with comments from the researcher such as "Remember, tell me what you are thinking."

Think-aloud procedures are clearly more task-specific than most interviews in which metacognitive knowledge about management of a great many tasks is probed. The purpose for eliciting the concurrent verbalizations, however, is much the same as that for eliciting the retrospective verbalizations in interviews: to learn what subjects know and do in interesting problem-solving situations. The think-aloud method is usually selected in preference to other methods because of its yield of rich data about processes "that are invisible to other methods" (Hayes & Flower, 1983, p. 218).

The procedure is applied in a series of steps. First, the think-aloud report is elicited, either with rather general instructions (e.g., "Tell me what you are thinking as you complete this task") or with more specific interspersed probes (e.g., "What are you studying now?" or "What background information did you need to solve that particular problem?" or "What is your next step?"). As the subject verbalizes thoughts and actions in sequence, his or her remarks are recorded, sometimes on videotape but more often on audiotape. The researcher takes notes on both nonverbal signs of problem-solving and contextual information (e.g., timing of specific probe questions). As Afflerbach and Johnston (1984) suggest, features of spoken discourse, such as sarcasm, need to be noted. Data from tapes and the researcher's notes are transcribed. The resulting transcripts are called "protocols." Kail and Bisanz (1982) point out that accurate transcription can be an arduous task in itself. Garbled speech and ambiguous gestures, for instance, make interpretive decisions necessary.

The next step in the sequence also presents difficulties. At this point, data are categorized. Much of the information in the protocols proves to be irrelevant; only information that fits into theoretically relevant a priori categories or into "emerging" categories is considered. Inter-rater agreement on categorization is assessed. Disagreements in categorization are resolved in the standard fashion, with a conference between raters or with invoking of a decision from a third rater.

When categories have been established and data have been clustered, the distribution of verbal responses across categories for different groups of learners (usually experts and novices in a particular domain) is examined. In some instances, verbal responses are compared to computer simulation models for the purpose of corroboration of a particular model of cognitive activity.

Think-aloud techniques have been used in a variety of ways to study a variety of problems. Two protocol samples are given here. In Figure 4.1, a "water jug problem" resolution (Hayes & Flower, 1980) is provided with intermittent comments from the experimenter. In Figure 4.2, a planning episode (Hayes-Roth & Hayes-Roth, 1979), a college graduate's uninterrupted protocol, is presented in abbreviated form. Some discussion of what we learn about what subjects know and do is provided for each protocol.

Hayes and Flower (1980) provide some analysis of the protocol presented in Figure 4.1. They note, for instance, that (a) the division route pursued in comment 1 is a "dead end," and the subject does not pursue this route for long; (b) the tactic used changes from adding 9s or 6s separately (lines 4 and 5) to combining 9s and 6s together and attempting subtraction of the combinations from 42 (lines 6 through 10); (c) the subject fails to note, at this juncture, that 6 + 6 + 9 solves the problem; (d) lines 12 through 14 contain many statements of low confidence in multiplication skills; (e) in lines 18–19, the subject realizes that if he could subtract 3 quarts from 24 quarts, he could solve the problem; (f) in line 20, the experimenter slips from a noncommittal stance, and provides approval of the line of thinking being pursued by the subject; (g) between lines 21 and 24, a shift in thinking from subtracting from 24 quarts to adding to 18 quarts appears; and (h) the problem is solved in line 25.

Hayes and Flower (1980) summarize these processes as an initial phase of forward search (i.e., search suggested by the problem statements alone) through a sequence of increasingly complex arithmetic procedures, followed by a phase of means-ends analysis where the subject assesses distance from the goal (in this case, subtracting 3 quarts) and where a solution is found. Hayes and Flower note that protocols are incomplete in the sense that many processes are not reported by subjects. The psychologist's task, according to them, is taking the incomplete record together with knowledge of the task and of human capabilities and

Figure 4.1.   Protocol of a water jug problem (Hayes & Flower, 1980, p. 5)

The Problem

Given Jug A, which contains 9 quarts, Jug B, 42 quarts, and Jug C, 6 quarts, measure out exactly 21 quarts. (The jugs are non-calibrated.)

The Protocol
  1. Uh, the first thing that's apparent is half of B, is uh, the
  2. amount that you want.
  3. E: Uh huh.
  4. Um, you can't get 21 from just multiplying up A or C.
  5. You get 18 and 18 respectively, that's as close as you can get,
  6. I guess. Um, so I'll try to think of the different combinations that
  7. might . . . come up with a surplus . . . or deficit of the 21 quarts . . . and
  8. 9 and 6 are, 15 . . . if you took two 9's and two 6's, you'd have 30 which
  9. would leave you . . . and pour them into the 42 container, you'd have a,
 10. an open space of a, 12, which means nothing. How about . . . see . . . now I'm
 11. trying to think of how close to 42 you can get with a 9 and the 6 quantities.
 12. You can get . . . I forget the 7 table. It's been a long time since I've
 13. had to multiply or anything so you'll have to give me some time. Um,
 14. 9 times 5 is 45 . . . hm, 6 times 7 is 42, I think. Is that right?
 15. E: Uh huh.
 16. OK, so you can, uh . . . fill B with C, evenly . . .
 17. E: You could . . .
 18. So . . . if you were to take . . . 36 . . . hm, oh, uh, 6 times 4 is 24, and if you, uh
 19. What I'm trying to get rid of is, is 3 quarts there . . .
 20. E: Good.
 21. So if you were to, um . . . still 24. I, I was trying to think possibly,
 22. some way of . . . the difference between the 6 and 9 is 3 quarts. I
 23. was trying to think of . . . a way to uh . . . Oh how about . . . you put the 3, 6
 24. quart quantity into the 42 bottle, which is 18, then the runoff from
 25. pouring a 9 into a 6 which is 3 and 18 is 21.
 26. E: Good.

inferring from these a model of the underlying psychological processes by which the subject has performed the task. They compare analyzing a protocol to "following the tracks of a porpoise, which occasionally reveals itself by breaking the surface of the sea" (Hayes & Flower, 1980, p. 9). We will return to this point when we discuss concerns about the application of think-aloud procedures. We turn now to an errand-planning task.

This protocol has 47 segments in all, of which the initial 10 appear in Figure 4.2. Hayes-Roth and Hayes-Roth (1979) provide analysis of the protocol. They note, about sections 1–10, for instance, that (a) segments 1–4 are devoted to using world knowledge to classify errands as things that must be accomplished ("primaries") or things that can be put off ("secondaries"), and to noting that given time constraints, the goal will be difficult to achieve; (b) in segments 5–7, the subject notes the initial loca-

Figure 4.2.   Protocol for an errand-planning task (Hayes-Roth & Hayes-Roth, 1979, pp. 277–278)

The Problem

You have just finished working out at the health club. It is 11:00 and you can plan the rest of your day as you like. However, you must pick up your car from the Maple Street parking garage by 5:30 and then head home. You'd also like to see a movie today, if possible. Show times at both theaters are 1:00, 3:00, and 5:00. Both movies are on your "must see" list, but go to whichever one most conveniently fits into your plan. Your other errands are as follows: 1) pick up medicine for your dog at the vet, 2) buy a fan belt for your refrigerator at the appliance store, 3) check out two of the three luxury apartments, 4) meet a friend for lunch at one of the restaurants, 5) buy a toy for your dog at the pet store, 6) pick up your watch at the watch repair, 7) special order a book at the bookstore, 8) buy fresh vegetables at the grocery, 9) buy a gardening magazine at the newsstand, and 10) go to the florist to send flowers to a friend in the hospital. [Not all errands were expected to be completed. A map depicting a hypothetical town was available during planning.]

The Protocol

1. Let's go back down the errand list. Pick up medicine for the dog at veterinary supplies. That's definitely a primary, anything taking care of health. Fan belt for refrigerator. Definitely a primary because you need to keep the refrigerator. Checking out two out of three luxury apartments. It's got to be a secondary, another browser. Meet the friend at one of the restaurants for lunch. All right. Now, that's going to be able to be varied, I hope. That's a primary though because it is an appointment, something you have to do. Buy a toy for the dog at the pet store. If you pass it, sure. If not, the dog can play with something else. Movie in one of the movie theaters. Better write that down, those movie times, 1, 3, or 5. Write that down on my sheet just to remember. And that's a primary because it's something I have to do. Pick up the watch at the watch repair. That's one of those borderline ones. Do you need your watch or not? Give it a primary. Special order a book at the bookstore.
2. We're having an awful lot of primaries in this one. It's going to be a busy day.
3. Fresh vegetables at the grocery. That's another primary. You need the food. Gardening magazine at the newsstand. Definitely secondary. All the many obligations of life.
4. Geez, can you believe all these primaries?
5. All right. We are now at the health club.
6. What is going to be the closest one?
7. The appliance store is a few blocks away. The medicine for the dog at the vet's office isn't too far away. Movie theaters — let's hold off on that for a little while. Pick up the watch. That's all the way across town. Special order a book at the bookstore.
8. Probably it would be best if we headed in a southeasterly direction. Start heading this way. I can see later on there are a million things I want to do in that part of town.

Figure 4.2. *(Continued)*

9. No we're not. We could end up with a movie just before we get the car. I had thought at first that I might head in a southeasterly direction because there's a grocery store, a watch repair, a movie theater all in that general area. Also a luxury apartment. However, near my parking lot also is a movie, which would make it convenient to get out of the movie and go to the car. But I think we can still end up that way.

10. All right. Apparently the closest one to the health club is going to be the vet's shop. So I might as well get that out of the way. It's a primary and it's the closest. We'll start . . .

tion and begins to sequence close errands, not clustering errands or taking the final location into consideration; (c) a strategy change occurs in segment 8, when a group of errands in the southeast corner of town are noticed; and (d) the subject vacillates between a sequencing of individual errands backward from the final location (segment 9) and beginning with the closest errand (segment 10).

Hayes-Roth and Hayes-Roth (1979) note that across all 47 segments the subject frequently plans low-level sequences of errands or routes in the absence, and sometimes in violation, of a prescriptive high-level plan. They also point out that the ability to simulate execution of a plan mentally and to use the results to guide additional planning is important for successful completion of the errand-planning task.

Concerns About Think-Aloud Data

The think-aloud method is not free from criticism. It is true that memory failure is not a problem, for the distance between process and report is one of seconds rather than of days or weeks. It is also true that knowledge-use discrepancies are rather improbable, as the report is a blow-by-blow description of what resources are actually being used; product data such as water jug arithmetic or errands divided into primary and secondary categories accompany the process report and provide corroborative data on processing. Furthermore, the highly specific tasks given subjects cannot be described as either "hypothetical" or "general," so those concerns that apply to interviews do not pose difficulties for think-aloud procedures. Finally, both consistency in coding of verbal output and consistency of output over time (the inter-rater agreement and subject response reliability issues, respectively) are not problems for the think-aloud method; agreement information is collected routinely and subjects are asked to solve a series of problems for which solution behavior is examined.

Three concerns mentioned as problematic for interviews, however, remain as problems for the think-aloud method. Inadvertent cuing is one. Investigators can cue entire protocols with specific directed comments at the outset of the activity. A blatant example would be eliciting the errand-planning protocol with a directive such as "Here is a list of errands you want to accomplish. Here is a map. Use the map to cluster errands by proximity if you wish. Plan how you will complete your errands, and tell me what you are thinking as you go along." A second sort of cuing that can occur is deviation from a noncommittal stance during task completion. The investigator evaluating the water jug protocol did this when he said "good" in line 20 (see Figure 4.1), thereby providing approval of the subject's new line of thinking, and probably altering subsequent thoughts and verbalizations.

A second problem inherent in the use of think-aloud procedures is verbal facility confounding results. When we get a skimpy protocol, we do not know whether limited cognitions, limited language skills, or some combination is the cause. Whether young children can even be instructed to provide sustained verbalizations, a rather unnatural parallel processing activity, is in doubt. Scardamalia and Bereiter (1983) suggest that encouragement, prodding of continuous verbalization, and practice sessions (perhaps while subjects perform a nonverbal activity such as drawing a picture) are essential in collecting think-aloud data from young children. Nearly all of the research to date has been conducted with adult subjects operating with very sophisticated domain-specific knowledge on complex tasks. (I avoided sophisticated physics and engineering thermodynamics examples in favor of more real-world measuring and planning tasks in this chapter.)

The third problem that interviews and think-aloud methods share is that of basic accessibility. Processes that have become automated are not any more available for reporting concurrently than they are retrospectively. Both accuracy and completeness of protocols are threatened by a preponderance of cognitive activity at below-conscious level. When we examine the protocols, we must remember they are but "clues for the underlying processes" (Meichenbaum, 1980, p. 276). This surely is what Hayes and Flower (1980) had in mind when comparing interpretation of a protocol to tracking a mostly submerged propoise.

Still another problem presented by the think-aloud method does not occur in interviewing. That is the potentially serious problem of process disruption and distortion. As Ballstaedt and Mandl (1984) put it, "It has not been clarified whether the unusual task of verbalizing has an effect on the ongoing processes" (p. 334). There are two possible reasons why disruption and distortion of processing might occur: First, moving thought to language may require processes that otherwise would not occur in task resolution, and second, the need for additional processing capacities may interfere with normal processing. The result in either case, of course, is undesirable. Either some operations that do not accurately reflect knowledge and activity beyond the research setting appear in the data, or some important knowledge and activity are not represented in the data. In other words, we get either too much or too little.

Schoenfeld (1983) provides an interesting discussion of the seriousness of the disruption/distortion problem, when he responds to Simon's point (Ericcson & Simon, 1980; Simon, 1979) that "blandly" enticed think-alouds about information readily available to subjects do not change the course or structure of processing. Schoenfeld (1983, p. 347) presented the following problem to college students:

> Estimate, as accurately as you can, how many cells might be in an average-sized adult human body. What is a reasonable upper estimate? A reasonable lower estimate? How much faith do you have in your figures?

Some students generated solo think-alouds, and some students were paired for reporting. Schoenfeld reports that the solo protocols were filled with extraordinarily detailed body-volume computations, whereas the pair protocols were not. Rather than attribute the meticulous, if largely irrelevant, solo work to students' cognitive confusion about bodies and volume, Schoenfeld (1983) suggests that the students were initially bewildered by the task and felt on trial to produce something for a mathematics professor, with no assistance available. Volume computations ad nauseam were the result. Had the protocols been analyzed as veridical representations of allocation of strategic resources, rather than as outcomes of a particular research situation, misinterpretation would surely have resulted. Schoenfeld's example illustrates how processes can be distorted by thought-to-language and contextual demands of the think-aloud method.

Application of the Think-Aloud Method to Reading

Olshavsky (1976–1977) applied the think-aloud technique to reading, in an effort to identify comprehension strategies of good and poor 10th-grade readers. In this study, a continuous protocol was not elicited. Rather, each subject was required to provide a think-aloud response after reading each clause of a short story. Practice was provided. Though the processing of the story was interrupted frequently, no experimenter intrusion occurred after the introduction to the task.

Strategies noted in protocols a minimum of five times were tallied and labeled. The 10 strategies that met this frequency criterion were: personal identification, use of context, synonym substitution, stated failure to understand a word, rereading, inference, addition of information, hypothesis, stated failure to understand a clause, and use of information about the story. There was no evidence in the study that good readers and poor readers used different sets of strategies. Frequency of strategy use did not differ significantly across groups either, although low sample size ($N = 24$), rather than the absence of real differences, may account for this finding. Though results of this study were inconclusive, the investigation represented a first effort to use the think-aloud method in reading research.

Two somewhat similar studies followed Olshavsky's (1976–1977) investigation, one with adults and one with children. Garner and Alexander (1982) also used a reading interruption paradigm, but with interruptions at less frequent intervals. They asked college students to read a *Smithsonian* article of about 4,000 words, stopping four times across the eight pages of text to think aloud (in writing this time) about how they were reading and preparing to answer an announced post-reading question. Garner and Alexander were interested in finding out if any of the students would report attempting to discern the specifics of the question, "psyching out" the instructor, so to speak. Garner and Alexander suggest that this is a very useful strategy to employ in school in instances in which the instructor has not provided the question(s) before reading, and an objective test is to follow the reading.

Half of the adult subjects verbalized trying to figure out what the question might be. These subjects were more accurate in answering the question than subjects who did not verbalize such efforts. Garner and Alexander (1982) note that either a general active style of reading or specific activation of related strategies (e.g., rehearsal of information expected in the question, rereading of particularly important parts of text for this question) could account for the superior performance of question formulators.

Hare and Smith (1982) also used protocol analysis in an investigation of seventh-grade students' strategy verbalizations while reading either a narrative or expository text of about 250 words. Approximately every 50 words, subjects stopped and talked about what they were doing and thinking to help them remember the material. After reading was complete, each subject was told the following: "Okay. You told me some things you did to help remember what you were reading. I showed this story to some other students and they told me things that helped them remember what they were reading. I wanted to know if you did any of these things while you were reading the story I just showed you." The strategies presented in this recognition segment were rehearsing, rereading, skipping parts of the passage, "imaging," changing reading speed, and relating parts of the passage to one's own experience.

Rereading was the strategy most frequently produced and recognized, with approximately equal frequencies of mention for narrative and expository texts. Hare and Smith (1982) suggest that think-aloud techniques have the potential of yielding important diagnostic information about individual readers.

Most think-aloud work has been done with adults. Hare and Smith's (1982) study is one exception. Alvermann's (1984) study with much younger children is still another. Alvermann asked second-grade children to read aloud basal-reader stories and to think aloud after each sentence about what they were thinking and doing while reading. It is important to note that these young children were given individual 30-minute practice sessions in thinking aloud prior to data collection. For this practice work, investigators modeled think-aloud behaviors for a story that was very familiar to the children.

The protocols of these young children differ from the protocols of the older learners who attempted to solve the water jug and errand-planning problems, in that they provide less information about thinking and doing while reading and more information about what is being read; the young children's protocols are, in other words, quite close to text in content. This is apparent in the sample sentences (S) and responses (R) from three different children reading a story called "The Little Hippo."

Child 1

9.   (S) He could not stop crying.
      (R) Know why he couldn't stop crying? 'Cause she—'cause he wants his mother.
10. (S) "Why are you crying?" asked a ladybug.
      (R) Hum, now she thinks a ladybug can cheer him up. (Looks confused) What can she do to cheer him up?
23. (S) "Look at the surprise I brought you!" said Little Hippo's mother.
      (R) Hmm, I wonder what it's gonna be.

Child 2

5.   (S) They took Little Hippo's mother away.
      (R) I'd be upset if *I* was the hippo.
15. (S) "She's been gone a whole year," said Little Hippo.
      (R) It ought to be different from what he says.
16/17. (S) "When did she leave?" asked the ladybug. "Yesterday!" said Little Hippo.
      (R) I wouldn't call *that* a whole year.

Child 3

5.   (S) They took Little Hippo's mother away.
      (R) Well, I could almost see him—okay—him or her, whatever—uh, kind of being sad or kind of weep—kind of crying or weeping, whatever hippopotamuses do.
15. (S) "She's been gone a whole year," said Little Hippo.
      (R) Well, I can see why the ladybug would really feel sad now. I've never really been left alone that long.

These three children give evidence of being very actively involved in reading the story about the hippopotamus. They express empathy, they predict content to come, and the second child even detects an inconsistency in the length of time that the mother hippo has been gone. What they do not do is mention their cognitive processing activities in any very explicit way. They do not say such things as "I'm trying to imagine what the baby hippo must feel like" or "I'm going to make a guess about what the mother hippo brought."

Alvermann (1984) has suggested that the think-aloud method may have instructional applications. Noting that the children in her study had been instructed in imagery strategies by their classroom teachers, she is not surprised to find frequent mention of visualizing the hippo weeping and so forth in the protocols. A teacher could perform a think-aloud activity to demonstrate points at which text stimulates "imaging." If Alvermann is correct about instructional potential for this activity, we will then have three applications for the think-aloud procedure: in research, to find differences among groups of learners in (verbalized) strategy use; in diagnosis, to find deficiencies among particular learners in strategy use; and in instruction, to model appropriate strategy use for reading or a host of other complex cognitive tasks.

Hare and Milligan (1984) provide the intriguing suggestion that teachers might model finding main ideas in text, a task we know can be quite difficult for elementary school children (see Baumann, 1982), by thinking aloud through a series of texts to find main ideas that may or may not be explicitly presented by authors. The idea is similar to Paris, Cross, and Lipson's (1984) notion of using class discussions to make strategy use "public," so that students can learn from one another about strategic options.

The think-aloud method is not the only alternative to interviews for discovering knowledge learners have about their own cognitive activity. Studies employing two alternative procedures have already been discussed in chapter 3; the methods used will be discussed here briefly. In addition, a third method will be discussed in some detail.

Other Methodological Alternatives to Interviews

One method already discussed is cross-age tutoring (Garner, Macready, & Wagoner, 1984; Garner et al., 1983). Garner and her colleagues asked subject-tutors to help younger children read a text and answer very detailed questions about the material. In both investigations they were interested in documenting tutors' encouragement of text reinspection behaviors in the younger children. They point out that if the older learners know something about rereading of texts to find information once read but not now remembered, and if they are in charge of the task completion (no adult assistance was available to the pairs), they would be likely to externalize their knowledge through direction or reinforcement of tutees.

It can be argued, furthermore, that memory failure poses no problem for this method, as the task is directly at hand. As the younger children often needed fairly extensive strategic directives and modeling of strategy use, verbalized knowledge in the absence of any use was unlikely as well. Cuing from investigators was avoided by audiotaping tutoring exchanges and recording nonverbal behaviors at a distance. Neither could the situation be termed either hypothetical or general; the teaching task, to show someone something, was quite real and quite specific. Finally, the situation seemed to be highly motivating to subject-tutors.

The method was applied with some knowledge of the literature on tutoring to improve learning outcomes (see, for instance, Allen, 1976; Allen & Feldman, 1976; Feldman, Devin-Sheehan, & Allen, 1976; Feshbach, 1976). That meant that tutoring pairs were same sex and same race, and those tutored were two years younger than tutors. An effort was made to avoid pairing close friends.

In the Garner, Macready, and Wagoner (1984) study, the tutored subjects were confederates trained to feign strategy deficits. For instance, they were trained not to answer questions and not to look back to text, awaiting a prompt from tutors to do so. The confederate system was incorporated in this study to diminish the likelihood of variability in style (e.g., asking questions of tutors versus awaiting all directions) among the younger children, variability that could affect encouragement of strategy use by subject-tutors.

Garner and her colleagues submit that the tutoring method is particularly useful for externalizing what is normally covert cognitive and metacognitive strategy knowledge and use. One serious problem that is not avoided by this paradigm is underestimating what subject-tutors know due to their meager verbal (and nonverbal) encouragement of strategy use. With this method, as with interviews and think-aloud procedures, "there is no guarantee that children express all that they know about the strategy" (Cavanaugh & Perlmutter, 1982, p. 19).

Another alternative method presented in chapter 3 is the optimal-nonoptimal product method in which subjects are asked to produce good and bad versions of text. As it was applied in the original Bracewell (1983) writing work and in the Garner (1985) summarization adaptation, subjects needed to be able to generate fairly long pieces of connected discourse. In these applications, then, only older children and adults would be likely to have the prerequisite composing skills to participate.

Bracewell (1983) wanted to investigate the mental and physical activities that lead to the production of text. He tried to think of a situation for which the presence of certain behaviors would make it reasonable to infer deliberate use of a particular cognitive process. He asked subjects to produce both optimal and nonoptimal versions of text on the same topic. Bracewell suggests that a metacognitively sophisticated learner should be able to provide differing versions.

Garner (1985) asked high school and college students to read a *Scientific American* passage on the topic of broadly held misconceptions about objects in motion. She then asked them to prepare good and bad short summaries of the passage, based on their notions of what makes a short summary acceptable. Both summaries from each subject were assessed for number of judged-important ideas included, number of words used, and integration level for judged-important information (this last measure was a measure of deviation from the copy-delete pattern discussed in chapter 3).

Garner tested two different, though not wholly discrete, explanations for summarization difficulties among older learners: (a) that learners are not aware of what makes a short summary acceptable, or (b) that learners are generally aware of features of acceptable short summaries, but cannot produce them. She predicted that younger subjects (in grades 9 and 11) would show both awareness and production gaps (i.e., they would not discriminate the two products in number of important ideas included, number of words used, and amount of integration provided *and* they would not approach ceiling level on these three measures for the "good" summary), and that older subjects (in college) would be unlikely to display either awareness or production problems.

In fact, as mentioned in chapter 3, all subjects demonstrated a high degree of awareness about including important ideas, and very few subjects demonstrated either awareness or production ability for integrating those ideas. The youngest and oldest subjects differed in production of important ideas and in production of succinct summaries.

It may be possible to adapt this method for use with young children. Perhaps to assess awareness of rapid information loss, as Kreutzer et al. (1975) did, children might be presented with a telephone, note paper, pencil, and props representing potential distractions (e.g., a television, sports equipment). Children might be asked to act out what a "smart person" or "a person who knows a lot about remembering and forgetting" would do if given a phone number he or she had to use to make an important call. Then the children might be asked to act out what a "less smart person" or "a person who doesn't know much about remembering and forgetting" would do.

If children produced appropriately differentiated routines for the smart and not-so-smart people, they would be demonstrating awareness of strategies to combat rapid information loss. If they acted out a great many strategic responses for the smart/knowledgeable person, they would be demonstrating production strengths. Separating awareness from production problems is perhaps most important if we are interested in providing instructional remedies with some specificity.

With both older and younger children, the optimal-nonoptimal task can also be presented in a recognition situation (see Garner, Belcher, Winfield, & Smith, 1985, for an example). Learners can be asked to say which among a set of essays or summaries or strategic routines is superior, and to provide reasons for the particular judgment made. With this method, proximity to expert production cannot be assessed, but depth of awareness of strategic options can be evaluated.

A third method also offers an alternative to standard interviews. It is really a hybrid of an interview and a think-aloud session. It is the "stimulated-recall" technique. Peterson, Swing, Braverman, and Buss (1982) used the method to study cognitive processes of fifth- and sixth-grade students participating in two 1-hour lessons on the topic of probability. During the lessons, student behavior was coded by three observers for a series of 20-second segments. All lessons were videotaped.

Following each lesson, small groups of students viewed one of five segments of the lesson, and then each student reported individually to an interviewer what he or she was doing and thinking at the time. Standardized prompts were used by interviewers.

A number of interesting results emerged from the study. First, observed off-task behavior was not related to either students' reports of attending or scores on a mathematics achievement test. (Peterson et al., 1982, note, however, that a ceiling effect due to uniformly high attending behavior precluded the possibility of high, positive correlations here.) Second, students who reported that they understood all of the material tended to perform well, both on assigned seatwork and on the mathematics achievement test. This result is a clear comprehension monitoring display. Third, and critical from a metacognitive perspective, students who did not provide detailed explanations of what/why they had trouble understanding tended to do poorly on seatwork and on the achievement test. Fourth, verbalization of a strategy labeled "trying to understand the teacher or problem," which involved general problem-solving steps applied to the task at hand, was positively related to both seatwork and achievement test performance.

Peterson et al. (1982) note that "the viewing of the videotaped segment was a nondirective retrieval cue that served to enhance the veridicality of the reports" (p. 546). Surely they are correct in assuming that by reducing the likelihood of memory failure, a problem for most interviews, they have also reduced the potential of inaccuracy, incompleteness, and interference in the verbal-report data. In addition, they have avoided the disruption of actual processing, a problem for most think-aloud procedures. Thus, stimulated recall diminishes some concerns we have expressed about both of these other methods. There is the technical problem of positioning the camera during videotaping of lessons in such a way that maximum cues to be used for the viewing and reporting phase are recorded.

For investigation of strategy use in noninstructional settings, the method would probably be much less useful. A videotape record of a learner reading a book, for instance, would be unlikely to provide a series of cues that would stimulate recall any more effectively than interview probes would. External cues for internal cognitive activity would be infrequent in most instances such as this.

With the think-aloud method and a number of other techniques available to augment interviews, where does our discussion in this chapter leave researchers who want to assess differences in metacognitive knowledge among learners? Should they avoid interviews? Should they avoid application of think-aloud procedures with young children? Should they try one of the more recently adopted techniques, perhaps tutoring or stimulated recall?

I would suggest that interview data can be highly informative. Interviews should not be avoided; rather, they should be structured to reduce the likelihood of confounding of results from the set of factors discussed in this chapter. The list of eight suggestions presented earlier in the chapter, if followed, would make collection of accurate, complete interview data more likely.

The use of think-aloud techniques with young children poses several problems. Little of this research has been attempted with children, though Hare and Smith's (1982) and Alvermann's (1984) work suggests that children can be instructed to provide sustained verbalizations about problem-solving efforts. We should not assume that in adopting this method we have eliminated all confounding factors; verbal facility and distortion of process are particularly problematic for this method.

Finally, we surely should try tutoring, optimal-nonoptimal production, or stimulated-recall techniques in an effort to get rich data about metacognitive knowledge bases. We also should use multiple methods within an investigation, the better to seek converging information about "true" knowledge with the effects of memory overload, glib or halting verbalization, cuing, automatic processing, and process distortion differentially diminished by each approach. As Kail and Bisanz (1982) note, "Hypotheses about cognitive functions need to be tested with multiple methods that independently converge on an answer" (pp. 252–253).

Turning from learners' metacognitive knowledge to their meta-cognitive experiences, we continue our discussion of problems associated with paradigms available in current research. Chapter 5 presents an examination of the error-detection method, its flaws, and some methodological alternatives.

Chapter 5

Methodological Concerns: Error-Detection Research

In chapter 3, "error detection" was cited as the dominant research paradigm used to investigate individual differences in cognitive monitoring. The results of the research discussed in that chapter are quite consistent: Young children and poor readers perform detection tasks less well than older children and good readers, respectively. Obviously, researchers are not particularly interested in learners' detection of lexical or logical flaws in contrived instructions or texts. They want to infer something about learners' sensitivity to comprehension obstacles in both oral and written texts they encounter in school and out.

Unfortunately, just as critics have pointed out that interviews may give us information about what learners can or cannot tell, rather than about what they know or do not know, critics have suggested that perfectly adept cognitive monitors may perform badly on error-detection tasks. That is, just as interview results may lead us to underestimate subjects' knowledge, error-detection results may lead us to underestimate the prowess with which students in nonexperimental settings monitor and remedy obstacles to a variety of cognitive operations.

In this chapter, we will examine detection results under conditions that varied in some respects from those imposed in the body of research already discussed. We will see that under these new conditions, detection rates often improve quite dramatically, even for less experienced and less proficient readers. Five conditions will be discussed: (a) explicit directions to locate errors; (b) inclusion of blatant errors; (c) use of relatively naturalistic research settings; (d) use of nonverbal measures of detection; and (e) provision of standards for the error-detection task.

Explicit Directions to Locate Errors

As noted in chapter 3, Markman (1979) warned some children in grades 3 and 6 that there was a problem, something tricky or confusing, in the essays that were going to be read to them. The majority of informed third-grade subjects (10 of 16) still failed to detect informational inconsistencies on at least two of three essays, but very few informed sixth-grade subjects (2 of 16) failed to locate the problems. These successful detection rates (i.e., 6 of 16 and 14 of 16) can be compared to those for uninformed peers: 4 of 16 and 8 of 16 for third graders and sixth graders, respectively. These differences between children who were told that there were problems to be found and children who were told only to inform the experimenter of any problems found were statistically significant. It seems that simply informing subjects (particularly older subjects) of the presence of errors improves error-detection performance.

Why should this be? It certainly results at least in part from the nature of oral and written communication. We are used to getting meaning from somewhat problematic messages. As language users in the real world, in contrast to error detectors in the laboratory, we are used to ignoring some of the problems with the messages we receive. Danks, Bohn, and Fears (1983), talking about the "robustness of human communication" (p. 193), list garbled speech, scrawled handwriting, vague references, and ambiguous phrasing as common events in communication, events listeners and readers manage rather easily, often without labeling them as communication problems. Fillmore (1982) talks about passages included in standardized tests of reading comprehension as "seriously flawed texts, texts which frequently require of their readers an uncommon degree of tolerance and cooperation" (p. 251). As those tests are frequently encountered by school-age learners, the uncommon degree of tolerance and cooperation is quite commonly exercised in schools. Flavell (1978) has said that coming to cognitive maturity in a culture such as ours requires, among other things, learning how to follow senseless-sounding directions and rules. Listeners and readers, in other words, get used to a certain amount of flawed material in messages, and they are unlikely to make much of this unless urged to do so.

A related matter is the inviolability of text. Readers in general often suppose text to be a formal, autonomous, finished piece (see Olson, 1977; Olson & Torrance, 1981); one tampers with "the very words" (Hildyard & Olson, 1982) at great risk. If Tierney and LaZansky (1980) are correct in saying that there exists an implicit allowability contract governing the production roles of writers and the comprehension roles of readers, then certain liberties (e.g., critiquing informational gaps or inconsistencies) may not be considered options by readers who judge most of the text to be relevant, sincere, and informative. (We must remember, in this regard, that the errors in experimental materials in error-detection studies are often single-word or single-phrase problems embedded in multiparagraph texts.) Again, if the texts are *generally* acceptable, the readers asked to evaluate them may gloss over the small problem areas, unless they are explicitly encouraged to attend to those areas by researchers' directives.

If readers in general suppose a text to be a finished piece to be held in awe, not under scrutiny, poor readers and young children surely suppose that to an even greater degree. As Capelli (1982) argues, these learners, because their cognitive skills are not yet fully developed and because they have had less experience, fail to understand many things that proficient adults understand. Because older, wiser people seem to understand things, because these things appear in generally reliable materials, these learners are reluctant to expose their miscomprehension, either because they presume they are in a very small minority or because they assume a researcher inquiring about comprehensibility wants an objective, not subjective, standard applied. In either case, poor readers and young children would be unlikely to announce error detection of this sort unless told that errors are really there to be found, even by successful adult learners.

Baker (1985c) tested a form of this reluctance-to-expose-miscomprehension explanation. She noticed a discrepancy in two findings: poor identification by fourth graders of nonsense words in passages (Paris & Myers, 1981) versus successful identification by fifth and sixth graders of difficult vocabulary words in passages (Garner, 1981). She hypothesized that the discrepancy may have arisen because the sets of "words" used in the Paris and Myers study (e.g., *kales, leet*) and in the Garner study (e.g., *expeditiously, multifarious*) differed in length. She suggests that learners may feel they should know short words and may be reluctant to admit they do not. They may be more comfortable reporting that they do not know five-syllable words.

She asked learners at two reading-skill levels in each of grades 3 and 5 to read a series of short paragraphs. Each child read eight paragraphs with one-syllable nonsense words embedded and eight paragraphs with three-syllable nonsense words embedded. The children were asked to report anything that might be hard for another child to understand.

The finding of interest here is that all children were less likely to report a word-comprehension problem when the nonsense words contained one syllable rather than three (38% versus 58% "detection" rate). Baker suggests that this result supports her notion of a response bias that produces underreporting of short "words" in a word-comprehension detection task. Had Baker (1985c) informed subjects of the existence of errors prior to reading, perhaps reader reluctance to report comprehension obstacles would have diminished.

Recently, Grabe and Mann (1984) employed a clever procedure both to inform subjects of errors and to provide a highly motivating situation for error-detection assessment. Fourth- and fifth-grade children at two reading-proficiency levels were asked to assume the role of detective and find the "criminals" by spotting people "who say things that sound mixed up or confused" (Grabe & Mann, 1984, p. 137). An example of one of the "mixed-up" statements is the following:

> All the people that work on this ship get along very well. The people that make a lot of money and the people that don't make much are still friends. The officers treat us like dirt. We often eat our meals together. I guess we are just one big happy family. (Grabe & Mann, 1984, p. 136)

At first glance, this short passage appears similar to many used in the studies discussed in chapter 3. However, in this instance subjects were not editors looking for possible flaws in presumably sincere and informative texts; they were detectives looking for crooks who "try to fool or mislead you" (Grabe & Mann, 1984, p. 137). The existence of errors was announced. To add to the motivational impact of the task, detectives "met" suspects via the computer terminal. The computer randomly selected the culprit, ordered the suspects, and selected which suspects would produce which statements.

Subjects' performance in identifying inconsistent statements did not improve from pretest to posttest; one might argue that limited practice without direct instruction is insufficient to improve spontaneous error-detection performance. Perhaps more important for the present discussion is the novelty of the detective procedure, a procedure that encourages subjects not to tolerate "mixed-up" text. Not only are subjects made comfortable reporting confusions; the whole point of the gamelike task is to do so.

We should note at this point and throughout this chapter that monitoring differences between age and reading-achievement groups do not disappear as conditions for error-detection demonstration are altered. On the contrary, the differences are maintained, but performance of all subjects is enhanced. For instance, Markman (1979) found that informing subjects of the existence of errors improved third-grade performance somewhat and sixth-grade performance substantially. Baker (1985c) found reluctance to report comprehension obstacles across age and skill groups, but also found predictable significant differences in reporting favoring more skilled over less skilled readers. Finally, Grabe and Mann (1984) also found predictable skill-group detection differences favoring better readers.

Inclusion of Blatant Errors

Winograd and Johnston (1982) have noted that specifying the kind and degree of target error for studies of error detection in text can be a problem. Researchers have used omissions, inconsistencies, unclear reference, inappropriate transitions, disorganized passages, anomalous sentences, spelling errors, and grammatical errors in their materials. Placement of the errors (i.e., high or low in the text structure) has varied. Perhaps most important of all, blatancy or magnitude of the errors has varied. That is, the errors have been differentially apparent and differentially "damaging" to the meaning of the texts. It seems intuitively obvious that use of quite blatant errors from maximally disruptive categories (for instance, informational inconsistencies as opposed to disorganized material) should enhance error-detection performance. These errors do such violence to the texts that they cannot be treated very readily with "tolerance and cooperation."

Some evidence in support of this intuition comes from a study conducted by Garner and Anderson (1981–1982). They replicated part of the Garner (1981) study discussed in chapter 3. They asked remedial readers in grades 5 and 6 to read a short narrative passage in which two sentences, one early in the passage and one late, provided inconsistent information. Subjects were then asked, as the original subjects had been, to comment on whether there was anything in the story that did not make sense. Subject selection and study procedure were essentially the same in both studies. The only distinction was in blatancy of errors in the texts. The two inconsistent passages are provided below for comparison purposes:

Garner (1981)
The train stopped in Centerville every day at both one o'clock and five o'clock. Dr. Jones needed to travel from Centerville to Milltown on business. He decided to go by train. He packed his bags. He caught a train at seven o'clock, and was in Milltown in time for his meeting.

Garner and Anderson (1981–1982)
The Anderson family stayed at the cabin in the woods. There was no electricity in the cabin. It did have a large fireplace and lots of space. The children spent their days climbing trees and swimming. Mrs. Anderson enjoyed hiking in the woods. Mr. Anderson fished in the lake near the cabin. Every evening after dinner, Mr. and Mrs. Anderson read their books. The children plugged in the television and watched their favorite shows. It was a great vacation for everyone.

It should be mentioned that 17 of 18 adult readers detected the departure-time disparity in the first text, and all 22 adult readers detected the discrepancy about electricity in the second text; in both cases they were explicitly informed of the existence of errors and asked to locate them. The children who were subjects in the two studies were not so explicitly informed, however, and their detection rates for the two texts differed dramatically: 0% for the train passage and 50% for the cabin passage.

Given that subjects and procedure were comparable, experimental materials appear to have made a difference. Both passages present the same kind of error: inconsistency. The placement of the key sentences is about the same in each text (one early, one late). Actually, in regard to placement, the train text may be slightly easier in one regard: Only three sentences separate the inconsistency-bearing material in that text, whereas five separate this material in the cabin text. A strict working memory analysis of text proposition integration (and then error detection) might suggest an advantage for the train passage.

That advantage did not materialize, of course, and I suggest differences in blatancy to explain the disparate results of the two studies. I would suggest that readers can "fix up" the problem in the train passage in ways that they cannot in the cabin passage. They can assume, for instance, that the five o'clock train sat on the tracks for 2 hours. They can decide that a special train ran that day to accommodate travelers to Milltown. They can suppose that Dr. Jones drove to another town and caught a seven o'clock train. None of these inferences based on background knowledge about trains and towns and meetings is outlandish, and none is directly excluded as a possibility by the text.

It is much harder to draw permissible inferences to explain away the electricity problem. There was no electricity in the cabin, and yet the children supposedly plugged in the television to watch their favorite shows. A battery of some sort seems the only obvious "fix-up," but "plugged in" does not seem the right language for an author to use when talking about a battery-operated television.

There is additional evidence to support the view that stimulus factors affect rates of error detection, and that blatancy or magnitude of error is a critical factor in this category. Patterson, O'Brien, Kister, Carter, and Kotsonis (1981), for instance, presented highly ambiguous and only slightly ambiguous messages to children in kindergarten and grades 2 and 4. Comprehension monitoring was assessed in a referential communication task. After an adult speaker had produced messages varying in degree of ambiguity, the child was asked to judge whether or not he or she knew enough to select a card that the speaker had described. If children said they needed more clues, they were asked what they needed to know before they would be certain of the appropriate referent. Scores were number of correct answers about sufficiency of clues. Success on such a task demands that the child recognize that not only must a message correspond to an intended referent; it must do so uniquely (Bonitatibus, 1984).

More effective comprehension monitoring was displayed for the highly ambiguous messages than for the slightly ambiguous ones. Degree of message inadequacy, in other words, affected monitoring performance. In addition, predictable age effects favoring the older children appeared in the study.

A related investigation was conducted by Beal and Flavell (1982). Kindergarten children were told that a girl named Sheri had made some block buildings and had recorded directions about how to make a building just like each of hers. Each subject's task was to listen to Sheri's instructions and to build a building like hers. The children were not forewarned about inadequate instructions. After the children had made their building, they were asked if their buildings looked like Sheri's and were asked about the adequacy of the instructions.

Children all received a series of ambiguous and unambiguous instructions. Detection of message inadequacy was indicated by (a) verbal and motor expressions of problem detection during building (e.g., subvocal speech, exclamations such as "huh," puzzled facial expressions, questioning looks at the investigator); and (b) comments about possible variation from Sheri's structure and negative evaluation of instructions during the postbuilding inquiry session.

The children showed frequent signs of ambiguity detection during the building phase of the study, but most reported that the instructions were adequate. The most important result for our present purposes is a relatively minor one in the Beal and Flavell (1982) study. After a number of the children had been tested, it was clear to the investigators that positive evaluations of the inadequate instructions would be the norm. Therefore, a final task was added for some of the children to determine if they would under any circumstances pronounce a message to be inadequate. The instructions for this task were impossible to execute, for the target block was not provided. Again, children were asked about the adequacy of instructions.

For this "impossible" task, over 70% of the children involved said the instructions were not adequate or that the block was missing. Just as in the Garner and Anderson (1981–1982) study, when the problem in the message could not be readily "fixed up," when the message was blatantly flawed, moderate to high rates of detection of message inadequacy resulted.

Use of Relatively Naturalistic Research Settings

Psychologists and educators frequently observe that a child knows more or is more adept than he or she shows in a given context. The literature admonishes researchers to study tasks "cultivated in the richly varied real world of the children" (Griffin, Cole, & Newman, 1982, p. 124); to *"maximize the similarity* between the conditions in which they study behavior and those other conditions, whatever they may be, to which researchers may ultimately wish to make inferences" (Shulman, 1970, p. 377); to estimate children's competencies "in naturally occurring situations" (Brown & DeLoache, 1978, p. 27). There is no reason to suppose that context effects hold less for error-detection phenomena than they do for any other psychological phenomena.

Revelle, Wellman, and Karabenick (1985) studied comprehension monitoring by preschool children, using what the authors call a "quasi-naturalistic" method. By this they mean that task, stimuli, and situation were simple and familiar to the children. Each child participated in what seemed to be two natural play interactions with an adult (i.e., sandbox play, preparations for a pretend tea party). Certain aspects of the situations and dialogue, however, had been structured in advance. In the course of the play sessions, the adult made a series of requests of the child, some of which posed comprehension or compliance dilemmas. The requests could be divided into three categories: those for which comprehension and compliance were easy, those presenting comprehension problems, and those for which compliance was difficult or impossible. A set of control requests was also presented.

Comprehension problems were of three types: referential ambiguity, unintelligibility, and memory overload. For referential ambiguity, the investigator requested an object (e.g., a cup) for which multiple objects in the room would satisfy the request. For unintelligibility, the investigator yawned while requesting the item, completely obscuring its name. For memory overload, five items were requested together. Compliance problems were of two types: unbringable items and absent items. For unbringable items, the investigator requested that an object present in the room but too heavy for the child to carry (e.g., a refrigerator) be brought. For absent items, the investigator requested an item that the child knew was not in the room. Revelle et al. (1985) report that, though much of the conversation in the play sessions was spontaneous and unstructured, the wording and ordering of the problem and control requests was invariant.

From videotapes of each play session, transcripts were made of all verbalizations. Nonverbal compliance attempt and search behaviors were coded as well. Seven categories of verbalizations that could indicate a child's detection of a comprehension or compliance problem were identified. Those seven categories and sample verbalizations for each appear below:

1. Requests for repetition: general ("What?" "Huh?")
2. Requests for repetition: specific ("What else?" "Did I forget something?")
3. Requests for confirmation: before object is found ("The rabbit?" "The dog, too?")
4. Requests for confirmation: with reference to an object in the room ("This one?" "This fish?" "The red one?")
5. Requests for specification ("Which one?" "The big one or the little one?")
6. Requests for elaboration ("Where is it?" "How can I bring it?")
7. Statements specifying the comprehension problem or expressing an inability to comply with the request ("I can't hear you." "I don't remember what else you want." "I don't know which one you want." "I don't see one." "I can't get it.")

The important finding from this study for our present purposes is that 3- and 4-year-old children displayed substantial facility at discriminating between requests that posed problems and those that did not. There were age effects. The younger children were adept at monitoring the yawn, the unbringable item, and the absent item. The older preschool children were adept at monitoring all problem requests. Both younger and older children showed through nonverbal and verbal means that they evaluated the unbringable item mentally, instead of trying to comply and then discovering that they could not.

The results of this investigation stand in sharp contrast to many of the studies discussed in chapter 3 in which school-age children by and large were reported to display low levels of cognitive monitoring. The results can be used to argue specifically against Markman's (1977) suggestion that first-grade children fail at spontaneous monitoring demonstrations because they do not execute activities mentally, and therefore do not notice problems until they attempt to perform tasks (see chapter 3). Revelle et al. (1985) found evidence of children as young as 3 years of age evaluating messages before attempting to act on them.

Revelle and her colleagues account for the discrepant results across these studies by pointing to the features in their study that have been highlighted here: familiar and simple stimuli, natural interactions, a familiar setting. These features characterize an "ecologically valid" study (Bronfenbrenner, 1979), which is conducted in a natural setting and involves objects and activities from everyday life. Revelle et al. (1985) add that the relatively easy performance task of a child's attempting to comply with an adult's request to bring an object to the adult is surely less difficult to execute than a judgment task that requires the child to state that a message is problematic, and then to specify the nature of the problem. Most of the error-detection studies discussed in chapter 3 did in fact present judgment tasks of this sort to subjects.

Use of Nonverbal Measures of Detection

In both the Beal and Flavell (1982) and Revelle et al. (1985) studies, nonverbal indicators of problem detection were sought. In both investigations, these nonverbal data showed that young children can detect blatantly flawed messages.

Other studies have included nonverbal data as a source of information about children's "taking their own 'mental temperatures' spontaneously" (Paris & Lindauer, 1982, p. 343). One is an investigation conducted by Patterson, Cosgrove, and O'Brien (1980) with children in preschool, kindergarten, and grades 2 and 4. Patterson et al. suggest that children who produce systematically different patterns of nonverbal behavior in response to informative and uninformative messages are demonstrating that they can discriminate between the two types of messages. These researchers were interested in studying the relationship between verbal and nonverbal indicants of comprehension and noncomprehension.

Patterson et al. (1980) asked the children to listen to an adult who produced messages about pictures of shapes on cards that varied in their informational adequacy. Some messages gave information about two critical attributes of a shape; these were informative messages. Partially informative messages gave information about only one attribute. Uninformative messages gave no information that would distinguish the target shape from all other shapes pictured. Half the children at each age level were trained to ask questions to obtain additional information when messages were not sufficiently informative. All children were then given a similar set of informative, partially informative, and uninformative messages.

The children's performances for this communication task were videotaped. Nonverbal behaviors in six categories were coded from the videotape records. The six categories were as follows: response time between the speaker's ending a message and the listener's selecting a referent; eye contact; body movement; hand movement; open mouth (with no audible noise); and verbalizations, including grunts, laughs, and groans, as well as questions posed.

In pretraining trials, preschool, kindergarten, and second-grade children asked very few questions, even when the speaker's messages were uninformative. Fourth-grade subjects, on the other hand, asked questions of the speaker, both before and after training. After training, children in kindergarten and grade 2 did request clarification of ambiguous messages, but preschoolers did not.

Given these results, the researchers turned their attention to the matter of interest here: nonverbal indicators of sensitivity to message inadequacy in the absence of verbal responses. For this analysis, data for the fourth graders were not informative; attention was focused on pretraining data from preschool, kindergarten, and second-grade children under the conditions of informative and uninformative messages.

Patterson et al. (1980) found that these children took longer to respond, made more eye contact with the speaker, shifted their bodies more frequently, and moved their hands more often in response to uninformative messages than to informative ones. In addition, they found that for reaction time, body movement, and hand movement, the relationship between verbal and nonverbal responses was additive. Patterns of nonverbal responding to informativeness of messages, in other words, were unaffected by initiation of verbal responses. Verbal responses were simply added to the existing nonverbal reactions. Patterson et al. suggest that we cannot be certain if the younger children in their study would be able to verbalize awareness of the uninformative nature of some of the messages if informed of problems and asked to elaborate (the point addressed earlier in this chapter). What we do know from this study is that the nonverbal data provide a picture of rudimentary detection of message inadequacy that the verbal data base does not give us.

Another study that included a nonverbal data base rich in information is one conducted by Flavell, Speer, Green, and August (1981). In this study, children in kindergarten and second grade were told that a girl named Kiersten (actually a 12-year-old confederate) had constructed a number of buildings out of blocks and had recorded her directions for constructing each one on a tape cassette. Each child was asked to make a building just like Kiersten's on the basis of her taped instructions. The children were taught how to press the cassette player replay button if they wanted to hear an instruction again. When the building activity was completed, the children were asked if they thought their buildings looked just like Kiersten's or not, and they were asked to evaluate Kiersten's instructions. The design of the study is quite similar to that of the Beal and Flavell (1982) study discussed earlier.

As in the Beal and Flavell (1982) study, some messages given to the subjects were adequate and some were inadequate. The children were not forewarned that some directions for construction would be problematic. The messages with problems could be characterized as inaudible, containing unknown key words, ambiguous, contradictory, incomplete, impossible to execute with available materials, or excessively demanding of comprehension or memory abilities of subjects.

The children's performances were videotaped. During preliminary viewing of a subset of the videotaped performances, a system of coding the tapes was devised. The initial coding system included 146 scoring categories, which were subsequently reduced to 75. A sample of the scoring categories, selected partially on the basis of particularly high inter-rater agreement, follows:

31. Problem-solving replay: replaying tape for the apparent purpose of obtaining or clarifying information relating to a detected problem
32. Verifying replay: replaying only to verify or double-check that the structure that was built is the correct one
33. No building is constructed, apparently because child believes it is difficult or impossible to build as specified by the instructions
34. Destroys building: disassembles part or all of structure in evident dissatisfaction with it as a solution to a detected problem, and does not subsequently rebuild
39. Verbal, defensible: an explicit statement of the nature of a plausible or "defensible" problem that we had not foreseen or intended
58. Compares present task with a prior one judged to be problematic, e.g., "she didn't mess it up like last time"
68. Changes the building during inquiry

In both age groups, each of seven key indices of problem detection during building (e.g., item 31 above) was significantly more frequent for inadequate instructions than for adequate. However, not surprisingly, the second-grade children gave more signs during the building activity than the kindergarten children of detecting problems in inadequate messages. Kindergartners were also more likely than second graders to say their buildings looked just like Kiersten's, though the most common response in both age groups to the "look alike" question was that they looked the same. The older children were about six times as likely as the younger children to express uncertainty about the adequacy of Kiersten's instructions.

Flavell et al. (1981) suggest that some of the young children in the study either may have been only momentarily aware of message problems while building or may not even have been aware that they were confused and were expressing puzzlement while they attempted to follow problematic instructions. The researchers further suggest the children may have initially recognized that Kiersten might have meant A or B, and they may have expressed this recognition with some sort of problem-detection sign. However, they may have arbitrarily decided she meant A, built accordingly, and then forgotten their initial confusion by the time they were asked to evaluate Kiersten's instructions. These lines of thinking provide possible explanations for the disjunction between nonverbal displays of detection and verbal data that show minimal detection, particularly for the younger children in the study.

Flavell and his colleagues (1981) do not think their subjects were reticent to criticize Kiersten. For one thing, she was described as a peer, not an adult authority figure. For another, she was not physically present. And finally, the children were told from time to time that other children had criticized Kiersten's instructions. Instead, they suggest that children "may have only fleeting and semiconscious experiences of comprehension difficulties which, to a degree surprising to an adult, they may ignore or dismiss as meaningless and unimportant" (Flavell et al., 1981, p. 53). Once again we have evidence that children's cognitive monitoring skills appear at different ages, but that this appearance interacts with task demands and situation, so that the abilities are manifest in some circumstances, but not in others (Pace, 1981).

Provision of Standards for the Error-Detection Task

As mentioned in chapter 3, Markman (1979) has suggested that children may examine texts primarily for empirical truth, not for logical consistency. If the error to be detected in a message is one of inconsistency across sentences, that error may go undetected as children accept each individual true statement and neglect to make any comparisons among statements. Markman and Gorin (1981) found that spurious questioning of truth occurred far more frequently than spurious questioning of consistency. Garner (1981) found a similar imbalance in spontaneous application of standards for text acceptability in a reading task; in this case, learners overused a word-understanding standard to the exclusion of an internal consistency standard.

In each of these three studies, subjects indicated a preference for a particular standard for evaluating message acceptability. In each of the three studies, the preferred standard could be applied without making cross-proposition assessments of the material's sense. In each of the studies, subjects' performance revealed tacit views of message evaluation that were incomplete. Finally, in each of the studies, these tacit views handicapped subjects' performance, because they did not match the researchers' views of message inadequacy, which included logical inconsistency.

Baker (1984b) maintains that message evaluation is a "multidimensional process, requiring the use of a variety of standards or criteria"

(p. 290). She points out that finding inconsistencies in a passage in nonadjacent text segments (applying an internal consistency standard to text) differs from finding either nonsense words or difficult vocabulary (applying a lexical standard), which in turn differs from finding violations of prior knowledge (applying an external consistency standard). She claims that the standards impose different cognitive processing demands and for that reason differ in ease of application. She argues that failure to apply one standard (e.g., internal consistency in the three studies mentioned above) does not indicate failure to apply all other standards. In fact, we know from the three studies that children ranging in age from 8 to 12 do show some strengths in application of lexical and external consistency standards.

Baker (1984b) designed a study to investigate spontaneous and instructed use of multiple standards of evaluation more fully. Children in grades 4 and 6, at two reading-proficiency levels within each grade, were assigned to one of two conditions: being informed of the existence of problems in passages, or being informed with more specificity plus being given two examples of each type (i.e., lexical, external consistency, internal consistency). Each type of problem appeared in four separate passages. A few nonproblematic passages were used as well. An example of each type of problem is as follows:

Lexical: It is so hot that most brugens would melt there.

External consistency: They used sand from the trees to make many things.

Internal Consistency: The temperature on Venus is much higher than boiling water. Venus is about the same size as Earth. But it is much too cold for us to live there.

Children were instructed to underline anything they thought was problematic while reading, and were then asked to rate the comprehensibility of each passage by circling one of four faces: a face with a big smile (no problems), a face with a small smile (small problems only), a face with a small frown (a problem affecting comprehension), or a face with a big frown (a big problem making the passage very hard to understand). Children explained their choices and their reasons for underlining.

It is interesting that subjects rarely circled either frowning face. They made distinctions between nonproblematic and problematic passages by selecting either the big or small smile. This finding is quite similar to Garner's (1980) finding that subjects very rarely rated a consistent or inconsistent passage as "difficult to understand" (see chapter 3). Rather, the good readers described consistent passages as "very easy to understand" and inconsistent ones as "okay."

The children in Baker's (1984b) study were credited with identifying a problem if they underlined the target information and gave an adequate explanation of the problem. The expected main effects of age and reading proficiency emerged; older children and better readers detected more problems than did younger children and poorer readers, respectively. In addition, children given examples of problems detected more errors than did children informed only generally that problems existed. This improvement with additional instruction was particularly strong for the better readers. Finally, children identified more nonsense words than either of the other two sorts of problems.

Baker (1984b) also checked for evidence of the subjects' applying one of the three standards exclusively. With one exception, the internal consistency standard was never used exclusively. The external consistency standard was applied exclusively by fewer than 5% of the children, all poor readers. The lexical standard, however, was used exclusively by more than one quarter of the children, more frequently in the less specific instructional condition, and more frequently among younger children and poorer readers. This finding of overreliance on the lexical standard among upper elementary school less successful readers is very consistent with Garner's (1981) results (see chapter 3).

Baker (1984b) draws three conclusions from this study. One is that children are responsive to external guidance about application of standards. That is, given a bit more direction (here about standards), children can monitor their cognitive processes (here reading comprehension) with more success than they do without such information.

A second conclusion is that there are learner-group and individual differences in the spontaneous application of various standards. Some children rely exclusively on a single standard, virtually always the lexical standard, while others have richer repertoires of standards.

A third conclusion is that there are robust developmental differences among learners in error detection, in "treating language itself as an object of thought, as opposed to simply using it to comprehend and produce sentences" (Tunmer, Nesdale, & Pratt, 1983, p. 97). These differences do not disappear with provision of guidance about standards. Older readers and better readers in Baker's (1984b) study identified more problems and used more different standards than did younger readers and poorer readers.

Baker's work in the area of standards for comprehensibility of text makes an important contribution. With this work, Baker has refined the notion of what it means to fail to detect a researcher-generated error in a text. It may in fact mean that the subject did not notice that particular assault on comprehensibility, and that he or she seldom notes assaults on comprehensibility. In other words, it may mean that this subject is not an adept comprehension monitor. However, this nondetection result might also mean something quite different. It might mean that the subject applied a lexical or an external consistency standard to a text in which an internal inconsistency was embedded. In this case, we would be in error to conclude that the subject is not an adept comprehension monitor in some instances, specifically in instances in which difficult vocabulary or knowledge gaps interfere with understanding.

The picture is complicated still further by standards such as structural cohesiveness (see Baker, 1985b) that have not been considered here, but that wise readers might well consider as they evaluate texts; by misapplication of standards that might be construed by researchers as nonapplication; and by insufficiently rigorous application of standards that might also be construed as nonapplication. With regard to the point about misapplication, subjects might, for instance, have insufficient prior knowledge to know that sand does not come from trees. These subjects would be unlikely to "detect" the external consistency error given earlier in this chapter, not because of inability to apply an external consistency standard, but rather because of insufficient knowledge about sand and trees. This distinction is important as we draw conclusions about monitoring competencies, particularly among young children who have less experience and, as a result, less schematic knowledge than older learners. With regard to the point about insufficiently rigorous application, subjects may apply a range of standards, but may use lax comprehension criteria, so that unwarranted inferences are drawn and retained despite the presence of disconfirming information in subsequent text segments (Capelli & Markman, 1982).

The Future of Error-Detection Research

Facilitating Conditions

It is clear from our discussion in this chapter that children's cognitive monitoring performance on error-detection tasks is much affected by task demands and situations we have described, and probably by others left unmentioned. Given the discussion in this chapter, we may want to reframe the conclusions drawn from the work described in chapter 3; we may want to say, "The X group of learners is more likely to monitor cognitive processes than the Y group of learners, but conditions of Z enhance the performance of both groups."

A question arises: Do we then draw our conclusions about "realworld" competencies of learners under conditions of Z or non-Z? Do we present error-detection tasks under conditions that have been demonstrated conclusively to enhance performance, or do we present them under what may be more "real" conditions, at least in school, where children are unlikely to get detailed information about a variety of blatant text problems in familiar stimuli, and as assessed by a range of measures? The best answer is probably that we do both. Certainly we want information about wholly spontaneous, unassisted performance, but surely we also want to know something about the outer limits of assisted performance. We want to know what sorts of assistance move fleeting, semiconscious, rudimentary skill displays to more sophisticated and deliberate ones.

Methodological Alternatives

Let us begin consideration of possible alternative methods by remembering what researchers have tried to accomplish with the dominant method of error detection. As noted in chapter 3, ordinary listeners and readers processing ordinary messages (usually texts) in ordinary settings encounter a number of difficulties such as unknown words, insufficient background knowledge, apparent contradictions, and a lack of unity in the message. We cannot observe those encounters as researchers. Sometimes learners complain, grunt, groan, sigh, scratch their heads, squirm, or provide some other verbal or nonverbal indication of comprehension failure, but often we do not get those gross external signs of internal processing difficulty.

Messages with embedded errors have been the preferred solution for this dilemma. The reasoning has been that if we know an error of some sort exists in a message (because we created it), and if learners' behavior indicates that they have detected it, then we can infer that they may also detect vocabulary problems, background knowledge gaps, and the rest in ordinary messages in ordinary processing settings. When detection takes place, we are optimistic about cognitive monitoring beyond the research setting. When detection does not appear to take place, either we can be pessimistic about cognitive monitoring or we can claim a potent effect of research conditions such as those discussed in this chapter.

In this section, two alternative methods that are used to produce external signs of internal processing events will be discussed. I am somewhat dubious about this particular application of the first method, and cautiously optimistic about the second.

The first method has been with us for some time. It is miscue analysis. Goodman and Goodman (1977, 1979) have argued that the qualitative analysis of oral reading miscues (i.e., unexpected responses, text–oral rendering discrepancies, what would typically be labeled "errors") offers an opportunity to study reader processing with uncontrived texts. As Beebe (1980) notes, three of the Goodmans' observations about processing have gained wide acceptance: (a) that miscues differ in impact on comprehension (i.e., some are disruptive and some are not); (b) that mis-cues are a normal part of the reading process, even for good readers; and (c) that regressions (repeated readings of input segments) are more posi-tive than negative because they usually occur when a reader realizes something has gone wrong.

The Goodmans claim that all the phenomena of silent reading are pres-ent or have their counterparts in oral reading, which has the advantage of displaying accessible data (e.g., omissions, insertions, substitutions, cor-rected miscues in any of these categories, uncorrected miscues) as silent reading cannot. When a reader omits a word or substitutes a graphically or semantically similar word for the actual text input, researchers gain "a window on the reading process," Goodman and Goodman argue (1977, p. 319).

This is an appealing idea. Instead of staring at readers staring at text-book pages, we can eavesdrop on readers' oral output, compare that to text input, and draw conclusions about a multitude of processing events, including cognitive monitoring. Particularly appealing is the possibility of using uncontrived texts and then tracking what actually causes prob-lems for particular readers, rather than examining the detection or nondetection of what is embedded in text by researchers.

There is a problem, however. Once again we are studying one thing to find out about another, and we must accept the isomorphic nature of the two things for this activity to have merit. In this case, one must accept that silent reading (what, outside of diagnostic, dramatic, and beginning reading situations, we mean by "reading") and oral reading are mostly the same in their processing requirements. Goodman and Goodman (1977) do in fact accept this. They note that the two forms of reading differ in function, but not in "intrinsic characteristics" (p. 322), and that "a single process underlies all reading" (p. 327).

A different argument can be made. One could say that the important distinctions in function make for important distinctions in intrinsic char-acteristics, that ultimately make for two related, but far from isomorphic, processes. Danks et al. (1983) elaborate this argument. They note that in silent reading a reader must satisfy comprehension demands. In oral reading, however, a reader must attempt to satisfy both verbal perform-ance demands ("Read with expression!" primary-grade teachers chide) and comprehension demands; the press of the immediate verbal per-formance demands is greater, Danks et al. submit.

A very interesting study conducted recently by Danner, Hiebert, and Winograd (1983) documents that even elementary school children are aware of differences in oral and silent reading demands. In this study, children in grades 2, 4, and 6 were given four short passages written at very different readability levels. The children were asked to indicate which passage they would choose to read out loud and which they would choose to read silently.

Children at all grade levels tended to choose a passage for oral reading that was at or below their current level of reading ability. For "private reading," however, they tended to choose a passage above that level. These children, even at the youngest age, seem aware of the danger of humiliation that exists in the public, but not the private, activity. Even Goodman and Goodman acknowledge that audience-conscious oral readers may take fewer risks in guessing at unknown words or in constructing tentative messages as they read than they would if they were reading silently.

These distinctions in process should make us wary of using oral reading as a route to inferences about cognitive monitoring in silent reading. Because the two forms of reading differ in nontrivial ways, I would advocate use of error-detection procedures with contrived texts in preference to miscue procedures with uncontrived ones.

A second method affords some of the advantages of both error-detection and miscue procedures, and I am cautiously optimistic about its broader application. This method is much more recent. It is on-line assessment of silent reading processing. With this method, we have external data (a record of interactions at the computer terminal), we can use uncontrived texts, and we can study the process of interest, silent reading. Tobias (1984) asked college students to read a 49-paragraph passage on the topic of data processing and computer programming, as it was displayed on microcomputer screens. Sentences in the passage were numbered and appeared on the screen one at a time. When students finished a sentence and pressed the space bar that sentence was erased, but the space it had occupied and its number remained on the screen.

Students had a number of options. They could (a) review any sentence or group of sentences; (b) preview any sentence or group of sentences; (c) consult an alternate text written with easier vocabulary at the end of any paragraph; (d) review the alternate text; (e) preview the alternate text; (f) take notes on the computer system; (g) review their notes; (h) request an organizational display that provided all headings in the main and alternate texts and sentence numbers covered by each heading; and (i) view a "menu" of these options. The students received pretraining and practice in using each option.

In one study conducted with this high-option procedure, college-age subjects were assigned to conditions of merely reading the data-processing passage; of reading the passage and responding to adjunct questions; or of reading, answering adjunct questions, and receiving feedback about response accuracy. In general, Tobias (1984) found that the group receiving feedback used the options least and the adjunct-question group used them most. Great variability existed within conditions in frequency of option use.

Tobias (1984) suggests that the students may not have known which strategies to employ when they encountered comprehension/learning difficulties. He suggests that some students' excessive option use may indicate an essentially trial-and-error approach to option sampling in time of difficulty. It may also be an artifact of the presentation of a relatively novel task: reading text on a computer terminal and selecting from a large set of assisting options, some of which have no real parallel in the noncomputer situation. For our present purposes, we should note that a computer presentation of text to be read and managed with so many options available can yield a great deal of information about difficulties detected and difficulties remedied.

Such a presentation also has instructional potential. In a more recent study, Tobias (1985) has prescribed reviewing of either just-read text or an easier version of that text in instances in which adjunct-question responses were incorrect. This is reminiscent of Alessi et al. (1979) (see chapter 3) in which college students were induced to review portions of text when question responses indicated a comprehension/memory failure. In comparing performance of college students for whom reviewing was either optional or required, Tobias found that the two "required-reviewing" groups had significantly higher scores on posttest items related to adjunct questions. These "required-reviewing" students, once again, were not particularly efficient in their use of text. They reread a great deal more text than was needed. These students, in other words, did not display text sampling (Garner et al., 1983) as discussed in chapter 3. Perhaps they needed more explicit instruction on application of the text-reinspection strategy.

It is to instruction in metacognitive activities, particularly strategy use, that we now turn our attention. Having documented the needs of less experienced and less proficient learners in chapter 3, needs that are not much diminished, it turns out, by methodological concerns examined in chapters 4 and 5, we turn to intervention efforts in chapter 6.

Chapter 6

Training Students to Use Strategies

In the past few years there has been a great deal of research activity devoted to strategy training. Strategies taught have generally been academically fundamental (i.e., all students appear to need them) and differentially exercised (i.e., some students appear not to use them spontaneously). Kail (1983) points out that reading is one of the areas where academically fundamental activities that are differentially exercised are common. This is surely one reason why so much of the recent cognitive instructional research has been focused on reading and reading-related strategies.

Why do investigators undertake strategy training studies? There are two distinct reasons, one theoretical and one practical. If, according to a theory of cognitive processing, a particular activity is an important component, then teaching people who do not use that component to do so should improve their performance. Such improvement provides support for the theoretical formulation. Just as important, perhaps, is the potential improvement of performance for academically poor students on academically fundamental tasks. Positive results in the experimental setting provide impetus for instructional interventions by educational practitioners (Brown et al., 1986; Dansereau et al., 1979; Weinstein & Underwood, 1985).

The two purposes for conducting strategy training studies can be made clearer if we refer to two specific strategies discussed in chapter 3. For the text reinspection strategy, Garner, Macready, and Wagoner (1984) proposed that four separate components—undifferentiated rereading, text sampling, question differentiation, and text manipulation—are exercised by strategy users. They found evidence of a particular component-acquisition order for both successful and unsuccessful readers. To satisfy the theoretical reason for conducting a training study, then, Garner and her colleagues might have taught the four components to non–strategy users in both the "preferred" sequence and alternative sequences. Finding improved text reinspection and question-answering performance for subjects taught the "preferred" sequence, but not for those taught alternative sequences, would provide further support for the theoretical formulation of a particular linear hierarchy of component acquisition. To satisfy the practical reason for conducting a training study, the researchers might have taught the strategy components in the "preferred" sequence to nonusers. Finding improved performance, the researchers could suggest how teachers might implement strategy instruction. Garner, Hare, Alexander, Haynes, and Winograd (1984) conducted the latter sort of study. This study will be discussed in some detail in this chapter.

A second specific strategy that was discussed in chapter 3 is the text summarization strategy. It will be recalled that Brown and Day (1983) proposed six rules for summarizing text; two deletion rules, two superordination rules, and two topic sentence rules. They found age differences in application of the six rules to expository text. To satisfy the theoretical reason for conducting a training study, then, Brown and her colleagues might have taught all six rules and subsets of the rules to nonproficient summarizers. Finding improved summarization performance for subjects taught all six rules, and either less improved or unimproved performance for subjects taught just some of the rules, would provide support for the Brown and Day (1983) theoretical formulation of rule-driven summarizing. To satisfy the practical reason for conducting a training study, the researchers might have taught the entire set of rules to nonproficient summarizers. Finding improved performance, they could advise teachers on summarization instruction. Both Day (Brown et al., 1981; Day, 1980) and Hare and Borchardt (1984) have conducted the latter sort of study. This work as well will be discussed later in this chapter.

Campione and Armbruster (1984) note that intervention research designed for theoretical or practical purposes tends to focus on either modification of learning materials or modification of learner activities. These two categories of interest are sometimes labeled "text engineering" and "human cognitive engineering" (Reif, 1980). When researchers modify texts, they make them more concrete, more explicit, more likely to trigger prior knowledge structures of readers (Pressley, 1983); that is, they reduce the amount of information processing required. When researchers modify learner activities, they extend strategy use and ultimately increase the learners' capacity to process information effectively. They make learners less dependent on future instruction (Frederiksen, 1984). It is only the modification of learner activities that will concern us in this chapter.

Hundreds of efforts to modify learner activities for theoretical or practical purposes have appeared in the recent literatures in psychology and education. Many of these efforts have produced some immediate behavioral change in the recipients of the training. For many of the efforts, however, we have little information about how learners performed tasks (whether successfully or unsuccessfully), about possible variations in target performance, about performance long after training was concluded, or about the adeptness with which the learners monitored and evaluated the success of their task completion.

In this chapter, only examples of training efforts that provide this sort of information will be presented. The focus will be on academically fundamental, differentially exercised activities related to reading. First, a list of the sorts of information needed about strategy interventions will be presented. Next, five specific training studies will be examined. Finally, the issue of appropriate relinquishing of strategic responsibility from instructor to learner will be discussed in the context of Vygotsky's (1978) "zone of proximal development" construct.

Strategy Training Research: What Do We Need to Know?

As Belmont and Butterfield (1977) pointed out some time ago, one thing we need to know is what a person is thinking while performing a task. We need to employ the most direct measurement possible, they suggest, to reveal specific activities used by good performers, performers' following or not following directions, and spontaneously produced strategic activity that either inhibits or assists in successful task performance. If we do not collect information on processing with the absolute minimum of logical and temporal distance between the processing and the measuring, we are unable to explain immediate or long-term failures of training, and we may well explain training successes incorrectly.

Second, we need to know how a person *should* be thinking while performing a task (Belmont & Butterfield, 1977). This information comes as a result of careful task analysis, accomplished either intuitively or empirically. As Belmont and Butterfield note, task analysis is a "confrontation with individual differences, on the one hand, and regularities in relationships between strategies and task demands, on the other" (Belmont & Butterfield, 1977, p. 456). Tobias (1982) adds that this analysis must be sufficiently "fine-grained" so that a computer program can be generated to simulate successful task performance. Case (1978) adds that task analysis must produce a description of a detailed sequence of operations.

Third, we need to know how we can judge whether or not the training has been successful. Belmont and Butterfield (1977) again provide useful direction. They suggest that we must be able to specify what or how well a person must do to permit the conclusion that training worked. Immediate improvement of performance, durability of instructional effects, and transfer of the instructed activity to new situations are the accepted tests. Immediate improvement in performance could be evident either in qualitative change, such as learning to generate topic sentences, or in quantitative improvement, such as movement toward an established criterion such as approximation of adult performance. Durability of effects is measured by maintenance of acceptable performance over a time interval without further instruction. Successful transfer demands acceptable performance in situations that are related to but still different from the original training conditions (Belmont, Butterfield, & Ferretti, 1982).

Obviously, if performance is not improved initially by strategy training, marked improvement after more time has elapsed is unlikely. Furthermore, if a strategy is not durable, it is unlikely to generalize to new situations (Kendall, Borkowski, & Cavanaugh, 1980). Some evidence for acceptable transfer comes from intervention programs in which somewhat general activities were trained (Brown & Campione, 1978; Lodico, Ghatala, Levin, Pressley, & Bell, 1983). Brown, Campione, & Murphy (1977) have suggested that direct instruction in generalization of the activities might enhance transfer.

It also appears that self-control training assists in generalization of strategy instruction (Belmont & Butterfield, 1977; Ryan, 1981; Short & Ryan, 1984). Brown et al. (1981) discuss blind training studies, informed training studies, and self-control training studies (see chapter 2 of this volume). Only the last sort of intervention requires the learners to be fully "active conspirators in the training process" (Brown et al., 1981, p. 15). In self-control training, learners are instructed in the use of a strategy, and they are also explicitly instructed how to monitor and evaluate their strategy use. It appears that strategy-plus-control training produces enhanced initial performance and transfer of the instructed activity (Brown et al., 1981; Brown & Palincsar, 1982; Pressley, Borkowski, & O'Sullivan, 1984; Simon, 1980).

The generality of strategy use is of course related to flexibility of strategy application (see chapter 3). If learners do not acquire information about when and where, as well as how, to use strategies, they are likely to apply routines in rote fashion in both appropriate and inappropriate instances. Frese and Stewart (1984) give the example of an undergraduate student falling into a "skill trap" by thinking that the highly practiced routine of memorizing material will produce success in graduate school, where, instead, original ideas are expected from students. Bransford and Heldmeyer (1983) give a related example of students using "flowery" language, not scientific prose, as they move from composition in one domain to composition in a new, unrelated one.

In the context of generality of strategy use, the training work conducted by Meichenbaum and his colleagues should be mentioned. Meichenbaum and Asarnow (1979) call their method "cognitive-behavioral modification" (CBM) and describe it as teaching a learner to verbalize the component processes of academic or self-control problem solving. General problem-solving activities are modeled for the learner, who then engages in extended rehearsal during task completion. Direct instruction in generalization is offered (Meichenbaum, 1980). The emphasis in this method is on the process, not the products, of problem solving. K. R. Harris (1982) notes that CBM may be particularly appropriate for special education students, who may not spontaneously make use of verbal mediation processes.

Specific Strategy Interventions

The reading-related instruction to be discussed here has been reported in such a way that we do have information about what subjects thought, about task demands, and about a variety of specific performance outcomes. Many of the studies have included a self-control training component. The studies also share an adherence to well-established learning principles, such as those discussed recently by Pearson and his colleagues (Pearson, 1982; Pearson & Gallagher, 1983; Pearson & Tierney, 1983): proceeding in training from simple to complex activities; provision of plenty of guided practice; systematic use of thought-provoking questions. Another point to be made about the studies as a group is that these successful training efforts have been "prolonged" (Ryan, 1981, p. 245); that is, the interventions have been conducted over several days.

An interesting final point about these studies taken together is that the instruction provided was, in every case, very direct and very explicit. Doyle (1983) defines direct instruction as instruction in which academic tasks are carefully structured for learners; in which learners are told very explicitly how to accomplish the tasks and are systematically guided through a series of exercises leading to mastery; and in which opportunities for directed practice, assessment of progress, and corrective feedback are frequent. Rosenshine and Stevens (1984) noted many of the same features in the set of successful instructional studies they reviewed recently. Duffy, Book, and Roehler (1983) highlighted the importance of explicitness in instructor explanations, citing data in support of the view that explicit teacher explanation produces student awareness, which in turn stimulates student achievement. Verbal explicitness from teachers is particularly important, Duffy, Roehler, and Wesselman (1984) argue, for low-aptitude students who learn exactly "what the teacher says." Winograd and Hare (in press) have tried to delineate what effective explanations about reading strategies should in fact explain. Their list is as follows:

1. Why the strategy should be learned
2. What the strategy is
3. How to use the strategy
4. When and where the strategy is to be used
5. How to evaluate use of the strategy

The reason why this predominance of direct, explicit instruction among the studies to be examined is important is that we have recent evidence that, despite the widespread belief that "a classroom is a place where instruction is offered and received" (Durkin, 1981, p. 516), little direct instruction in reading comprehension actually seems to occur in elementary school. Durkin (1978–1979) found that less than 1% of some 17,997 minutes of instructional time in elementary school reading and social studies classes was devoted to direct comprehension instruction. In a follow-up study, she found that in five bestselling basal series' teacher manuals application and unguided practice exercises appeared far more frequently than did direct, explicit comprehension instructional suggestions. Pearson (1982) notes that Durkin's two studies reveal a teacher and text emphasis on "massive doses of unguided practice" (p. 12).

Goetz (1984) speculates that a number of reasons may account for the lack of direct instruction in reading comprehension in school: (a) the assumption that skills and strategies will emerge without instruction; (b) a focus on activity flow and control behaviors in classrooms; (c) a focus on domain-specific content; and (d) teachers' lack of knowledge about how to teach comprehension. Certainly successful training studies that provide algorithm-governed interventions that can be adapted for regular classroom use are important because they can extend teacher's knowledge about strategy instruction. Potentially, then, one of the negative factors discussed by Goetz diminishes in importance with dissemination of results from the body of research that we will sample now.

Text Summarization

As we noted in chapter 3, text summarization is a tool both for making cognitive progress and for monitoring it. As a cognitive strategy, it allows learners to synthesize information from multiple sources and diverse perspectives. This makes it a prerequisite tool for adept completion of such common academic tasks as writing reports, preparing study summaries of texts, and writing responses to essay examination questions. As a metacognitive strategy, it allows learners to attempt synopses of what has been read. If they cannot produce abbreviated versions of text, this is an indication to them that a remedy, perhaps rereading of the material, must be applied. Thus, text summarization is an extremely useful strategy in academic settings.

We have already discussed some of the evidence of differential exercise of this strategy in chapter 3. We know from work done by Brown and her colleagues that only deletion rules are used effectively by students as young as 11 years of age, and that even college students use the topic-sentence invention rule far less frequently than would be appropriate (Brown & Day, 1983). We know that students in grades 5, 7, and 11 and in college underutilize condensing and revising activities, particularly in the absence of space constraints (Brown, Day, & Jones, 1983).

In addition, we know that even high school and college students display minimal integration of information units in text (Garner, 1985); information integration is an important means to producing succinct summaries. We know that poor readers in grade 8 frequently do not match adults in their judgments of what information is important in text, what information, in other words, should be included in a summary of the text (Winograd, 1984). We know that grade 5 learners can recognize the superiority of concise summaries to long "copy-delete" examples, but few produce succinct summaries of their own (Garner et al., 1985). Finally, we know from very recent work that "text engineering" in the areas of enhanced semantic and lexical cuing of important information and reorganization of information is insufficient to produce exemplary summarization performance, even from college students (Garner & McCaleb, 1985). It seems that the need for training in text summarization is strong, even among older, relatively successful learners.

Based on Day's (1980) dissertation work in which she trained junior college students to apply the deletion, superordination, and topic-sentence rules for text summarization, Hare and Borchardt (1984) set out to teach slightly younger students the rules Day had taught, plus a paragraph-combining rule and a "polishing" (i.e., revising) rule. Low-income, minority high school juniors were assigned to conditions of inductive or deductive instruction. Instruction was delivered to both groups for 2 hours per day over 3 consecutive days.

Some of the procedural specifics were adaptations from Day's (1980) work. A "rulesheet," for instance, provided step-by-step assistance in checking comprehension of the original text and in planning, generating, and revising a summary of that text (see Figure 6.1 for the rules for generating and revising the summary). A series of expository texts, some used in Day's study and some naturally occurring high school passages, were used for pretesting, training, and posttesting. "Helpsheets" demonstrating application of the various summarization rules were pre-

Figure 6.1. Summarization rules (Hare & Borchardt, 1984, p. 66)

Four Rules for Writing a Summary

1. Collapse lists. If you see a list of things, try to think of a word or phrase name for the whole list. For example, if you saw a list like eyes, ears, neck, arms, and legs, you could say "body parts." Or, if you saw a list like ice skating, skiing, or sledding, you could say "winter sports."

2. Use topic sentences. Often authors write a sentence that summarizes a whole paragraph. It is called a topic sentence. If the author gives you one, you can use it in your summary. Unfortunately, not all paragraphs contain topic sentences. That means you may have to make up one for yourself. If you don't see a topic sentence, make up one of your own.

3. Get rid of unnecessary detail. Some text information can be repeated in a passage. In other words, the same thing can be said in a number of different ways, all in one passage. Other text information can be unimportant, or trivial. Since summaries are meant to be short, get rid of repetitive or trivial information.

4. Collapse paragraphs. Paragraphs are often related to one another. Some paragraphs explain one or more other paragraphs. Some paragraphs just expand on the information presented in other paragraphs. Some paragraphs are more necessary than other paragraphs. Decide which paragraphs should be kept or gotten rid of, and which might be joined together.

A Final Suggestion

Polish the summary. When a lot of information is reduced from an original passage, the resulting concentrated information often sounds very unnatural. Fix this problem and create a more natural-sounding summary. Adjustments may include but are not limited to paraphrasing, the insertion of connecting words like "and" or "because," and the insertion of introductory or closing statements. Paraphrasing is especially useful here, for two reasons: one, because it improves your ability to remember the material, and two, it avoids using the author's words, otherwise known as plagiarism.

---

pared for specific texts. Teachers for both inductive and deductive conditions used instructional scripts, and were observed for fidelity of their instruction to the guidelines.

For both a specially constructed test passage and a naturally occurring test passage, experimental subjects outperformed control subjects in rule use. Hare and Borchardt (1984) found two fairly predictable transition patterns among experimental subjects: Either they exhibited no use of a particular rule in pretesting and moved to inconsistent use in posttesting, or they exhibited inconsistent use of a rule in pretesting and moved to consistent use in posttesting. Generally, strategic gains in summarizing were maintained 2 weeks after the training had been concluded. Not surprisingly, the use of the difficult topic-sentence invention rule was not readily taught inductively or deductively. Perhaps somewhat surprisingly, no differences in rule use between subjects assigned to inductive and deductive conditions appeared in the study.

Both the Day (1980) and Hare and Borchardt (1984) studies seem to support the conclusion that text summarization can be taught. It appears that instruction similar to that offered in these two investigations could be given by teachers in classrooms.

Text Reinspection

Text reinspection is another useful, underutilized strategy that appears to be teachable. As noted in chapter 3, the reinspection strategy capitalizes on the permanence of print. Learners recognize that information once read is not now remembered, and they intentionally reaccess the portions of text that provide the needed information. The strategy is invaluable in situations in which at-hand, not exclusively in-head, information is called for, and in which memory overload is likely because of length or difficulty of text. It is particularly useful for responding to questions, the primary means of demonstrating what has been learned from text (Raphael & Pearson, 1982). As Rigney (1980) argues, however, general "looking-back skills" are used even by technicians making voltage measurements in a circuit, by computer programmers assessing current outcomes, and by many others who need to "maintain a history of processing up to the current place in the sequence that will serve as the basis for determining what comes next" (p. 338).

Much of the research presented in chapter 3 suggests that the text reinspection strategy is often not implemented, particularly by younger and less proficient readers. We know that these younger, less adept readers are unlikely to remedy memory failure with text lookbacks (Garner & Reis, 1981) and are unlikely to encourage still younger children whom they are tutoring to reaccess text to answer very detailed questions about the content (Garner et al., 1983). When these less proficient readers do use text reinspection, they tend to engage in "undifferentiated rereading" of the entire text in all instances in which an answer to a question is elusive, and they seldom look beyond a single sentence for information needed to answer a particular question (Garner, Macready, & Wagoner, 1984). Garner and her colleagues have suggested that during the normal course of schooling, learners acquire the notion that text reinspection is "illegal." Both children (see Garner, Hare, Alexander, Haynes, & Winograd, 1984) and adults (see Alexander et al., 1984), for instance, employ the text reinspection strategy less in a print-down condition as opposed to a print-up condition, with no prohibitions about reinspection having been given. Eliminating erroneous ideas about legality of strategy use may be a critical part of any text reinspection intervention.

Garner, Hare, Alexander, Haynes, & Winograd (1984) taught the strategy to upper elementary and middle school students enrolled in a remedial reading clinic. In 3 days of training, subjects read a series of 200-word expository passages and answered "text-based" questions (i.e., questions cuing text recall or reaccess) and "reader-based" questions (i.e., questions cuing use of reader knowledge base) for each passage. Each day, a different hint about appropriate use of the strategy was given. The hints about why, when, and where to use lookbacks were based on task analysis of text reinspection to answer questions. The hints appear in Figure 6.2.

Five days after training was concluded, the instructed students and control students were tested for strategy use. An adult who had not been involved in training presented subjects with two texts and told each child that he or she should read each article carefully and be prepared to answer three questions about the material. The pages of the first text were placed print down, whereas the pages of the second were left print up. In the latter condition, if a subject did not use text reinspection, the subject was prompted with the cue "You can look back at any part of the article to answer the questions." All test sessions were videotaped for eventual replaying and coding.

Both *how* the trained and control subjects processed (strategy use) and *how well* they processed (question-answering accuracy) were of interest in this study. A series of group comparisons showed no difference between trained subjects and control subjects on percent of correct answers from recall alone, but significant differences, favoring trained subjects in each case, on both percent of answers unrecalled but correct with lookbacks and percent of lookbacks used when needed. The first significant difference showed trained subjects answered more questions correctly when they could not immediately recall the information; they did so by using text reinspection. The second difference showed that these trained subjects used the strategy appropriately even when correct answers were not the outcome. It is noteworthy that of all text reinspection instances that occurred during testing, 100% of the control subjects' lookbacks appeared in the print-up condition, whereas only 33% of the trained subjects' lookbacks did. Additionally, all instances for control subjects were cued verbally, whereas only 13% of the instances for the trained subjects were so cued.

Garner, Hare, Alexander, Haynes, and Winograd (1984) conclude from this study that use of the text reinspection strategy can be improved with direct instruction, instruction that could be provided by teachers in classrooms to groups of learners in much the same way it was delivered to individuals in the clinic setting. At the very least, Garner and her colleagues argue, classroom discussion of the error of assuming that reinspection in nontest situations is "illegal" is sorely needed.

Figure 6.2. Text reinspection hints

Day 1

Most people do not remember everything they read in an article. That is *why* it is a good idea to look back at the article to find information needed to answer some questions. People who want to answer questions correctly often spend many minutes searching for the answers. Let's look at the first article you read. When you had (if you had had) some difficulty answering question ____ you (could have) looked back in the article and found the answer _____ here. Do you understand why looking back to the article for information works? (Good.) Now, as I ask you each of the questions for this article you've just read, I hope you'll decide if you should look back to part of the article to answer the question. Do you understand what to do? Tell me. (Good.)

Day 2

Before I ask you questions about today's article, I want to do two things. I want to remind you to use hint 1 that we reviewed a few minutes ago, and I want to give you a second hint. That hint is that some questions ask about what you think or what's in your head, not about what the author said or what's on the page. An example of this "do you think" kind of question for an article you've read is question ____. *When* you get a question like that, you should not spend a lot of time looking back at the article. Instead, you should give an answer based on what you know. Do you understand when you should look back to the article to answer questions, and when you should not? (Good.) Now, as I ask you the questions, I hope you'll decide if you should look back to part of the article to answer them. Do you understand what to do? Tell me. (Good.)

Day 3

Before I ask you the last set of questions, I want to do two things. I want to remind you to use the first two hints about why and when to look back to the article, and I want to give you one last hint. The last hint is about *where* to look for answers in articles. In the first article you read, one question we looked at earlier asked _____. If you knew you did not remember the answer, and you knew the question wasn't asking about what you think, you'd probably know you should look back to the article, but where? If you remembered that the answer was in either the first or second section, that would help somewhat. Skimming the entire article quickly to find the part that would be most helpful is a good idea. So for this question (a text-based one) for another article you've read, we might try that (modeled, with use of key words in the question). Notice that for that question, we needed to look in more than one sentence to get the complete answer. That is often the case. Do you understand where you should look back in an article for answers? (Good.) Now, as I ask you the questions, I hope you'll decide if you should look back to the article to answer them. Think about all three of the hints I've given you. Do you understand what to do? Tell me. (Good.)

Studying Text

Beginning in the upper elementary grades, studying textbook material occupies a large proportion of learners' time in school and out (Weinstein & Mayer, 1986). Much of the time expended on learning from text is spent independent of instructors, completing tasks assigned as homework (T. H. Anderson, 1979). If learners do not employ study strategies while completing assignments, they are likely to waste much time and learn little. T. H. Anderson and Armbruster (1984) point out that processing demands of textbook material are extensive. According to them, it is not unusual for a single page of exposition to have at least 50 separate idea units that are interrelated in complex ways. Chapters assigned by instructors for independent reading are often 20–50 pages long. T. H. Anderson and Armbruster (1984) note that "it is folly to think that a student could (or should) learn and remember all, or even most, of the content in a textbook chapter" (p. 660). Strategies that increase the likelihood of comprehension and retrieval of important content, given the finite resources available, are essential.

Rohwer (1984) notes that research efforts to date to investigate the relation between individual differences in studying and variations in academic achievement have been disappointing. The preferred method has been one of administering self-report inventories to large samples of students and then correlating scale scores for these reports with cumulative grade-point averages. Psychometric inadequacies and low correlations have been common. Rohwer suggests that these survey investigations have suffered from a pair of dubious assumptions: (a) that study activities are of uniform effectiveness regardless of task conditions, and (b) that students are consistently effective from situation to situation. He also suggests that we need to devise some relatively small-scale interview and observational studies to obtain information about how and how effectively students study under different conditions. Such studies could provide data about differential exercise of specific study strategies beyond the general deficits documented in the professional and lay literatures.

Adams, Carnine, and Gersten (1982) analyzed studying tasks in the literature and concluded that the following six tactics have been substantiated as increasing the likelihood of comprehension and retrieval of important content in textbooks:

1. Previewing the passage by reading the headings and subheadings
2. Reciting the first subheading
3. Asking oneself questions about what might be important to learn
4. Reading to find the important details
5. Rereading the subheading, reciting important details
6. Rehearsing (as a final review and check of test readiness)

Adams et al. (1982) then assigned fifth-grade students to one of three groups: one receiving direct instruction in studying, a second engaging in independent study with feedback provided by a teacher, and a third receiving no study skills instruction. The studying instruction given the first group was very similar to what might be offered in regular classrooms, in that a commercial social studies textbook was used, students were not allowed to mark in their books, and training time matched that of a typical class session (i.e., about 40 minutes per day for each of 4 days). Experienced teachers implemented the treatments.

The instruction presented the six steps given above after a daily vocabulary review. Use of each step was modeled by the teacher. Oral use of the method was faded gradually to silent studying by the last day of training. The independent study group also spent about 40 minutes daily, but only in reviewing vocabulary and then studying the 500–800 word social studies segments without any direction beyond being told to study "until important information had been learned." Both the studying instruction and independent study groups were administered quizzes on content at the end of each session. The group receiving no study skills instruction stayed in regular classrooms for the 4 training days.

Testing occurred on two occasions, the day after training was concluded and 2 weeks later. All students were asked to retell passage content and were given short-answer tests on the social studies content. Students given direct instruction outperformed students in the two comparison conditions on the short-answer tests, but not on the retelling task. This pattern held for both immediate and delayed testing. The direct-instruction subjects also studied longer for both immediate and delayed tests than did either of the other two groups of subjects. The students given direct instruction did not, however, use the study rules they were taught as frequently as the researchers might have hoped. Half of these students were observed to use the study rules on the immediate posttest, and only 20% were observed using them on the delayed posttest. A large proportion of the students did use an observable study strategy, if not the instructed ones. Adams et al. (1982) suggest that by the second posttest many of the instructed subjects had adopted more personalized study methods with which there was no decrement in test performance. Weinstein, Underwood, Wicker, and Cubberly (1979) have noted that development and modification of strategies to fit individual learners' learning processes and styles is to be desired.

Perhaps the most important finding of all from this study is the lack of performance differences between subjects given independent study with feedback and subjects given no study instruction at all. This result led Adams et al. (1982) to conclude that the common practice of giving students workbook assignments to be completed independently in the absence of any direct strategic instruction from teacher or text (see Venezky, 1982) is not a very effective way for most students to acquire systematic studying routines. More direct instruction seems to be needed, at least by fifth-grade students attempting to read and remember information from a social studies textbook.

Drawing Inferences from Text

A very basic component of comprehension of text is drawing appropriate inferences. Trabasso (1980) distinguishes between "text-connecting" inferences, in which readers find semantic or logical relations between propositions expressed in text, and "slot-filling" inferences, in which readers fill in missing information to make connections between events discussed in text. The making of both sorts of inferences is considered to be a mostly unconscious process (McCagg, 1984).

A large body of evidence supports the view that once we draw an inference, we represent what we have read and what we have inferred together in memory, failing to distinguish the source of the information (see, for example, Blachowicz, 1977–1978; Bransford & Johnson, 1973; Kintsch, 1983; Voss, Tyler, & Bisanz, 1982). When given a recognition task, then, we are at least as likely to recognize falsely a statement of inferred information as we are to recognize information that actually appeared in text. If writers could not rely on readers' inferencing, they would have to be tediously explicit in their writing. Note, for instance, the three sentences given below:

1. The man boarded the bus and fumbled in his pocket for the fare.
2. He pulled three nickels and two pennies from his pocket.
3. He got off the bus at the next stop.

Most readers would draw a series of inferences: The man had only 17¢ in his pocket, 17¢ was insufficient for the adult fare, the man was embarrassed as he exited the bus. In a false-recognition paradigm task, readers might well recognize having read a sentence such as "The man did not have enough money to ride the bus." Writers do not need to tell readers everything, for readers connect text events and fill slots with assumptions based on general knowledge of the objects and events discussed.

Children have more difficulty in answering "inferential" questions about text than they do in answering "literal" ones (Hansen & Pearson, 1980). That is, they seem to understand and remember explicit and implicit relations between propositions less well than they understand and remember explicit intraproposition information. It is not clear whether learner limitations for a difficult task or instructional emphasis or some combination is responsible for this situation (Gordon & Pearson, 1983). If learner limitations are to be held accountable, either meager general knowledge base (Resnick, 1983; Voss, 1984) or adherence to serial processing of single propositions with minimal integration (Paris & Lindauer, 1982) might be responsible for the pattern.

Hansen and Pearson (1983) provided explicit inference strategy training and substantial practice in drawing inferences to good and poor fourth-grade readers. Regular classroom teachers provided the instruction to experimental and control groups for 2 days each week over a 10-week period. For the experimental group, the first day each week was given over to strategy training. Students discussed the importance of comparing their own experiences to those in a text in order to help their comprehension; the children coined the phrase "using your own life" to describe this aspect of instruction. The second day of each week for the experimental group was allocated to discussion composed entirely of inferential questions. The control group's work on the first day was determined by the teacher's manual directions. The group's discussion on the second day was composed of literal and inferential questions in a ratio of 4:1.

For both comprehension worksheets completed after the discussion of each story and answering questions for new stories not used in training, training benefited the poor readers, whose inferential question-answering performance was superior to that of the poor readers in the control group. Good readers were not similarly assisted by their assignment to inference training. Hansen and Pearson (1983) suggest that good readers may figure out "inference game" rules on their own, whereas poor readers need direct instruction. The results of this study are consonant with that argument and provide hope to applied researchers wanting to document both that teachers can deliver explicit inference instruction and that poor readers can show improved performance as a result of that instruction.

Monitoring and Resolving Text Comprehension Obstacles

By far the most ambitious of the five strategy interventions discussed in this chapter is the Informed Strategies for Learning (ISL) program devised by Paris and his colleagues (see, for example, Paris, Cross, DeBritto, Jacobs, Oka, & Saarnio, 1984; Paris, Cross, & Lipson, 1984; Paris & Jacobs, 1984). The "protracted period and varied conditions of procedural acquistion in natural settings" (Rohwer & Litrownik, 1983, p. 809) provide quite a contrast to the large number of relatively short-term experiments in the literature. Paris and his colleagues began with the research base presented in chapter 3 of this volume; that is, they knew that many

children, particularly younger children and less able readers, are surprisingly tolerant of obstacles to text comprehension (Paris & Wixson, in
press), and many, if they do notice comprehension problems, do not possess the strategic resources to remedy the problems. These nonmonitoring, minimally strategic children operate at a serious disadvantage in
school, particularly in situations demanding self-directed, independent
approaches to learning. Paris and his colleagues believe that reading
strategies can be explained directly to children.

Three principles of effective instruction guided the group's efforts: (a)
students need to know about declarative (propositional), procedural
("how-to"), and conditional (flexible application) knowledge; (b) students can share their thoughts and feelings about what they are learning;
and (c) students need to be "coached" from a position of other-regulation
to one of self-regulation of learning. The five techniques used in the lessons that evolved from these principles were informed teaching, metaphors for strategies and bulletin boards, group dialogue, guided practice,
and "bridging" to content-area reading.

Informed teaching meant that teachers told students what a strategy
was, how to use it, and when and why it should be used (note the similarity to the list for effective explanations in Winograd and Hare, in press).
Metaphors (e.g., comparing prereading and planning a trip, or comparing summarizing and participating in a roundup) gave concrete cues
for recall, discussion, and visual display of strategy components. Group
dialogue allowed student confusion or depth of understanding to emerge
(an assessment function) and also allowed modeling of effective strategic
behavior to occur (an instructional function). Guided practice meant that
direct instruction, reading, and discussion of strategic applications for a
particular selection were followed by use of worksheets, for which the
students needed to use the strategies. The bridging was accomplished
through periodic lessons in which teachers applied the instructed strategies to science and social studies texts.

The instruction, provided for approximately 4 months, included 20
modules designed for grades 3 through 5. Direct instruction lessons of 30
minutes each were given twice a week for the 4-month period. Each mod-
ule of the 20 emphasized one comprehension strategy. The modules were
grouped into four clusters. The 20 modules and accompanying metaphors appear in Figure 6.3.

Two third-grade classes and two fifth-grade classes received the instruction, and two other classes at each grade level served as control
groups. All children were pretested in October and posttested in April
and May, 1 month after the ISL intervention had ended. Measures used
were a standardized comprehension subtest, a standardized paragraph-
reading subtest, cloze tasks, and error-detection tasks. Paris, Cross, and

Figure 6.3.   ISL modules (Paris, Cross, DeBritto, Jacobs, Oka, & Saarnio, 1984)

I.   Awareness of Reading Goals, Plans, and Strategies
    1. Goals and purposes of reading ("Hunting for reading treasure")
    2. Evaluating the reading task ("Be a reading detective")
    3. Comprehension strategies ("A bag full of tricks for reading")
    4. Forming plans ("Planning to build meaning")
    5. Review
II.   Components of Meaning in Text
    6. Kinds of meaning and text content ("Turn on the meaning")
    7. Ambiguity and multiple meanings ("Hidden meaning")
    8. Temporal and causal sequences ("Links in the chain of events")
    9. Clues to meaning ("Tracking down the main idea")
    10. Review
III.   Constructive Comprehension Skills
    11. Making inferences ("Weaving ideas")
    12. Preview and review of goals and task ("Surveying the land of reading")
    13. Integrating ideas and using context ("Bridges to meaning")
    14. Critical reading ("Judge your reading")
    15. Review
IV.   Strategies for Monitoring and Improving Comprehension
    16. Comprehension monitoring ("Signs for reading")
    17. Detecting comprehension failures ("Road to reading disaster")
    18. Self-correction ("Road repair")
    19. Text schemas and summaries ("Round up your ideas")
    20. Review

Lipson (1984) note that the first two tests are conventional measures of comprehension, while the last two tasks require readers to apply cognitive strategies presumably taught in the ISL program: supplying missing words in text and monitoring meaning in text.

Using pretest scores as a covariate and posttest scores as the dependent variable, Paris and his colleagues tested for grade and treatment effects. For the conventional comprehension measures, neither main effects nor interactions were statistically significant. For the cloze measure and the error-detection measure, however, both main effects reached conventional levels of significance, with fifth-grade subjects' performance superior to that of third-grade subjects on both tasks, and the experimental group's performance superior to that of control subjects on both tasks.

Paris, Cross, and Lipson (1984) have tried to explain the incongruity of results for conventional measures and more instruction-specific measures. One possibility, they acknowledge, is that strategies taught in the ISL program were too esoteric to be relevant to general comprehension performance, but Paris and his colleagues do not accept this line of argument. They suggest an alternative: Standardized tests devised to maximize discrimination among students of varied reading proficiency are based on generalized traits, not specific knowledge, strategies, or curricula. Such tests, they submit, are highly correlated with general intelligence measures and are relatively insensitive to variations in specific learning experiences.

Given that some measures yielded results of superior performance for instructed students, attention needs to be paid to this strategic intervention. ISL is driven by theory, and yet it is "packaged" in such a manner that, even given the "complexities and constraints of classroom life" (Duffy, 1982, p. 359), trained teachers were able to train groups of students to monitor and resolve comprehension obstacles in text in the natural social world of classrooms. Bronfenbrenner (1979) has described a mass of laboratory experiments conducted by psychologists as "the science of the strange behavior of children in strange situations with strange adults for the briefest possible periods of time" (p. 19). None of the criticisms inherent in Bronfenbrenner's description applies to the ISL program. In this program, teachers taught students in their classrooms a wide variety of strategies that applied to their texts over about half a year's time. In discussing Goetz's (1984) analysis of the absence of direct instruction of this sort, I suggested that sound, well-packaged programs can make an important practical contribution in schools. The ISL intervention may be just such a program.

Strategic Responsibility Shifts

A serious problem for some strategy training research has been the relatively low durability of trained strategic behaviors. That is, learners improve their text-processing performance or other cognitive performance after instruction, but neither the strategic behaviors nor the improved performance is maintained for very long after instruction ends. This dilemma has been described as follows: "The critical breakdown seems to occur when beginning learners or children are left to their own devices" (Paris & Cross, 1983, p. 149), and such learners "frequently revert to their immature strategies when no longer explicitly constrained to play the instructor's programs" (Belmont & Butterfield, 1977, p. 465).

One possible solution to the dilemma of low durability is to provide for a gradual release of responsibility for strategy use from instructor to student *during training*. A student who performs in a particular fashion as a self-directed learner, rather than as a merely compliant one, might be expected to continue to do so. It can be argued that all of the strategy interventions discussed in this chapter did provide for substantial participation by learners, particularly in the later stages of training. Two lines of inquiry suggest that this idea of instructors relinquishing some strategic responsibility to students may have merit.

One is the work of Vygotsky (1978) and of those who have extended his notion of a "zone of proximal development." Vygotsky suggested that cognitive functions appear first on the social (interpsychological) level and only later on the individual (intrapsychological) level. He used a method of presenting children in experimental contexts with tasks beyond the children's present capabilities. They were allowed to solve these tasks with adult guidance. The performance of the "interacting system" (Maccoby, 1982, p. 160) was assessed.

Vygotsky (1978) explained that "what children can do with the assistance of others might be in some sense even more indicative of their mental development than what they can do alone" (p. 85). His zone of proximal development, then, is the distance between the level of independent problem-solving and the level of problem solving in collaboration with an adult or a more capable peer. Vygotsky suggested that "good learning" is always learning in advance of development, that the quality of mediated learning that a child experiences determines that child's cognitive growth to a large extent.

Wertsch and his colleagues (Wertsch, 1978, 1979; Wertsch, McNamee, McLane, & Budwig, 1980; Wertsch & Stone, 1979) have extended Vygotsky's work. They devised a puzzle-making task that mothers and their 2- to 4-year-old children were to complete together. The puzzle depicted a truck carrying a cargo of six square boxes. For the cargo portion of the puzzle, there was only one correct solution, as shown in a model puzzle placed near the children. The children's task was to make the copy look exactly like the model. A complication was that extra pieces not needed to complete the copy were provided as well.

Each mother-child dyad was shown the model and the intact copy. Then the copy was dismantled, and mothers were instructed to help their children as they thought necessary. Sessions were videotaped. Of particular interest in the coding of tapes from the sessions were the mothers' utterances and nonverbal behaviors (e.g., eye gazes to the model) used to regulate children's performance.

Wertsch and his colleagues have identified levels of child performance in this puzzle-making task. At the first level, the children seemed to interpret the adult utterances as discrete statements unrelated to the building of the copy. At a second level, at least the utterance-task connection was made by the children. At a third level, however, the children took on a much larger share of the strategic responsibility, and the mothers functioned largely as givers of reassurance that all was proceeding well. At the final level, the children took over total problem-solving responsibility and were functioning on the intrapsychological plane. The first three levels described by Wertsch and his colleagues were all in the zone of proximal development.

Some important implications for instruction emerge from this body of work. For instance, Wertsch (1979) notes that mothers did not restrict their directives to ones their children could respond to flawlessly. Neither did the mothers give up when children failed to respond or responded inappropriately. It seems that they provided challenging directives and then "coached" the children through the steps necessary to respond. An example is a mother's asking "What do we need next?" and then pointing to the correct piece in the model when the child failed to respond.

Wertsch and Stone (1979) point out that this sort of interaction requires continual monitoring of a child's strategic needs and constant adjustment of the strategic assistance provided (see also Brown & French, 1979; Rogoff, Ellis, & Gardner, 1984). Wertsch (1978) emphasizes that the task for this interaction must fall within a limited range of complexity; it must be difficult enough so that it has not already been mastered, but simple enough so that it will not be impossible for the child to understand anything done in the interactive problem-solving. The child, in other words, must not be required to do too much alone or be denied any degree of participation (Ellis & Rogoff, 1982).

Palincsar and Brown's (1983) "reciprocal teaching" method applies many of Vygotsky's and Wertsch's ideas to reading and reading-related tasks. In this work, summarizing, questioning, clarifying, and predicting were taught as both cognitive and metacognitive activities (i.e., seventh-grade students were taught to use them both to make cognitive progress and to monitor it). In one study, investigators delivered instruction; in another, classroom and resource room teachers provided the instruction. The reciprocal teaching intervention involved an interactive learning game in which instructor and student took turns in leading a dialogue about particular text segments. The "teacher" for each segment first asked a question, then summarized, and offered predictions and clarification as appropriate. The role the student played was expanded over time in training from mostly respondent to mostly instruction giver. The intervention proved to be a powerful method for improving comprehension, in both the resource room and the classroom, in cases of investigator instruction and teacher instruction (Brown, Palincsar, & Armbruster, 1984; Palincsar, 1984).

A second, quite different line of inquiry that nonetheless provides some support for strategic responsibility shifts from instructor to student in Bandura's (1977) work on "self-efficacy" that I will mention only briefly here. Bandura describes an efficacy expectation as "the conviction that one can successfully execute the behavior required to produce the outcomes" (p. 193). Such an expectation is derived from social learning. Such an expectation affects both initiation and persistence of problem-solving behaviors. The stronger the perceived self-efficacy, the more active the problem-solving efforts.

As Oka and Paris (in press) note, to the extent that pursuing an activity seriously threatens self-worth, low motivation to pursue is a more adaptive response than high motivation. For this reason, Corno and Mandinach (1983) argue that the strength of belief in one's ability to perform is a more critical influence on behavior in many situations than either task incentives or actual personal skill.

It appears that changes in self-efficacy require development of capabilities followed by removal of external aids, so that personal efficacy is verified (Bandura, 1977), and so that facility at managing personal and situational resources is expanded (Covington, 1983, 1985). This pattern of removal of assistance is quite similar to the shift in responsibility discussed by Wertsch and his colleagues.

Final Notes on Strategy Training

It appears that there is cause for some optimism among researchers and educational practitioners as a result of the strategy training studies that have been discussed in this chapter. It seems that strategies can be taught to students who do not employ them spontaneously. Two cautions must be sounded, however.

One has been voiced by Paris (in press). He argues that strategies are tools for learning, not ends in themselves. Learning how to use a strategy is only part of the point of training. The second, more important part is the functional and *enduring* use of the strategy for purposes of enhancing learning (for instance, learning from text). Paris suggests that researchers should track how trained strategies are modified or abandoned through experience. We know from the Adams et al. (1982) study discussed earlier that modifications do in fact occur. I think Paris is correct in charging that some strategy training investigations are atheoretical, decontextualized efforts to teach sanctified procedures, with minimal information about flexible application over time being provided to the recipients of the training.

J. H. Flavell (personal communication, January 22, 1985) has suggested that in addition to tracking learners' modification and abandonment of strategies, researchers should examine *why* learners do not use strategies they should use, strategies they have been taught to use. He suggests that backsliding in strategy use may turn out to be very much like backsliding in other areas, such as resisting substance abuse. Maintaining effortful, difficult activities may be much the same, whether the maintenance involves text processing or good health. Flavell goes so far as to suggest that it may be worthwhile to teach learners about circumstances that will tempt them not to bother to invoke strategies. This may involve training them to believe that they cause their behavior and that they can change the nature of that behavior (see McCombs, 1984).

A second caution also has to do with application of trained strategies. Peterson and Swing (1983) note that even if training can be adapted to group instruction for classroom implementation, in classrooms students' cognitive processing "must be done in real time" (p. 275). This means that, given the nature of activity flow of most classrooms, students cannot slow down their processing to incorporate the use of unpracticed cognitive and metacognitive strategies. The reality is that students who worry about "being left behind" in task completion are likely to revert to possibly less mature, but presumably more rehearsed, routines (see Pressley, Ross, Levin, & Ghatala, 1984). This seems a good time to reiterate Pearson's (1982) point mentioned earlier: that plenty of guided practice needs to be part of strategy training. Such practice makes strategies both more personalized and more routinized. Obviously, if strategies are not applied to learning tasks because of either factor just mentioned, the whole point of training students in how to perform a particular strategic routine must be questioned. In the next chapter, learning and use of strategies in classrooms will be discussed further.

Chapter 7

Applications of Metacognitive Research to Classroom Instruction

What insights does the metacognitive literature discussed in chapters 2–6 offer for current views of reading comprehension presented in chapter 1? One of the important contributions recent metacognitive research has made to our understanding of reading is the provision of rich descriptions of ways in which younger and less successful readers differ from older and more proficient readers. We can say with some certainty that less effective readers have misconceptions about the reading process, fail to monitor their comprehension, and underutilize sophisticated cognitive and metacognitive strategies to make and monitor reading progress. To lists of both "bottom-up" and "top-down" factors which distinguish readers of high and low reading proficiency, then, we can now add metacognitive knowledge, cognitive monitoring, and strategy use.

Recent instructional research, much of it conducted under the rubric of metacognition, has also made an important contribution to our understanding of reading. It is this body of work (presented, in part, in chapter 6) that tells us that some factors "are potential objectives for instruction" (Resnick, 1984, p. 435), that they can be taught to learners, and that improvement in general reading performance is the result.

Though awareness and monitoring change have been implicit components of many of the training programs (see, especially, the discussion of the ISL program in chapter 6), the core of this instructional work has been the teaching of text-processing strategies. The content of the instruction has been academically fundamental strategic components, and the recipients of the instruction have been those learners who apparently have failed to adopt spontaneously the strategies for their daily text-processing routines. In this chapter, I want to continue the discussion begun in the last chapter about implementation of strategy training *in classrooms*. I

have in mind a scenario of teachers, not researchers, training strategic behaviors. I also have in mind training that is delivered over many months,
not for a brief intervention period with little or no follow-up.

This does not imply "atheoretical foraging" about (Light & Pillemer,
1984, p. ix) for tactics. Instead, I picture implementation of strategies already documented to meet two criteria: (a) that some students have some
difficulty (or a great deal of difficulty) applying them, and (b) that the
strategies are teachable, and the outcomes, both immediate and long-
term, for learning from text are good. In other words, decisions about instructing learners should be made on the basis of the descriptive and instructional metacognitive research literature of the past few years. If a
strategy matters for school learning, if it is not uniformly successfully exercised, if it is teachable with good results, it is a candidate for classroom
instruction.

Candidate Strategies

Two clusters of strategies already discussed at length in this volume meet
the selection criteria readily. They are text reinspection and text summarization. I refer to them as clusters of strategies here because a number of
"strategic cousins" exist for each, and these not-so-distant relatives all
seem to meet the criteria.

For text reinspection, for instance, one can have in mind the version of
the strategy discussed in many parts of this volume: the intentional reaccessing of portions of text to locate information once read but not remembered, a strategy usually exercised by proficient readers when they need
to answer a question after reading. However, one can also have in mind
backtracking *while reading* (see Scardamalia & Bereiter, 1984) at a point of
detected comprehension difficulty. A reader might note what appears to
be an external inconsistency (a violation of prior knowledge), an internal
inconsistency (a logical violation between nonadjacent text segments), or
lexical anomaly (an unfamiliar or seemingly nonsensical word) and might
reread the troublesome portion or portions of text to resolve the confusion, or perhaps to prompt additional strategic action such as seeking information from an external source.

Both the during-reading and post-reading examples of text reinspection require reaccessing of selected text segments under particular
conditions. Though the impetus for looking back to text varies (i.e., detected comprehension failure versus detected memory failure), both examples of strategic use of text permanence follow successful cognitive
monitoring. That is, readers have an "aha" that something is wrong with
the cognitive enterprise, and they decide to take action. As Brown (1980)

notes, a reader's tolerance for feelings of failure to understand (or remember) is related to the importance of the immediate reading or studying goal. As noted repeatedly in this volume, engaging in strategies takes time and effort. A reader is unlikely to bother to invoke the reinspection strategy or any other strategy unless both skill and will to do so are present (Paris & Cross, 1983; Paris et al., 1983).

Text summarization can also be thought of as a family of related strategies. One can think of the strategy in the form that has been presented at some length in this volume: judging which ideas are central in a text, applying condensation rules, and then generating an abbreviated new written text. This is a strategy usually used by proficient readers after reading is completed, either to monitor understanding or to produce a synthesis of information (i.e., either as a metacognitive or a cognitive strategy). However, one can also think, once again, of a *during-reading* application. A reader might consciously create a meaningful gist, superordinate to a particular cluster of propositions (see Scardamalia & Bereiter, 1984). This is probably most fruitfully done after each paragraph in a short text or just prior to a new heading in a longer text. Just as with the post-reading application of the strategy, if an adequate synopsis cannot be generated either orally or in writing and if the reading goal is sufficiently important, remedial action (perhaps text reinspection) is called for. Generating a single topic sentence or even a single thematic title for a text segment is simply a variation of the theme "judge importance in linguistic input—condense—generate linguistic output" (see Williams, Taylor, & de Cani, 1984).

Text reinspection and text summarization, then, are clusters of strategies employed in a cognitive monitoring context. Metacognitive knowledge and content-schematic knowledge are important to their use. Metacognitive knowledge of text-processing tasks is particularly critical. Readers need to know that seldom will they want to recall every piece of information in a text, and in any case they will be unlikely to be able to do so (Goetz & Armbruster, 1980). One should not reinspect for trivial details, and one should not include trivia in one's oral or written summary. Knowing that certain pieces of information are central to a text and others are not and that the former should receive greater attention in processing is very important to successful application of these two strategies. It may well be that much inefficient cognitive performance should be attributed to an unsophisticated metacognitive knowledge base.

Content-schematic knowledge is important, for if a text presents such unfamiliar information that main points and minor points are mostly indistinguishable, both reinspection and summarization are likely to be done poorly if they are done at all. That is, an adaptive response from a reader mired in text about a wholly unfamiliar domain might well be to skip attempts at deep and active processing altogether in favor of seeking out an alternative source of information.

It has occurred to me recently that those of us conducting research on development and use of strategies that depend on learners' knowing something about expository text structure (strategies such as reinspection and summarization) may have failed to ask some preliminary questions in favor of leaping to some more intermediate ones. Expository texts have many important features about which highly proficient readers have tacit knowledge. Three of the most important are topical relationship, super-ordination, and cohesion. That is, texts, unlike random sentence strings, are composed of sentences that are topically related, with some constraints on their arrangement. For example, a superordinate statement often precedes subordinate statements that expand or provide embellishment for the main point, and sentences are "tied" together by pronoun reference, substitution, conjunction, and other cohesive devices. Texts, in other words, are neither randomly selected nor randomly arranged sentence sets.

I am not certain that we can assume that children have tacit knowledge of these critical expository text features. The reader will recall that I discussed a series of studies in chapter 1 that found gaps in structural knowledge in learners ranging in age from the very young to adult level. I think that the whole matter of structural knowledge has been underinvestigated in favor of examination of text-processing strategies for which this knowledge is probably prerequisite. When a researcher asks a child to reinspect text, the researcher does not intend for the child to reread the entire text from start to finish. In many instances, the researcher hopes the child will look back to more than a single sentence, for a full response to a question may demand just that. In during-reading exercises, a researcher may be interested in whether or not a child can self-correct an oral rendering of a text segment that states something wholly irrelevant to the topic at hand (e.g., a rendering of "Crustaceans usually are found in the water" as "Crusts usually are found in the water"). A child must know something about where important information in a text is most likely to be found, must spot situations where ideas flow from one connected sentence to another, and must detect a topic-irrelevant statement. A child must, in other words, know something about superordination, cohesion, and topical relationship in text.

The same sort of prerequisite knowledge about expository text features is important for completion of text summarization tasks. When a researcher asks a child to summarize a text, the researcher does not expect that the child will include important *and* unimportant information in the summary. For certain texts, the researcher will expect adept summarizers to integrate related ideas. For most texts, a researcher will be interested in whether or not a child collapses lists of topically related information bits in an effort to produce a succinct summary. Again, a child must know something about where important information in a text is most likely to be found, must note intersentence connections, and must detect topical relatedness.

I am suggesting that we need to examine directly children's tacit knowledge of structural features of expository text. We have just begun to investigate tacit knowledge for structure of short expository texts among adults and students in grades 3, 5, and 7 (Garner et al., 1986). We expect to find that intermediate-level findings of poor performance from some learners at these ages (e.g., failure to sample just important segments of text and failure to combine ideas across sentence boundaries for text reinspection; failure to select/invent topic sentences and failure to devise superordinate category labels for lists for text summarization) will be accompanied by more preliminary-level findings of an unsophisticated text structure knowledge base.

To return to the three criteria for selection of strategies to be implemented in classrooms stated earlier: These two strategies matter for completion of school tasks, they are not uniformly successfully exercised, and they are teachable with good results. How, then, should strategy instruction in classrooms proceed?

On the basis of the strategy instruction literature (much of it presented in chapter 6) and my recent experience directing a university-sponsored summer remedial reading clinic devoted wholly to small-group instruction in strategies, I propose six guidelines for effective strategy instruction in classrooms. The guidelines are based on sustaining clear successes described in the literature or experienced in the reading clinic.

Guideline #1: Process Instruction

Teachers must care about the processes involved in reading and studying, and must be willing to devote instructional time to them. Brown (1981) is only one of many instructional analysts who have noted that reading and study *products* (i.e., demonstration of content knowledge in specific subject areas), not *processes*, currently command the larger share of classroom attention. Van Dijk and Kintsch (1983), noting the origins of the word *strategy* in the Greek *strategia*, the organization of military actions to reach a particular goal, remind us that employment of a strategy involves not only reaching a goal, but reaching it in some optimal way. I believe strongly that the way the goal is reached must be analyzed and presented explicitly to learners.

One way to make strategy thinking public (Paris, Cross, & Lipson,

1984), to "bring more of the cognitive processes out into the open where teachers and students can examine and try to understand them" (Scardamalia & Bereiter, 1983, pp. 62–63), is for the teacher to render the covert cognitive and metacognitive processes in overt form by thinking aloud while modeling task completion. This is an instructional tactic proposed by Hare and Milligan (1984; see chapter 4, this volume), among others. Just modeling task completion is insufficient, for strategic activity will be largely unobservable, and the product, not the process, will again be receiving the greater emphasis (see Bransford, Arbitman-Smith, Stein, & Vye, 1985).

There are at least two different styles of modeling. One would involve presenting a sophisticated form of the strategy under consideration. The teacher would first establish the context (i.e., why the strategy is useful), would then think aloud about how the strategy is applied and how it is evaluated, and would finally discuss when and where the strategy is most useful. The teacher would provide more than one instance of strategy use on more than one occasion. Students would attempt to use the strategy immediately following the teacher's modeling and thinking aloud.

A second style of teacher modeling would involve use of a contrastive method. Both a sophisticated form and a very immature form of the strategy under consideration would be presented via think-alouds, and their relative effectiveness would be assessed by the class. The content of the immature form could be an amalgam of ineffective activities actually used by students in the class (either as students reported use or as use was observed by the teacher). Again, students would attempt to use the sophisticated strategy immediately following the teacher's modeling of the text strategy pair.

For either text reinspection or text summarization strategies, there might be a benefit in using the second approach. A teacher could, for instance, think aloud trying to answer a question by reinspecting an entire text versus skimming the text to find just the information-rich segment. Only the latter sophisticated form of the strategy would allow a reader to reach a goal (i.e., locating the information in text) in optimal fashion (i.e., quickly, without undue expenditure of strategic energy and without excessive frustration). Similarly, a teacher could think aloud generating a summary by including a great deal of both important and unimportant information, adhering in general to the wording of the original text, versus deleting less salient information and providing only the salient material in reduced form. Again, only the latter attack on the problem would allow a reader to reach a goal (i.e., reduce a text to its gist) in optimal fashion (i.e., in a single attempt, without the need for successive reductions to make the summary product adequately succinct). Whether or not the second style of thinking aloud while modeling would in fact be superior to the first in promoting adept use of strategies by the students is, of course, an empirical question.

Guideline #2: Task Analyses

Teachers must do task analyses of strategies to be taught. It would be impossible for a teacher to engage in the thinking aloud discussed above if he or she had not thought in some detail about how a particular strategy is best applied and also about how it is applied in its immature forms. For information about the latter, a teacher can observe students in spontaneous problem-solving and can discuss their strategic activity immediately afterward. For information about the former, the teacher can refer to the research literature, can consider his or her own strategic activity, or can ask colleagues to think aloud about their expert reading/studying and strategic activity.

Case (1978) suggests a procedure for generating a sufficiently detailed sequence of strategic operations to be used in instruction. He suggests that someone (a teacher in our discussion) begin by breaking down a strategy into global steps. Next, each global step is broken down into a sequence of substeps. At this point, adequacy of the description can be tested by asking a colleague to perform the task by following the substeps, and doing only what he or she is explicitly told. If the colleague doing the problem solving wants to deviate from the step-by-step description, modification of the description may be in order.

Such a detailed description probably should include some self-statements in the behavioral realm by the time it is used instructionally. Meichenbaum and Asarnow (1979) suggest that self-evaluation ("I seem to be getting rid of a lot of unimportant information") and coping strategies ("I can't remember where the article said something about erosion effects, but I'll keep looking for the word 'erosion' ") should be presented along with problem-solving procedures.

Coping strategies such as the persistence example above may be particularly important. It may be the case that if students realize that trying to solve an academic problem in strategic fashion does not ensure rapid, trouble-free solution on the first effort in all instances, they will be less likely to abandon a strategy at the first sign of difficulty in independent reading and studying situations. This may be one way of informing students of circumstances that will tempt them not to bother to invoke strategies or not to persevere in applying them, information Flavell (see chapter 6, this volume) has suggested is important.

Guideline #3: Generalizing Strategy Application

Teachers must present strategies as applicable to texts and tasks in more than one content domain. Duffy et al., (1984) remind us that low-aptitude students learn exactly "what the teacher says." In fact, students at all aptitude levels often learn that strategy X works in class Y for text Z, because the teacher in Class Y (or for subject matter Y) taught strategy X for text Z and never mentioned or demonstrated that the strategy had broader applicability. The strategy is then welded to the original instructional setting (Brown, Bransford, Ferrara, & Campione, 1983). There is minimal transfer of the instructed activity to other strategy-appropriate situations in which students find themselves.

Suppose a teacher were to say something on the order of "Today, I'm going to show you one way to handle the confusion that sometimes arises when you're reading your social studies textbook and you encounter a completely unfamiliar word that 'stops you in your tracks.' I'll talk you through a step-by-step strategy for trying to figure out that word by using what you've already read rather than by interrupting your reading for a long time to come to ask me the meaning of the word or to stop to look up the meaning in a dictionary." Suppose, then, that the teacher engaged in a think-aloud exercise on this day with the social studies textbook, and on another day with a science textbook, and said on the second occasion something to the effect of "You see that this cost-efficient strategy works for more than one subject area and for more than one textbook. It doesn't always work, though. Sometimes we have to resort to more time-consuming alternative strategies. . . ." This last point could be embellished with information about relatively impoverished linguistic contexts and external-resource strategic alternatives. By demonstrating a variety of situations in which learners might profitably use this version of text reinspection, the probability that transfer would occur is increased (see Brown, Bransford, Ferrara, & Campione, 1983).

Related to the need for teachers to present strategies in many contexts is the need for them to present explicitly the variations on a particular strategic theme. This prevents students from generalizing strategy application in a rote fashion. For instance, if a teacher has presented the text summarization strategy and has demonstrated selection of important information in a particular paragraph as cued by a main idea explicitly stated in the first sentence of the paragraph, he or she should also demonstrate how one selects important information when a main idea statement must be invented by the reader or summary writer. If the teacher fails to do this, students are likely to falter when given texts that do not obey the "initial mention convention" (see chapter 1). This becomes a critical point when we learn that Baumann and Serra (1984) have reported that for 294 paragraphs appearing in social studies textbooks for grades 4, 6, and 8, only 1 in 4 presented an explicit main-idea statement at the beginning of the paragraph; 75% of the paragraphs, in other words, did *not* obey the "initial mention convention."

Guideline #4: An Entire Year's Instruction

Teachers must teach strategies over an entire year, not in just a single lesson or unit. This guideline pertains to all the preceding guidelines. It is commonly acknowledged (see, for instance, Bereiter, 1984) that subject-matter delivery commands most of the instructional energy in schools, and that non–subject matter information (e.g., learning how to learn or strategy instruction) is treated as "academic frill." The frill is often relegated to leftover school time before recess or just after the fire drill or is assigned to a "special segment"; in either case, it is delivered (and received by students) as isolated material unrelated to subject matter and to important learning from text. Bereiter suggests that strategy instruction needs to be an integral part of already accepted instructional objectives.

Once a teacher allows strategic instruction to permeate his or her curriculum, this is really rather easy. While teaching the crops of the Middle Atlantic states, Ms. Jones can demonstrate that clustering a long list of crops into conceptual categories of vegetables, fruits, and grains can assist in efficient learning. While Mr. Smith works through the multiplication tables, he can allude to what Flavell (1971, p. 276) has called the "storing nuts for the winter" character of memorizing. When one deliberately memorizes, one is doing something now that will pay off later, and Mr. Smith can tell his students that "learning the fours by heart" will mean that two- and three-digit computational problems will eventually be solvable quickly and without constant reaccessing of the fours tables at the back of the arithmetic book. Ms. Connors, in announcing a quiz the next day on Newtonian mechanics principles, can suggest to her science students that they skim the headings of the textbook segment on Newton, write questions that might appear on the quiz, and engage in self-testing of their ability to answer these questions. Mr. Johnson can give a pop quiz on the battles of World War II and the outcomes of each and can then announce that no grades will be recorded for this quiz. Instead, the performance information will be used only by the students themselves. The students should note which battles had particularly confused them and should spend more time studying those battles in preparation for a quiz 3 days hence. The results of that quiz will be recorded.

Ms. Jones, Mr. Smith, Ms. Connors, and Mr. Johnson are interested in subject matter. They are also interested in efficient learning of subject matter. They appear to believe that they should explicitly teach both content *and* the way to learn content efficiently. They have not done what Bereiter (1984) claims many teachers do, which is to list a few strategy rules, list a few examples (apart from the crops, fours, Newtonian principles, and World War II battles that the students know are what really matter in school, for that is what they will be tested on), and call that the lesson or unit on strategies.

Guideline #5: Guided Practice

Teachers must provide students with opportunities to practice strategies they have been taught. It is well established that cognitive processing capacity is not boundless. It has been argued for some time (see, for instance, Gough, 1981; Perfetti & Lesgold, 1979) that proficient reading comprehension depends on rapid, accurate, automatic decoding. In this view, processing capacities are taxed until extensive reading practice produces more efficient decoding skills that release cognitive resources from code breaking to comprehension. As Samuels (1979) puts it, "When decoding is automatic, attention may be focused on deriving meaning" (p. 352).

Also important is practice in moving strategic activity to a near automatic state. The reader might remember that in chapter 3 I argued that though subroutines of complex strategies are often learned to a point of automaticity, these strategies always retain a deliberate, planful element. I believe that some conscious attention is required for the activation of the complex reading and studying strategies discussed throughout this volume. It is because strategic subroutines can become automatic, however, that a variety of text-processing strategies can be engaged simultaneously without the process being overloaded (see Paris & Cross, 1983; van Dijk & Kintsch, 1983).

Learners come to use strategies concurrently and semiautomatically through temporally distributed practice. To ensure that students practice strategies, teachers must allocate some school time to the activity. This need not be time "borrowed" from social studies or science, for the students must practice strategy use *on* texts and tasks, and (this reiterates guideline #4) the content of the school curriculum is a logical vehicle for strategic learning.

Pearson (1982, 1984) reminds us that this sort of practice must be guided. Teachers must intersperse practice with more direct instruction (see guideline #1) and must give substantive feedback about strategy use during practice sessions. In other words, this prescription for practice is not to be confused with the teaching system that Durkin (1978–1979) observed in classrooms: giving a great many assignments for students to complete in the absence of any instructional guidance (see chapter 6, this volume).

As noted earlier, students for whom strategies are neither personalized nor routinized may well fail to use the strategies when they must be executed in the rushed activity flow of classrooms. For a teacher, activity flow means keeping students under control, whereas waiting for individual students to respond increases the frequency of discipline problems (Shulman & Carey, 1984). Activity flow dominates classroom life (Duffy, 1982). Students, then, worry about being "left behind" within teacher-established time constraints, and often, I suspect, opt for immature strategies that provide for task completion in less-than-optimal fashion, rather than employing sophisticated strategies that take time and effort and therefore slow down task completion. Practice makes preferred systems of processing more quickly executed, more automatic, and thus more likely to be applied in school settings.

Guideline #6: Children Teaching Children About Strategies

Teachers must be prepared to let students teach each other about reading and studying processes. One of the benefits of creating a classroom where cognitive processes are examined is that students can tell teachers and other students about special modifications of trained routines. As Paris, Cross, and Lipson (1984) note, discussions about strategic modifications give teachers information about instructional efficacy and about depth of strategy understanding for individual students. Further direct instruction can be planned on the basis of these two kinds of information.

Children in the summer reading clinic developed a classroom vernacular about the strategies they were taught. They talked about "finding the trick part" when they attempted to detect internal inconsistencies by integrating information across sentences. They tried to locate a "big idea" in the first sentence of paragraphs of exposition. They referred to "questions that tell you it's o.k. to look at the book" when they described text-based questions cuing text reinspection.

We capitalized a bit on this colorful language of strategy use by allowing children to demonstrate their strategy use to instructors in order to attain "teacher helper" (i.e., tutor) status. In order to become tutors, children needed to demonstrate understanding of why a strategy is useful, how it is applied and evaluated, and when and where it is best implemented. Use of spontaneously generated descriptions for the various procedures (e.g., "find the big idea first") was encouraged. Once tutoring status was conferred, these strategy experts were asked to tutor other (usually younger) children in strategy use.

This pairing system yielded three important benefits. First, children were motivated to learn about strategies so they could teach someone else about them. Second, the tutors' strategic repertoires were surely reinforced by the planning they did with younger children's text materials in preparation for tutoring. Third, adult instructors and children learned that a given student was not a uniformly "good" or "poor" strategy user; tutors for reinspection might be tutees for summarization.

A Final Note on Classroom Strategy Instruction

Teachers are harried, driven by published materials, and perhaps worst of all, very isolated from fellow professionals in the schools (Calfee, 1984). Asking them to undertake a whole new layer of instruction, strategies on top of content knowledge, would surely be futile. They would be worried about time constraints, would wonder *how* to teach strategies in the absence of a textbook, and would be concerned lest children in their classes be ill-prepared vis-à-vis children in classes down the hall to "take the test" on the required content for the year. They would be justifiably worried, for frenetic scheduling, instruction based almost exclusively on basal readers and textbooks, and evaluation of educational quality on relatively restricted standardized measures are facts of contemporary schooling.

The only way classrooms will become arenas for extensive strategy instruction is for the strategy instruction to be wholly intertwined with subject-area instruction in a manner like that I have described in the six guidelines. To fail to teach students strategies they do not use and from which they could benefit is to fail the students, to neglect to show them ways of reaching reading and studying goals in optimal ways. To teach crops and arithmetic facts and science principles and battles without teaching students how they can learn more about any of this or about other content is to risk that children will not become effective independent learners. This is, put simply, entirely unacceptable educational practice.

References

Adams, A., Carnine, D., & Gersten, R. (1982). Instructional strategies for studying content area texts in the intermediate grades. *Reading Research Quarterly, 18,* 27–55.

Afflerbach, P., & Johnston, P. (1984). On the use of verbal reports in reading research. *Journal of Reading Behavior, 16,* 307–322.

Alessi, S. M., Anderson, T. H., & Goetz, E. T. (1979). An investigation of lookbacks during studying. *Discourse Processes, 2,* 197–212.

Alexander, P. A., Hare, V. C., & Garner, R. (1984). The effects of time, access, and question type on response accuracy and frequency of lookbacks in older, proficient readers. *Journal of Reading Behavior, 16,* 119–130.

Allen, V. L. (1976). Children helping children: Psychological processes in tutoring. In J. R. Levin & V. L. Allen (Eds.), *Cognitive learning in children: Theories and strategies* (pp. 241–290). New York: Academic Press.

Allen, V. L., & Feldman, R. S. (1976). Studies on the role of tutor. In V. L. Allen (Ed.), *Children as teachers: Theory and research on tutoring* (pp. 113–129). New York: Academic Press.

Allington, R. L. (1980). Teacher interruption behaviors during primary-grade oral reading. *Journal of Educational Psychology, 72,* 371–377.

Allington, R. L. (1983). The reading instruction provided readers of differing reading abilities. *The Elementary School Journal, 83,* 548–559.

Alvermann, D. E. (1984). Second graders' strategic preferences while reading basal stories. *Journal of Educational Research, 77,* 184–189.

Alvermann, D. E., & Boothby, P. R. (1983). A preliminary investigation of the differences in children's retention of "inconsiderate" text. *Reading Psychology, 4,* 237–246.

Anderson, R. C. (1970). Control of student mediating processes during verbal learning and instruction. *Review of Educational Research, 40,* 349–369.

Anderson, R. C. (1977). *Schema-directed processes in language comprehension* (Tech. Rep. No. 50). Urbana: University of Illinois, Center for the Study of Reading.

Anderson, R. C. (1984). Some reflections on the acquisition of knowledge. *Educational Researcher, 13,* 5–10.

Anderson, R. C., & Freebody, P. (1979). *Vocabulary knowledge* (Tech. Rep. No. 136). Urbana: University of Illinois: Center for the Study of Reading.

Anderson, R. C., & Pearson, P. D. (1984). A schema-theoretic view of basic processes in reading comprehension. In P. D. Pearson (Ed.), *Handbook of reading research* (pp. 255–291). New York: Longman.

Anderson, R. C., & Pichert, J. W. (1978). Recall of previously unrecallable information following a shift in perspective. *Journal of Verbal Learning and Verbal Behavior, 17,* 1–12.

Anderson, R. C., Pichert, J. W., & Shirey, L. L. (1979). *Effects of the reader's schema at different points in time* (Tech. Rep. No. 119). Urbana: University of Illinois, Center for the Study of Reading.

Anderson, R. C., Reynolds, R. E., Schallert, D. L., & Goetz, E. T. (1977). Frameworks for comprehending discourse. *American Educational Research Journal, 14,* 367–381.

Anderson, R. C., Spiro, R. J., & Anderson, M. C. (1978). Schemata as scaffolding for the representation of information in connected discourse. *American Educational Research Journal, 15,* 433–440.

Anderson, T. H. (1979). Study skills and learning strategies. In H. F. O'Neil, Jr., & C. D. Spielberger (Eds.), *Cognitive and affective learning strategies* (pp. 77–97). New York: Academic Press.

Anderson, T. H. (1980). Study strategies and adjunct aids. In R. J. Spiro, B. C. Bruce, & W. F. Brewer (Eds.), *Theoretical issues in reading comprehension* (pp. 483–502). Hillsdale, NJ: Erlbaum.

Anderson, T. H., & Armbruster, B. B. (1984). Studying. In P. D. Pearson (Ed.), *Handbook of reading research* (pp. 657–679). New York: Longman.

Armbruster, B. B., & Anderson, T. H. (1981). *Content area textbooks* (Rdg. Ed. Rep. No. 23). Urbana: University of Illinois, Center for the Study of Reading.

August, D. L., Flavell, J. H., & Clift, R. (1984). Comparison of comprehension monitoring of skilled and less skilled readers. *Reading Research Quarterly, 20,* 39–53.

Ausubel, D. P. (1963). *The psychology of meaningful learning.* New York: Grune & Stratton.

Ausubel, D. P. (1980). Schemata, cognitive structure, and advance organizers: A reply to Anderson, Spiro, and Anderson. *American Educational Research Journal, 17,* 400–404.

Baker, L. (1979). Comprehension monitoring: Identifying and coping with text confusions. *Journal of Reading Behavior, 11,* 365–374.

Baker, L. (1984a). Children's effective use of multiple standards for evaluating their comprehension. *Journal of Educational Psychology, 76,* 588–597.

Baker, L. (1984b). Spontaneous versus instructed use of multiple standards for evaluating comprehension: Effects of age, reading proficiency, and type of standard. *Journal of Experimental Child Psychology, 38,* 289–311.

Baker, L. (1985a). Differences in the standards used by college students to evaluate their comprehension of expository prose. *Reading Research Quarterly, 20,* 297–313.

Baker, L. (1985b). How do we know when we don't understand? Standards for evaluating text comprehension. In D. L. Forrest-Pressley, G. E. MacKinnon, & T. G. Waller (Eds.), *Metacognition, cognition, and human performance* (Vol. 1, pp. 155–205). Orlando, FL: Academic Press.

Baker, L. (1985c, April). *When will children acknowledge failures of word comprehension?* Paper presented at the meeting of the Society for Research in Child Development, Toronto.

Baker, L., & Anderson, R. I. (1982). Effects of inconsistent information on text processing: Evidence for comprehension monitoring. *Reading Research Quarterly, 17,* 281–294.

Baker, L., & Brown, A. L. (1984a). Cognitive monitoring in reading. In J. Flood (Ed.), *Understanding reading comprehension: Cognition, language, and the structure of prose* (pp. 21–44). Newark, DE: International Reading Association.

Baker, L., & Brown, A. L. (1984b). Metacognitive skills and reading. In P. D. Pearson (Ed.), *Handbook of reading research* (pp. 353–394). New York: Longman.

Ballstaedt, S., & Mandl, H. (1984). Elaborations: Assessment and analysis. In H. Mandl, N. L. Stein, & T. Trabasso (Eds.), *Learning and comprehension of text* (pp. 331–353). Hillsdale, NJ: Erlbaum.

Bandura, A. (1977). Self-efficacy: Toward a unifying theory of behavioral change. *Psychological Review, 84,* 191–215.

Bartlett, F. C. (1932). *Remembering: A study in experimental and social psychology.* Cambridge, England: Cambridge University Press.

Baumann, J. F. (1982). Research on children's main idea comprehension: A problem of ecological validity. *Reading Psychology, 3,* 167–177.

Baumann, J. F., & Serra, J. K. (1984). The frequency and placement of main ideas in children's social studies textbooks: A modified replication of Braddock's research on topic sentences. *Journal of Reading Behavior, 16,* 27–40.

Beal, C. R., & Flavell, J. H. (1982). Effect of increasing the salience of message ambiguities on kindergartners' evaluations of communicative success and message adequacy. *Developmental Psychology, 18,* 43–48.

Beaugrande, R. de (1982). Psychology and composition: Past, present, and future. In M. Nystrand (Ed.), *What writers know: The language, process, and structure of written discourse* (pp. 211–267). New York: Academic Press.

Beebe, M. J. (1980). The effect of different types of substitution miscues on reading. *Reading Research Quarterly, 15,* 324–336.

Belmont, J. M., & Butterfield, E. C. (1977). The instructional approach to developmental cognitive research. In R. V. Kail, Jr., & J. W. Hagen (Eds.), *Perspectives on the development of memory and cognition* (pp. 437–481). Hillsdale, NJ: Erlbaum.

Belmont, J. M., Butterfield, E. C., & Ferretti, R. P. (1982). To secure transfer of training instruct self-management skills. In D. K. Detterman & R. J. Sternberg (Eds.), *How and how much can intelligence be increased* (pp. 147–154). Norwood, NJ: Ablex.

Bereiter, C. (1984). How to keep thinking skills from going the way of all frills. *Educational Leadership, 42,* 75–77.

Blachowicz, C. L. Z. (1977–1978). Semantic constructivity in children's comprehension. *Reading Research Quarterly, 13,* 188–199.

Blank, M. (1975). Eliciting verbalization from young children in experimental tasks: A methodological note. *Child Development, 46,* 254–257.

Bonitatibus, G. J. (1984). *Comprehension monitoring and the apprehension of literal meaning.* Unpublished doctoral dissertation, Stanford University.

Bonitatibus, G. J., & Flavell, J. H. (1985). Effect of presenting a message in written form on young children's ability to evaluate its communication adequacy. *Developmental Psychology, 21,* 455–461.

Borko, H., Shavelson, R. J., & Stern, P. (1981). Teachers' decisions in the planning of reading instruction. *Reading Research Quarterly, 16,* 449–466.

Bower, G. H. (1978). Representing knowledge development. In R. S. Siegler (Ed.), *Children's thinking: What develops?* (pp. 349–362). Hillsdale, NJ: Erlbaum.

Bracewell, R. J. (1983). Investigating the control of writing skills. In P. Mosenthal, L. Tamor, & S. A. Walmsley (Eds.), *Research on writing: Principles and methods* (pp. 177–203). New York: Longman.

Bransford, J. D., Arbitman-Smith, R., Stein, B. S., & Vye, N. J. (1985). Improving thinking and learning skills: An analysis of three approaches. In J. W. Segal, S. F. Chipman, & R. Glaser (Eds.), *Thinking and learning skills* (Vol. 1, pp. 133–206). Hillsdale, NJ: Erlbaum.

Bransford, J. D., & Heldmeyer, K. (1983). Learning from children learning. In J. Bisanz, G. L. Bisanz, & R. Kail (Eds.), *Learning in children: Progress in cognitive development research* (pp. 171–190). New York: Springer-Verlag.

Bransford, J. D., & Johnson, M. K. (1973). Considerations of some problems of comprehension. In W. G. Chase (Ed.), *Visual information processing* (pp. 383–438). New York: Academic Press.

Bronfenbrenner, U. (1979). *The ecology of human development: Experiments by nature and design.* Cambridge, MA: Harvard University Press.

Brown, A. L. (1975). The development of memory: Knowing, knowing about knowing, and knowing how to know. In H. W. Reese (Ed.), *Advances in child development and behavior* (Vol. 10, pp. 103–152). New York: Academic Press.

Brown, A. L. (1977). *Knowing when, where, and how to remember: A problem of metacognition* (Tech. Rep. No. 47). Urbana: University of Illinois, Center for the Study of Reading.

Brown, A. L. (1980). Metacognitive development and reading. In R. J. Spiro, B. C. Bruce, & W. F. Brewer (Eds.), *Theoretical issues in reading comprehension* (pp. 453–481). Hillsdale, NJ: Erlbaum.

Brown, A. L. (1981). Metacognition: The development of selective attention strategies for learning from texts. In M. L. Kamil (Ed.), *Directions in reading: Research and instruction* (pp. 21–43). Washington, DC: National Reading Conference.

Brown, A. L. (1984). Metakognition, Handlungskontrolle, Selbststeuerung und andere, noch geheimnisvollere Mechanismen [Metacognition, executive control, self-regulation and other even more mysterious mechanisms]. In F. E. Weinert & R. H. Kluwe (Eds.), *Metakognition Motivation und Lernen* (pp. 60–109). Stuttgart, West Germany: Kohlhammer.

Brown, A. L., Armbruster, B. B., & Baker, L. (1986). The role of metacognition in reading and studying. In J. Orasanu (Ed.), *Reading comprehension: From research to practice* (pp. 49–75). Hillsdale, NJ: Erlbaum.

Brown, A. L., Bransford, J. D., Ferrara, R. A., & Campione, J. C. (1983). Learning, remembering, and understanding. In J. H. Flavell & E. M. Markman (Eds.), *Handbook of child psychology* (Vol. 3, pp. 77–166). New York: Wiley.

Brown, A. L., & Campione, J. C. (1977). Training strategic study time apportionment in educable retarded children. *Intelligence, 1,* 94–107.

Brown, A. L., & Campione, J. C. (1978). Memory strategies in learning: Training children to study strategically. In H. L. Pick, H. W. Leibowitz, J. E. Singer, A. Steinschneider, & H. W. Stevenson (Eds.), *Psychology: From research to practice* (pp. 47–73). New York: Plenum.

Brown, A. L., Campione, J. C., & Day, J. D. (1981). Learning to learn: On training students to learn from text. *Educational Researcher, 10,* 14–21.

Brown, A. L., Campione, J. C., & Murphy, M. D. (1977). Maintenance and generalization of trained metamnemonic awareness by educable retarded children. *Journal of Experimental Child Psychology, 24,* 191–211.

Brown, A. L., & Day, J. D. (1983). Macrorules for summarizing texts: The development of expertise. *Journal of Verbal Learning and Verbal Behavior, 22,* 1–14.

Brown, A. L., Day, J. D., & Jones, R. S. (1983). The development of plans for summarizing texts. *Child Development, 54,* 968–979.

Brown, A. L., & DeLoache, J. S. (1978). Skills, plans, and self-regulation. In R. S. Siegler (Ed.), *Children's thinking: What develops?* (pp. 3–35). Hillsdale, NJ: Erlbaum.

Brown, A. L., & French, L. A. (1979). The zone of potential development: Implications for intelligence testing in the year 2000. *Intelligence, 3,* 255–273.

Brown, A. L., & Palincsar, A. S. (1982). *Inducing strategic learning from texts by means of informed self-control training* (Tech. Rep. No. 262). Urbana: University of Illinois, Center for the Study of Reading.

Brown, A. L., Palincsar, A. S., & Armbruster, B. B. (1984). Instructing comprehension-fostering activities in interactive learning situations. In H. Mandl, N. L. Stein, & T. Trabasso (Eds.), *Learning and comprehension of text* (pp. 255–286). Hillsdale, NJ: Erlbaum.

Brown, A. L., & Smiley, S. S. (1977). Rating the importance of structural units of prose passages: A problem of metacognitive development. *Child Development, 48,* 1–8.

Bruner, J. S. (1979). *On knowing: Essays for the left hand.* Cambridge, MA: Harvard University Press.

Calfee, R. (1981). Cognitive psychology and educational practice. In D. C. Berliner (Ed.), *Review of research in education* (Vol. 9, pp. 3–73). Washington, DC: American Educational Research Association.

Calfee, R. (1984). *Applying cognitive psychology to educational practice: The mind of the reading teacher.* Unpublished manuscript, Stanford University.

Campione, J. C., & Armbruster, B. B. (1984). An analysis of the outcomes and implications of intervention research. In H. Mandl, N. L. Stein, & T. Trabasso (Eds.), *Learning and comprehension of text* (pp. 287–304). Hillsdale, NJ: Erlbaum.

Capelli, C. A. (1982). *Factors affecting children's ability to evaluate their comprehension.* Unpublished manuscript, Stanford University.

Capelli, C. A., & Markman, E. M. (1982). Suggestions for training comprehension monitoring. *Topics in Learning and Learning Disabilities, 2,* 87–96.

Carr, T. H. (1981). Building theories of reading ability: On the relation between individual differences in cognitive skills and reading comprehension. *Cognition, 9,* 73–114.

Case, R. (1978). A developmentally based theory and technology of instruction. *Review of Educational Research, 48,* 439–463.

Cavanaugh, J. C., & Borkowski, J. G. (1980). Searching for metamemory-memory connections: A developmental study. *Developmental Psychology, 16,* 441–453.

Cavanaugh, J. C., & Perlmutter, M. (1982). Metamemory: A critical examination. *Child Development, 53,* 11–28.

Chi, M. T. H. (1985). Changing conception of sources of memory development. *Human Development, 28,* 50–56.

Chi, M. T. H., & Glaser, R. (1980). The measurement of expertise: Analysis of the development of knowledge and skill as a basis for assessing achievement. In E. L. Baker & E. S. Quellmalz (Eds.), *Educational testing and evaluation* (pp. 37–47). Beverly Hills, CA: Sage.

Christie, J. M., & Just, M. A. (1976). Remembering the location and content of sentences in a prose passage. *Journal of Educational Psychology, 68,* 702–710.

Corno, L., & Mandinach, E. B. (1983). The role of cognitive engagement in classroom learning and motivation. *Educational Psychologist, 18,* 88–108.

Covington, M. V. (1983). Motivated cognitions. In S. G. Paris, G. M. Olson, & H. W. Stevenson (Eds.), *Learning and motivation in the classroom* (pp. 139–164). Hillsdale, NJ: Erlbaum.

Covington, M. V. (1985). Strategic thinking and the fear of failure. In J. W. Segal, S. F. Chipman, & R. Glaser (Eds.), *Thinking and learning skills* (Vol. 1, pp. 389–416). Hillsdale, NJ: Erlbaum.

Danks, J. H., Bohn, L., & Fears, R. (1983). Comprehension processes in oral reading. In G. B. Flores d'Arcais & R. J. Jarvella (Eds.), *The process of language understanding* (pp. 193–223). New York: Wiley.

Danks, J. H., & End, L. J. (in press). Processing strategies for reading and listening. In R. Horowitz & S. J. Samuels (Eds.), *Comprehending oral and written language.* New York: Academic Press.

Danner, F. W. (1976). Children's understanding of intersentence organization in the recall of short descriptive passages. *Journal of Educational Psychology, 68,* 174–183.

Danner, F. W., Hiebert, E. H., & Winograd, P. N. (1983). *Children's understanding of text difficulty.* Unpublished manuscript, University of Kentucky.

Dansereau, D. F., Collins, K. W., McDonald, B. A., Holley, C. D., Garland, J., Diekhoff, G., & Evans, S. H. (1979). Development and evaluation of a learning strategy training program. *Journal of Educational Psychology, 71,* 64–73.

Day, J. D. (1980). *Teaching summarization skills: A comparison of training methods.* Unpublished doctoral dissertation, University of Illinois.

DeLoache, J. S., Cassidy, D. J., & Brown, A. L. (1985). Precursors of mnemonic strategies in very young children's memory. *Child Development, 56,* 125–137.

DiVesta, F. J., Hayward, K. G., & Orlando, V. P. (1979). Developmental trends in monitoring text for comprehension. *Child Development, 50,* 97–105.

Doyle, W. (1983). Academic work. *Review of Educational Research, 53,* 159–199.

Duffy, G. G. (1982). Fighting off the alligators: What research in real classrooms has to say about reading instruction. *Journal of Reading Behavior, 14,* 357–373.

Duffy, G. G., Book, C., & Roehler, L. R. (1983). A study of direct teacher explanation during reading instruction. In J. A. Niles & L. A. Harris (Eds.), *Searches for meaning in reading/language processing and instruction* (pp. 295–303). Rochester, NY: National Reading Conference.

Duffy, G. G., Roehler, L. R., & Wesselman, R. (1984, November). *Disentangling the complexities of instructional effectiveness: A line of research on classroom reading instruction.* Paper presented at the meeting of the National Reading Conference, St. Petersburg, FL.

Durkin, D. (1978–1979). What classroom observations reveal about reading comprehension instruction. *Reading Research Quarterly, 14,* 481–533.

Durkin, D. (1981). Reading comprehension instruction in five basal reader series. *Reading Research Quarterly, 16,* 515–544.

Ellis, S., & Rogoff, B. (1982). The strategies and efficacy of child versus adult teachers. *Child Development, 53,* 730–735.

Ericsson, K. A., & Simon, H. A. (1980). Verbal reports as data. *Psychological Review, 87,* 215–251.

Feldman, R. S., Devin-Sheehan, L., & Allen, V. L. (1976). Children tutoring children: A critical review of research. In V. L. Allen (Ed.), *Children as teachers: Theory and research on tutoring* (pp. 235–252). New York: Academic Press.

Feshbach, N. D. (1976). Teaching styles in young children: Implications for peer tutoring. In V. L. Allen (Ed.), *Children as teachers: Theory and research on tutoring* (pp. 81–98). New York: Academic Press.

Fillmore, C. J. (1982). Ideal readers and real readers. In D. Tannen (Ed.), *Analyzing discourse: Text and talk* (pp. 248–270). Washington, DC: Georgetown University Press.

Fischer, P. M., & Mandl, H. (1982). Metacognitive regulation of text processing: Aspects and problems concerning the relation between self-statements and actual performance. In A. Flammer & W. Kintsch (Eds.), *Discourse processing* (pp. 339–351). Amsterdam: North-Holland.

Fischer, P. M., & Mandl, H. (1984). Learner, text variables, and the control of text comprehension and recall. In H. Mandl, N. L. Stein, & T. Trabasso (Eds.), *Learning and comprehenson of text* (pp. 213–254). Hillsdale, NJ: Erlbaum.

Flavell, J. H. (1970). Developmental studies of mediated memory. In H. W. Reese & L. P. Lipsitt (Eds.), *Advances in child development behavior* (Vol. 5, pp. 181–211). New York: Academic Press.

Flavell, J. H. (1971). First discussant's comments: What is memory development the development of? *Human Development, 14,* 272–278.

Flavell, J. H. (1976). Metacognitive aspects of problem solving. In L. B. Resnick (Ed.), *The nature of intelligence* (pp. 231–235). Hillsdale, NJ: Erlbaum.

Flavell, J. H. (1978). Comments. In R. S. Siegler (Ed.), *Children's thinking: What develops?* (pp. 97–105). Hillsdale, NJ: Erlbaum.

Flavell, J. H. (1979). Metacognition and cognitive monitoring: A new area of cognitive-developmental inquiry. *American Psychologist, 34,* 906–911.

Flavell, J. H. (1981). Cognitive monitoring. In W. P. Dickson (Ed.), *Children's oral communication skills* (pp. 35–60). New York: Academic Press.

Flavell, J. H. (1984). Annahem zum Begriff Metakognition sowie zur Entwicklung von Metakognition [Speculations about the nature and development of metacognition]. In F. E. Weinert & R. H. Kluwe (Eds.), *Metakognition Motivation und Lernen* (pp. 23–31). Stuttgart, West Germany: Kohlhammer.

Flavell, J. H. (1985). *Cognitive development* (2nd ed.) Englewood Cliffs, NJ: Prentice-Hall.

Flavell, J. H., Friedrichs, A. G., & Hoyt, J. D. (1970). Developmental changes in memorization processes. *Cognitive Psychology, 1,* 324–340.

Flavell, J. H., Speer, J. R., Green, F. L., & August, D. L. (1981). The development of comprehension monitoring and knowledge about communication. *Monographs of the Society for Research in Child Development, 46,*(5, Serial No. 192).

Flavell, J. H., & Wellman, H. M. (1977). Metamemory. In R. V. Kail, Jr., & J. W. Hagen (Eds.), *Perspectives on the development of memory and cognition* (pp. 3–33). Hillsdale, NJ: Erlbaum.

Floden, R. E. (1981). The logic of information-processing psychology in education. In D. C. Berliner (Ed.), *Review of research in education* (Vol. 9, pp. 75–109). Washington, DC: American Educational Research Association.

Forrest, D. L., & Waller, T. G. (1980, April). *What do children know about their reading and study skills.* Paper presented at the meeting of the American Educational Research Association, Boston, MA.

Forrest-Pressley, D. L., & Gillies, L. A. (1983). Children's flexible use of strategies during reading. In M. Pressley & J. R. Levin (Eds.), *Cognitive strategy research: Educational applications* (pp. 133–156). New York: Springer-Verlag.

Forrest-Pressley, D. L., & Waller, T. G. (1984a). *Cognition, metacognition, and reading.* New York: Springer-Verlag.

Forrest-Pressley, D. L., & Waller, T. G. (1984b). Knowledge and monitoring abilities of poor readers. *Topics in Learning and Learning Disabilities, 3,* 73–80.

Frederiksen, N. (1984). Implications of cognitive theory for instruction in problem solving. *Review of Educational Research, 54,* 363–407.

Frese, M., & Stewart, J. (1984). Skill learning as a concept in life-span developmental psychology: An action theoretic analysis. *Human Development, 27,* 145–162.

Frick, T., & Semmel, M. I. (1978). Observer agreement and reliabilities of classroom observational measures. *Review of Educational Research, 48,* 157–184.

Gage, N. L. (1978). *The scientific basis of the art of teaching.* New York: Teachers College Press.

Garner, R. (1980). Monitoring of understanding: An investigation of good and poor readers' awareness of induced miscomprehension of text. *Journal of Reading Behavior, 12,* 55–64.

Garner, R. (1981). Monitoring of passage inconsistency among poor comprehenders: A preliminary test of the "piecemeal processing" explanation. *Journal of Educational Research, 74,* 159–162.

Garner, R. (1982). Verbal-report data on reading strategies. *Journal of Reading Behavior, 14,* 159–167.

Garner, R. (1983). Correcting the imbalance: Diagnosis of strategic behaviors in reading. *Topics in Learning and Learning Disabilities, 2,* 12–19.

Garner, R. (1985). Text summarization deficiencies among older students: Awareness or production ability? *American Educational Research Journal, 22,* 549–560.

Garner, R. (in press-a). Strategies for reading and studying expository text. *Educational Psychologist.*

Garner, R. (in press-b). Verbal-report data on cognitive and metacognitive strategies. In C. Weinstein, E. T. Goetz, & P. Alexander (Eds.), *Learning and study strategies: Assessment, instruction, and evaluation.* Orlando, FL: Academic Press.

Garner, R., & Alexander, P. (1982). Strategic processing of text: An investigation of the effects on adults' question-answering performance. *Journal of Educational Research, 75,* 144–148.

Garner, R., Alexander, P., Slater W., Hare, V. C., Smith, T., & Reis, R. (1986, April). *Children's knowledge of structural properties of text.* Paper presented at the meeting of the American Educational Research Association, San Francisco, CA.

Garner, R., & Anderson, J. (1981–1982). Monitoring-of-understanding research: Inquiry directions, methodological dilemmas. *Journal of Experimental Education, 50,* 70–76.

Garner, R., Belcher, V., Winfield, E., & Smith, T. (1985). Multiple measures of text summarization proficiency: What can fifth-grade students do? *Research in the Teaching of English, 19,* 140–153.

Garner, R., Hare, V. C., Alexander, P., Haynes, J., & Winograd, P. (1984). Inducing use of a text lookback strategy among unsuccessful readers. *American Educational Research Journal, 21,* 789–798.

Garner, R., & Kraus, C. (1981–1982). Good and poor comprehender differences in knowing and regulating reading behaviors. *Educational Research Quarterly, 6,* 5–12.

Garner, R., Macready, G. B., & Wagoner, S. (1984). Readers' acquisition of the components of the text-lookback strategy. *Journal of Educational Psychology, 76,* 300–309.

Garner, R., & McCaleb, J. L. (1985). Effects of text manipulations on quality of written summaries. *Contemporary Educational Psychology, 10,* 139–149.

Garner, R., & Reis, R. (1981). Monitoring and resolving comprehension obstacles: An investigation of spontaneous text lookbacks among upper-grade good and poor comprehenders. *Reading Research Quarterly, 16,* 569–582.

Garner, R., Wagoner, S., & Smith, T. (1983). Externalizing question-answering strategies of good and poor comprehenders. *Reading Research Quarterly, 18,* 439–447.

Gelman, R. (1979). Preschool thought. *American Psychologist, 34,* 900–905.

Gibson, E. J., & Levin, H. (1975). *The psychology of reading.* Cambridge, MA: MIT Press.

Glenberg, A. M., Wilkinson, A. C., & Epstein, W. (1982). The illusion of knowing: Failure in the self-assessment of comprehension. *Memory and Cognition, 10,* 597–602.

Goelman, H. (1982). Selective attention in language comprehension: Children's processing of expository and narrative discourse. *Discourse Processes, 5,* 53–72.

Goetz, E. T. (1984). The role of spatial strategies in processing and remembering text: A cognitive-information-processing analysis. In C. D. Holley & D. F. Dansereau (Eds.), *Spatial learning strategies: Techniques, applications, and related issues* (pp. 47–77). New York: Academic Press.

Goetz, E. T., & Armbruster, B. B. (1980). Psychological correlates of text structure. In R. J. Spiro, B. C. Bruce, & W. F. Brewer (Eds.), *Theoretical issues in reading comprehension* (pp. 201–220). Hillsdale, NJ: Erlbaum.

Golinkoff, R. M. (1975–1976). A comparison of reading comprehension processes in good and poor comprehenders. *Reading Research Quarterly, 11,* 623–659.

Goodman, K. S. (1970). Reading: A psycholinguistic guessing game. In H. Singer & R. B. Ruddell (Eds.), *Theoretical models and processes of reading* (pp. 259–271). Newark, DE: International Reading Association.

Goodman, K. S., & Goodman, Y. M. (1977). Learning about psycholinguistic processes by analyzing oral reading. *Harvard Educational Review, 47,* 317–333.

Goodman, K. S., & Goodman, Y. M. (1979). Learning to read is natural. In L. B. Resnick & P. A. Weaver (Eds.), *Theory and practice of early reading* (Vol. 1, pp. 137–154). Hillsdale, NJ: Erlbaum.

Gordon, C. J., & Pearson, P. D. (1983). *The effects of instruction in metacomprehension and inferencing on children's comprehension abilities* (Tech. Rep. No. 277). Urbana: University of Illinois, Center for the Study of Reading.

Gough, P. B. (1981). A comment on Kenneth Goodman. In M. L. Kamil (Ed.). *Directions in reading: Research and instruction* (pp. 92–95). Washington, DC: National Reading Conference.

Grabe, M., & Mann, S. (1984). A technique for the assessment and training of comprehension monitoring skills. *Journal of Reading Behavior, 16,* 131–144.

Griffin, P., Cole, M., & Newman, D. (1982). Locating tasks in psychology and education. *Discourse Processes, 5,* 111–125.

Hansen, J., & Pearson, P. D. (1980). *The effects of inference training and practice on young children's comprehension* (Tech. Rep. No. 166). Urbana: University of Illinois, Center for the Study of Reading.

Hansen, J., & Pearson, P. D. (1983). An instructional study: Improving the inferential comprehension of good and poor fourth-grade readers. *Journal of Educational Psychology, 75,* 821–829.

Hare, V. C., & Borchardt, K. M. (1984). Direct instruction of summarization skills. *Reading Research Quarterly, 20,* 62–78.

Hare, V. C., & Milligan, B. (1984). Main idea identification: Instructional explanations in four basal reader series. *Journal of Reading Behavior, 16,* 189–204.

Hare, V. C., & Smith, D. C. (1982). Reading to remember: Studies of metacognitive reading skills in elementary school-aged children. *Journal of Educational Research, 75,* 157–164.

Harris, K. R. (1982). Cognitive-behavior modification: Application with exceptional students. *Focus on Exceptional Children, 15,* 1–16.

Harris, P. L., Kruithof, A., Terwogt, M. M., & Visser, T. (1981). Children's detection and awareness of textual anomaly. *Journal of Experimental Child Psychology, 31,* 212–230.

Hayes, J. R., & Flower, L. S. (1980). Identifying the organization of writing processes. In L. W. Gregg & E. R. Steinberg (Eds.), *Cognitive processes in writing* (pp. 3–30). Hillsdale, NJ: Erlbaum.

Hayes, J. R., & Flower, L. S. (1983). Uncovering cognitive processes in writing: An introduction to protocol analysis. In P. Mosenthal, L. Tamor, & S. A. Walmsley (Eds.), *Research on writing: Principles and methods* (pp. 207–220). New York: Longman.

Hayes-Roth, B., & Hayes-Roth, F. (1979). A cognitive model of planning. *Cognitive Science, 3,* 275–310.

Hiebert, E. H. (1983). An examination of ability grouping for reading instruction. *Reading Research Quarterly, 18,* 231–255.

Hiebert, E. H., Englert, C. S., & Brennan, S. (1983). Awareness of text structure in recognition and production of expository discourse. *Journal of Reading Behavior, 15,* 63–79.

Hildyard, A., & Olson, D. R. (1982). On the structure and meaning of prose text. In W. Otto & S. White (Eds.), *Reading expository material* (pp. 155–184). New York: Academic Press.

Johnson, R. E. (1970). Recall of prose as a function of the structural importance of the linguistic units. *Journal of Verbal Learning and Verbal Behavior, 9,* 12–20.

Kail, R. (1983). Research strategies for a cognitive developmental psychology of instruction. In J. Bisanz, G. L. Bisanz, & R. Kail (Eds.), *Learning in children: Progress in cognitive development research* (pp. 85–104). New York: Springer-Verlag.

Kail, R. V., Jr., & Bisanz, J. (1982). Cognitive strategies. In C. R. Puff (Ed.), *Handbook of research methods in human memory and cognition* (pp. 229–255). New York: Academic Press.

Kantor, R. N., Anderson, T. H., & Armbruster, B. B. (1983). How inconsiderate are children's textbooks? *Journal of Curriculum Studies, 15,* 61–72.

Kellogg, R. T. (1982). When can we introspect accurately about mental processes? *Memory and Cognition, 10,* 141–144.

Kendall, C. R., Borkowski, J. G., & Cavanaugh, J. C. (1980). Metamemory and the transfer of an interrogative strategy by EMR children. *Intelligence, 4,* 255–270.

Kieras, D. E. (1978). Good and bad structure in simple paragraphs: Effects on apparent theme, reading time, and recall. *Journal of Verbal Learning and Verbal Behavior, 17,* 13–28.

Kieras, D. E. (1980). Initial mention as a signal to thematic content in technical passages. *Memory and Cognition, 8,* 345–353.

Kieras, D. E. (1982). A model of reader strategy for abstracting main ideas from simple technical prose. *Text, 2,* 47–81.

Kieras, D. E. (1985). Thematic processes in the comprehension of technical prose. In B. K. Britton & J. B. Black (Eds.), *Understanding expository text: A theoretical and practical handbook for analyzing explanatory text* (pp. 89–107). Hillsdale, NJ: Erlbaum.

Kintsch, W. (1979). On modeling comprehension. *Educational Psychologist, 14,* 3–14.

Kintsch, W. (1982). Text representations. In W. Otto & S. White (Eds.), *Reading expository material* (pp. 87–101). New York: Academic Press.

Kintsch, W. (1983). *Text structure and inference* (Tech. Rep. No. 123). Boulder: University of Colorado, Institute of Cognitive Science.

Kintsch, W., & van Dijk, T. A. (1978). Toward a model of text comprehension and production. *Psychological Review, 85,* 363–394.

Kintsch, W., & Yarbrough, J. C. (1982). Role of rhetorical structure in text comprehension. *Journal of Educational Psychology, 74,* 828–834.

Kintsch, W., & Young, S. R. (1984). Selective recall of decision-relevant information from texts. *Memory and Cognition, 12,* 112–117.

Kitchener, K. S. (1983). Cognition, metacognition, and epistemic cognition. *Human Development, 26,* 222–232.

Kleiman, G. M. (1982). *Comparing good and poor readers: A critique of the research* (Tech. Rep. No. 246). Urbana: University of Illinois, Center for the Study of Reading.

Kolers, P. A. (1970). Three stages of reading. In H. Levin & J. P. Williams (Eds.), *Basic studies on reading* (pp. 90–118). New York: Basic Books.

Kreutzer, M. A., Leonard, C., & Flavell, J. H. (1975). An interview study of children's knowledge about memory. *Monographs of the Society for Research in Child Development, 40*(1, Serial No. 159).

Kurtz, B. E., Reid, M. K., Borkowski, J. G., & Cavanaugh, J. C. (1982). On the reliability and validity of children's metamemory. *Bulletin of the Psychonomic Society, 19,* 137–140.

Larkin, J., McDermott, J., Simon, D. P., & Simon, H. A. (1980). Expert and novice performance in solving physics problems. *Science, 208,* 1335–1342.

Lesgold, A. M., & Perfetti, C. A. (1978). Interactive processes in reading comprehension. *Discourse Processes, 1,* 323–336.

Light, R. J., & Pillemer, D. B. (1984). *Summing up: The science of reviewing research.* Cambridge, MA: Harvard University Press.

Lodico, M. G., Ghatala, E. S., Levin, J. R., Pressley, M., & Bell, J. A. (1983). The effects of strategy-monitoring training on children's selection of effective memory strategies. *Journal of Experimental Child Psychology, 35,* 263–277.

Loman, N. L., & Mayer, R. E. (1983). Signaling techniques that increase the understandability of expository prose. *Journal of Educational Psychology, 75,* 402–412.

Maccoby, E. E. (1982). Organization and relationships in development. In W. A. Collins (Ed.), *The concept of development* (pp. 155–161). Hilsdale, NJ: Erlbaum.

Mandler, J. M., & Johnson, N. S. (1977). Remembrance of things parsed: Story structure and recall. *Cognitive Psychology, 9,* 111–151.

Markman, E. M. (1977). Realizing that you don't understand: A preliminary investigation. *Child Development, 48,* 986–992.

Markman, E. M. (1979). Realizing that you don't understand: Elementary school children's awareness of inconsistencies. *Child Development, 50,* 643–655.

Markman, E. M. (1981). Comprehension monitoring. In W. P. Dickson (Ed.), *Children's oral communication skills* (pp. 61–84). New York: Academic Press.

Markman, E. M., & Gorin, L. (1981). Children's ability to adjust their standards for evaluating comprehension. *Journal of Educational Psychology, 73,* 320–325.

Masur, E. F., McIntyre, C. W., & Flavell, J. H. (1973). Developmental changes in apportionment of study time among items in multitrial free recall task. *Journal of Experimental Child Psychology, 15,* 237–246.

Mayer, R. E. (1983). *Thinking, problem solving, cognition.* New York: Freeman.

McCagg, P. B. (1984). *An investigation of inferencing in second-language reading comprehension.* Unpublished doctoral dissertation, Georgetown University.

McCombs, B. L. (1984). Processes and skills underlying continuing intrinsic motivation to learn: Toward a definition of motivational skills training interventions. *Educational Psychologist, 19,* 199–218.

McNeil, J. D. (1984). *Reading comprehension: New directions for classroom practice.* Glenview, IL: Scott, Foresman.

Meichenbaum, D. (1980). A cognitive-behavioral perspective on intelligence. *Intelligence, 4,* 271–283.

Meichenbaum, D., & Asarnow, J. (1979). Cognitive-behavioral modification and metacognitive development: Implications for the classroom. In P. C. Kendall & S. D. Hollon (Eds.), *Cognitive-behavioral interventions: Theory, research, and procedures* (pp. 11–35). New York: Academic Press.

Meichenbaum, D., Burland, S., Gruson, L., & Cameron, R. (1979, October). *Metacognitive assessment.* Paper presented at the conference on the Growth of Insight, Wisconsin Research and Development Center, Madison, WI.

Meyer, B. J. F., Brandt, D. M., & Bluth, G. J. (1980). Use of top-level structure in text: Key for reading comprehension of ninth-grade students. *Reading Research Quarterly, 16,* 72–103.

Meyer, B. J. F., & Rice, E. (1984). The structure of text. In P. D. Pearson (Ed.), *Handbook of reading research* (pp. 319–351). New York: Longman.

Miller, P. H. (1983). *Theories of developmental psychology.* San Francisco, CA: Freeman.

Miller, P. H., & Bigi, L. (1979). The development of children's understanding of attention. *Merrill-Palmer Quarterly, 25,* 235–250.

Miyake, N., & Norman, D. A. (1979). To ask a question, one must know enough to know what is not known. *Journal of Verbal Learning and Verbal Behavior, 18,* 357–364.

Mosenthal, P. (1983). The influence of social situation on children's classroom comprehension of text. *The Elementary School Journal, 83,* 537–547.

Myers, M., & Paris, S. G. (1978). Children's metacognitive knowledge about reading. *Journal of Educational Psychology, 70,* 680–690.

Neisser, U. (1982). Memory: What are the important questions? In U. Neisser (Ed.), *Memory observed: Remembering in natural contexts* (pp. 3–19). San Francisco, CA: Freeman.

Nisbett, R. E., & Wilson, T. D. (1977). Telling more than we can know: Verbal reports on mental processes. *Psychological Review, 84,* 231–259.

Oka, E. R., & Paris, S. G. (in press). Patterns of motivation and reading skills in underachieving children. In S. J. Ceci (Ed.), *Handbook of cognitive, social and neuropsychological aspects of learning disabilities.* Hillsdale, NJ: Erlbaum.

Olshavsky, J. E. (1976–1977). Reading as problem solving: An investigation of strategies. *Reading Research Quarterly, 12,* 654–675.

Olson, D. R. (1977). From utterance to text: The bias of language in speech and writing. *Harvard Educational Review, 47,* 257–281.

Olson, D. R., & Torrance, N. (1981). Learning to meet the requirements of written text: Language development in the school years. In C. H. Frederiksen & J. F.

Dominic (Eds.), *Writing: Process, development and communication* (pp. 235–255). Hillsdale, NJ: Erlbaum.

Omanson, R. C. (1982). An analysis of narratives: Identifying central, supportive, and distracting content. *Discourse Processes, 5,* 195–224.

Owings, R. A., Petersen, G. A., Bransford, J. D., Morris, C. D., & Stein, B. S. (1980). Spontaneous monitoring and regulation of learning: A comparison of successful and less successful fifth graders. *Journal of Educational Psychology, 72,* 250–256.

Pace, A. J. (1981, April). *Comprehension monitoring by elementary students: When does it occur?* Paper presented at the meeting of the American Educational Research Association, Los Angeles, CA.

Palincsar, A. S. (1984, April). *Reciprocal teaching: Working within the zone of proximal development.* Paper presented at the meeting of the American Educational Research Association, New Orleans, LA.

Palincsar, A. S., & Brown, A. L. (1983). *Reciprocal teaching of comprehension-monitoring activities* (Tech. Rep. No. 269). Urbana: University of Illinois, Center for the Study of Reading.

Paris, S. G. (in press). Theories and metaphors about learning strategies. In C. Weinstein, E. T. Goetz, & P. Alexander (Eds.), *Learning and study strategies: Assessment, instruction, and evaluation.* Orlando, FL: Academic Press.

Paris, S. G., & Cross, D. R. (1983). Ordinary learning: Pragmatic connections among children's beliefs, motives, and actions. In J. Bisanz, G. L. Bisanz, & R. Kail (Eds.), *Learning in children: Progress in cognitive development research* (pp. 137–169). New York: Springer-Verlag.

Paris, S., Cross, D., DeBritto, A. M., Jacobs, J., Oka, E., & Saarnio, D. (1984, April). *Improving children's metacognition and reading comprehension with classroom instruction.* Paper presented at the meeting of the American Educational Research Association, New Orleans, LA.

Paris, S. G., Cross, D. R., & Lipson, M. Y. (1984). Informed strategies for learning: A program to improve children's reading awareness and comprehension. *Journal of Educational Psychology, 76,* 1239–1252.

Paris, S. G., & Jacobs, J. E. (1984). The benefits of informed instruction for children's reading awareness and comprehension skills. *Child Development, 55,* 2083–2093.

Paris, S. G., & Lindauer, B. K. (1982). The development of cognitive skills during childhood. In B. W. Wolman (Ed.), *Handbook of developmental psychology* (pp. 333–349). Englewood Cliffs, NJ: Prentice-Hall.

Paris, S. G., Lipson, M. Y., & Wixson, K. K. (1983). Becoming a strategic reader. *Contemporary Educational Psychology, 8,* 293–316.

Paris, S. G., & Myers, M. (1981). Comprehension monitoring, memory, and study strategies of good and poor readers. *Journal of Reading Behavior, 13,* 5–22.

Paris, S. G., & Wixson, K. K. (in press). The development of literacy: Access, acquisition, and instruction. In D. Bloome (Ed.), *Literacy, language, and schooling.* Norwood, NJ: Ablex.

Patterson, C. J., Cosgrove, J. M., & O'Brien, R. G. (1980). Nonverbal indicants of comprehension and noncomprehension in children. *Developmental Psychology, 16,* 38–48.

Patterson, C. J., O'Brien, C., Kister, M. C., Carter, D. B., & Kotsonis, M. E. (1981). Development of comprehension monitoring as a function of context. *Developmental Psychology, 17,* 379–389.

Pearson, P. D. (1982). *A context for instructional research on reading comprehension* (Tech. Rep. No. 230). Urbana: University of Illinois, Center for the Study of Reading.

Pearson, P. D. (1984). Direct explicit teaching of reading comprehension. In G. G. Duffy, L. R. Roehler, & J. Mason (Eds.), *Comprehension instruction* (pp. 222–233). New York: Longman.

Pearson, P. D., & Gallagher, M. C. (1983). The instruction of reading comprehension. *Contemporary Educational Psychology, 8,* 317–344.

Pearson, P. D., Hansen, J., & Gordon, C. (1979). The effect of background knowledge on young children's comprehension of explicit and implicit information. *Journal of Reading Behavior, 11,* 201–209.

Pearson, P. D., & Tierney, R. (1983). In search of a model of instructional research in reading. In S. G. Paris, G. M. Olson, & H. W. Stevenson (Eds.), *Learning and motivation in the classroom* (pp. 39–60). Hillsdale, NJ: Erlbaum.

Perfetti, C. A., & Lesgold, A. M. (1977). Discourse comprehension and sources of individual differences. In M. A. Just & P. A. Carpenter (Eds.), *Cognitive processes in comprehension* (pp. 141–183). New York: Wiley.

Perfetti, C. A., & Lesgold, A. M. (1979). Coding and comprehension in skilled reading and implications for reading instruction. In L. B. Resnick & P. A. Weaver (Eds.), *Theory and practice of early reading* (Vol. 1, pp. 57–84). Hillsdale, NJ: Erlbaum.

Peterson, P. L., & Swing, S. R. (1983). Problems in classroom implementation of cognitive strategy instruction. In M. Pressley & J. R. Levin (Eds.), *Cognitive strategy research: Educational applications* (pp. 267–287). New York: Springer-Verlag.

Peterson, P. L., Swing, S. R., Braverman, M. T., & Buss, R. (1982) Students' aptitudes and their reports of cognitive processes during direct instruction. *Journal of Educational Psychology, 74,* 535–547.

Phifer, S. J., & Glover, J. A. (1982). Don't take students' word for what they do while reading. *Bulletin of the Psychonomic Society, 19,* 194–196.

Piché, G. L., & Slater, W. H. (1983). Predicting learning from text: A comparison of two procedures. *Journal of Reading Behavior, 15,* 43–57.

Pichert, J. W., & Anderson, R. C. (1977). Taking different perspectives on a story. *Journal of Educational Psychology, 69,* 309–315.

Pressley, M. (1983). Making meaningful materials easier to learn: Lessons from cognitive strategy research. In M. Pressley & J. R. Levin (Eds.), *Cognitive strategy research: Educational applications* (pp. 239–266). New York: Springer-Verlag.

Pressley, M., Borkowski, J. G., & O'Sullivan, J. T. (1984). Memory strategy instruction is made of this: Metamemory and durable strategy use. *Educational Psychologist, 19,* 94–107.

Pressley, M., Ross, K. A., Levin, J. R., & Ghatala, E. S. (1984). The role of strategy utility knowledge in children's strategy decision making. *Journal of Experimental Child Psychology, 38,* 491–504.

Raphael, T. E., & Pearson, P. D. (1982). *The effect of metacognitive training on children's question-answering behavior* (Tech. Rep. No. 238). Urbana: University of Illinois, Center for the Study of Reading.

Reif, F. (1980). Theoretical and educational concerns with problem solving: Bridging the gaps with human cognitive engineering. In D. T. Tuma & F. Reif (Eds.), *Problem solving and education: Issues in teaching and research* (pp. 39–50). Hillsdale, NJ: Erlbaum.

Resnick, L. B. (1981). Instructional psychology. *Annual Review of Psychology, 32,* 659–704.

Resnick, L. B. (1983). Toward a cognitive theory of instruction. In S. G. Paris, G. M. Olson, & H. W. Stevenson (Eds.), *Learning and motivation in the classroom* (pp. 5–38). Hillsdale, NJ: Erlbaum.

Resnick, L. B. (1984). Comprehending and learning: Implications for a cognitive theory of instruction. In H. Mandl, N. L. Stein, & T. Trabasso (Eds.), *Learning and comprehension of text* (pp. 431–443). Hillsdale, NJ: Erlbaum.

Revelle, G. L., Wellman, H. M., & Karabenick, J. D. (1985). Comprehension monitoring in preschool children. *Child Development, 56,* 654–663.

Rigney, J. W. (1980). Cognitive learning strategies and dualities in information processing. In R. E. Snow, P. A. Federico, & W. E. Montague (Eds.), *Aptitude, learning, and instruction* (Vol. 1, pp. 315–343). Hillsdale, NJ: Erlbaum.

Robinson, E. J. (1981). The child's understanding of inadequate messages and communication failure: A problem of ignorance or egocentrism? In W. P. Dickson (Ed.), *Children's oral communication skills* (pp. 167–188). New York: Academic Press.

Rogoff, B., Ellis, S., & Gardner, W. (1984). Adjustment of adult-child instruction according to child's age and task. *Developmental Psychology, 20,* 193–199.

Rohwer, W. D., Jr. (1984). An invitation to an educational psychology of studying. *Educational Psychologist, 19,* 1–14.

Rohwer, W. D., Jr., & Litrownik, J. (1983). Age and individual differences in the learning of a memorization procedure. *Journal of Educational Psychology, 75,* 799–810.

Rosenshine, B., & Stevens, R. (1984). Classroom instruction in reading. In P. D. Pearson (Ed.), *Handbook of reading research* (pp. 745–798). New York: Longman.

Rothkopf, E. Z. (1982). Adjunct aids and the control of mathemagenic activities during purposeful reading. In W. Otto & S. White (Eds.), *Reading expository material* (pp. 109–138). New York: Academic Press.

Rothkopf, E. Z. (in press). Perspectives on study skills training in a realistic instructional economy. In C. Weinstein, E. T. Goetz, & P. Alexander (Eds.), *Learning and study strategies: Assessment, instruction, and evaluation.* Orlando, FL: Academic Press.

Rubin, A. (1980). A theoretical taxonomy of the differences between oral and written language. In R. J. Spiro, B. C. Bruce, & W. F. Brewer (Eds.), *Theoretical issues in reading comprehension* (pp. 411–438). Hillsdale, NJ: Erlbaum.

Rumelhart, D. E. (1977). Toward an interactive model of reading. In S. Dornic (Ed.), *Attention and performance* (Vol. 6, pp. 573–603). Hillsdale, NJ: Erlbaum.

Rumelhart, D. E. (1980). Schemata: The building blocks of cognition. In R. J. Spiro, B. C. Bruce, & W. F. Brewer (Eds.), *Theoretical issues in reading comprehension* (pp. 33–58). Hillsdale, NJ: Erlbaum.

Ryan, E. B. (1981). Identifying and remediating failures in reading comprehension: Toward an instructional approach for poor comprehenders. In G. E. Mackinnon & T. G. Waller (Eds.), *Reading research: Advances in theory and practice* (Vol. 3, pp. 223–261). New York: Academic Press.

Ryan, E. B., Ledger, G. W., Short, E. J., & Weed, K. A. (1982). Promoting the use of active comprehension strategies by poor readers. *Topics in Learning and Learning Disabilities, 2*, 53–60.

Samuels, S. J. (1979). How the mind works when reading: Describing elephants no one has ever seen. In L. B. Resnick & P. A. Weaver (Eds.), *Theory and practice of early reading* (Vol. 1, pp. 343–368). Hillsdale, NJ: Erlbaum.

Samuels, S. J., Dahl, P., & Archwamety, T. (1974). Effect of hypothesis/test training on reading skill. *Journal of Educational Psychology, 66*, 835–844.

Samuels, S. J., & Kamil, M. L. (1984). Models of the reading process. In P. D. Pearson (Ed.), *Handbook of reading research* (pp. 185–224). New York: Longman.

Scardamalia, M., & Bereiter, C. (1983). Child as coinvestigator: Helping children gain insight into their own mental processes. In S. G. Paris, G. M. Olson, & H. W. Stevenson (Eds.), *Learning and motivation in the classroom* (pp. 61–82). Hillsdale, NJ: Erlbaum.

Scardamalia, M., & Bereiter, C. (1984). Development of strategies in text processing. In H. Mandl, N. L. Stein, & T. Trabasso (Eds.), *Learning and comprehension of text* (pp. 379–406). Hillsdale, NJ: Erlbaum.

Schoenfeld, A. H. (1983). Beyond the purely cognitive: Belief systems, social cognitions, and metacognitions as driving forces in intellectual performance. *Cognitive Science, 7*, 329–363.

Schwarz, M. N. K., & Flammer, A. (1981). Text structure and title—Effects on comprehension and recall. *Journal of Verbal Learning and Verbal Behavior, 20*, 61–66.

Short, E. J., & Ryan, E. B. (1984). Metacognitive differences between skilled and less skilled readers: Remediating deficits through story grammar and attribution training. *Journal of Educational Psychology, 76*, 225–235.

Shulman, L. S. (1970). Reconstruction of educational research. *Review of Educational Research, 40*, 371–396.

Shulman, L. S., & Carey, N. B. (1984). Psychology and the limitations of individual rationality: Implications for the study of reasoning and civility. *Review of Educational Research, 54*, 501–524.

Simon, H. A. (1979). Information processing models of cognition. *Annual Review of Psychology, 30*, 363–396.

Simon, H. A. (1980). Problem solving and education. In D. T. Tuma & F. Reif (Eds.), *Problem solving and education: Issues in teaching and research* (pp. 81–96). Hillsdale, NJ: Erlbaum.

Simon, H. A. (1981). *The sciences of the artificial* (2nd ed.). Cambridge, MA: MIT Press.

Slater, W. H., Graves, M. F., & Piché, G. L. (1985). Effects of structural organizers on ninth-grade students' comprehension and recall of four patterns of expository text. *Reading Research Quarterly, 20,* 189–202.

Smith, F. (1977). Making sense of reading—and of reading instruction. *Harvard Educational Review, 47,* 386–395.

Smith, F. (1982). *Understanding reading* (3rd ed.). New York: Holt, Rinehart, & Winston.

Spilich, G. J., Vesonder, G. T., Chiesi, H. L., & Voss, J. F. (1979). Text processing of domain-related information for individuals with high and low domain knowledge. *Journal of Verbal Learning and Verbal Behavior, 18,* 275–290.

Spiro, R. J. (1979). Etiology of reading comprehension style. In M. L. Kamil & A. J. Moe (Eds.), *Reading research: Studies and applications* (pp. 118–122). Clemson, SC: National Reading Conference.

Spiro, R. J., & Tirre, W. C. (1980). Individual differences in schema utilization during discourse processing. *Journal of Educational Psychology, 72,* 204–208.

Stanovich, K. E. (1980). Toward an interactive-compensatory model of individual differences in the development of reading fluency. *Reading Research Quarterly, 16,* 32–71.

Steffensen, M. S., Joag-dev, C., & Anderson, R. C. (1979). A cross-cultural perspective on reading comprehension. *Reading Research Quarterly, 15,* 10–29.

Stein, N. L., & Glenn, C. G. (1979). An analysis of story comprehension in elementary school children. In R. O. Freedle (Ed.), *New directions in discourse processing* (pp. 53–120). Norwood, NJ: Ablex.

Stein, N. L., & Nezworski, T. (1978). The effects of organization and instructional set on story memory. *Discourse Processes, 1,* 177–193.

Sternberg, R. J. (1984). What should intelligence tests test? Implications of a triarchic theory of intelligence for intelligence testing. *Educational Researcher, 13,* 5–15.

Taylor, B. M. (1979). Good and poor readers' recall of familiar and unfamiliar text. *Journal of Reading Behavior, 11,* 375–380.

Taylor, B. M., & Samuels, S. J. (1983). Children's use of text structure in the recall of expository material. *American Educational Research Journal, 20,* 517–528.

Thorndyke, P. W. (1977). Cognitive structures in comprehension and memory of narrative discourse. *Cognitive Psychology, 9,* 77–110.

Tierney, R. J., & LaZansky, J. (1980). The rights and responsibilities of readers and writers: A contractual agreement. *Language Arts, 57,* 606–613.

Tobias, S. (1982). When do instructional methods make a difference? *Educational Researcher, 11,* 4–9.

Tobias, S. (1984, April). *Macroprocesses, individual differences and instructional methods.* Paper presented at the meeting of the American Educational Research Association, New Orleans, LA.

Tobias, S. (1985). *Optional and required text review strategies and their interaction with student characteristics.* (Tech. Rep. No. 5). New York: City College of New York, Instructional Research Project.

Trabasso, T. (1980). *On the making of inferences during reading and their assessment*

(Tech. Rep. No. 157). Urbana: University of Illinois, Center for the Study of Reading.

Tulving, E., & Gold, C. (1963). Stimulus information and contextual information as determinants of tachistoscopic recognition of words. *Journal of Experimental Psychology, 66,* 319–327.

Tunmer, W. E., Nesdale, A. R., & Pratt, C. (1983). The development of young children's awareness of logical inconsistenciess. *Journal of Experimental Psychology, 36,* 97–108.

van Dijk, T. A. (1979). Relevance assignment in discourse comprehension. *Discourse Processes, 2,* 113–126.

van Dijk, T. A., & Kintsch, W. (1983). *Strategies of discourse comprehension.* New York: Academic Press.

Venezky, R. L. (1982). The origins of the present-day chasm between adult literacy needs and school literacy instruction. *Visible Language, 16,* 113–127.

Voss, J. F. (1984). On learning and learning from text. In H. Mandl, N. L. Stein, & T. Trabasso (Eds.), *Learning and comprehension of text* (pp. 193–212). Hillsdale, NJ: Erlbaum.

Voss, J. F., Tyler, S. W., & Bisanz, G. L. (1982). Prose comprehension and memory. In C. R. Puff (Ed.), *Handbook of research methods in human memory and cognition* (pp. 349–393). New York: Academic Press.

Vygotsky, L. S. (1978). *Mind in society: The development of higher psychological processes.* Cambridge, MA: Harvard University Press.

Wagner, R. K., & Sternberg, R. J. (1983). *Executive control of reading.* Unpublished manuscript.

Wagoner, S. A. (1983). Comprehension monitoring: What it is and what we know about it. *Reading Research Quarterly, 18,* 328–346.

Weinstein, C. E., & Mayer, R. E. (1986). The teaching of learning strategies. In M. C. Wittrock (Ed.), *Handbook of research on teaching* (3rd ed., pp. 315–327). New York: Macmillan.

Weinstein, C. E., & Underwood, V. L. (1985). Learning strategies: The *how* of learning. In J. W. Segal, S. F. Chipman, & R. Glaser (Eds.), *Thinking and learning skills* (Vol. 1, pp. 241–258). Hillsdale, NJ: Erlbaum.

Weinstein, C. E., Underwood, V. L., Wicker, F. W., & Cubberly, W. E. (1979). Cognitive learning strategies: Verbal and imaginal elaboration. In H. F. O'Neil, Jr., & C. D. Spielberger (Eds.), *Cognitive and affective learning strategies* (pp. 45–75). New York: Academic Press.

Wellman, H. M. (1978). Knowledge of the interaction of memory variables: A developmental study of metamemory. *Developmental Psychology, 14,* 24–29.

Wellman, H. M. (1983). Metamemory revisited. In M. T. H. Chi (Ed.), *Trends in memory development research* (pp. 31–51). Basel, Switzerland: Karger.

Wellman, H. M., Collins, J., & Glieberman, J. (1981). Understanding the combination of memory variables: Developing conceptions of memory limitations. *Child Development, 52,* 1313–1317.

Wertsch, J. V. (1978). Adult-child interaction and the roots of metacognition. *The Quarterly Newsletter of the Institute for Comparative Human Development, 2,* 15–18.

Wertsch, J. V. (1979). From social interaction to higher psychological processes: A clarification and application of Vygotsky's theory. *Human Development, 22,* 1–22.

Wertsch, J. V., McNamee, G. D., McLane, J. B., & Budwig, N. A. (1980). The adult-child dyad as a problem-solving system. *Child Development, 51,* 1215–1221.

Wertsch, J. V., & Stone, C. A. (1979, March). *A social interactional analysis of learning disabilities remediation.* Paper presented at the meeting of the Association for Children with Learning Disabilities, San Francisco, CA.

White, P. (1980). Limitations on verbal reports of internal events: A refutation of Nisbett and Wilson and of Bem. *Psychological Review, 87,* 105–112.

Wilkinson, A. C. (1980). Children's understanding in reading and listening. *Journal of Educational Psychology, 72,* 561–574.

Williams, J. P. (1984). Categorization, macrostructure, and finding the main idea. *Journal of Educational Psychology, 76,* 874–879.

Williams, J. P., Taylor, M. B., & de Cani, J. S. (1984). Constructing macrostructure for expository text. *Journal of Educational Psychology, 76,* 1065–1075.

Williams, J. P., Taylor, M. B., & Ganger, S. (1981). Text variations at the level of the individual sentence and the comprehension of simple expository paragraphs. *Journal of Educational Psychology, 73,* 851–865.

Winograd, P. N. (1984). Strategic difficulties in summarizing texts. *Reading Research Quarterly, 19,* 404–425.

Winograd, P. N., & Hare, V. C. (in press). Direct instruction of reading comprehension strategies: The role of teacher explanation. In C. Weinstein, E. T. Goetz, & P. Alexander (Eds.), *Learning and study strategies: Assessment, instruction, and evaluation.* Orlando, FL: Academic Press.

Winograd, P. N., & Johnston, P. (1982). Comprehension monitoring and the error detection paradigm. *Journal of Reading Behavior, 14,* 61–76.

Wittrock, M. C. (1979). The cognitive movement in instruction. *Educational Researcher, 8,* 5–11.

Young, D. R., & Schumacher, G. M. (1983). Context effects in young childen's sensitivity to the importance level of prose information. *Child Development, 54,* 1446–1456.

Yussen, S. R., & Bird, J. E. (1979). The development of metacognitive awareness in memory, communication, and attention. *Journal of Experimental Child Psychology, 28,* 300–313.

Yussen, S. R., Mathews, S. R., & Hiebert, E. (1982). Metacognitive aspects of reading. In W. Otto & S. White (Eds.), *Reading expository material* (pp. 189–218). New York: Academic Press.

Author Index

A

Adams, A., 116, 117, 125, *139*
Afflerbach, P., 69, *139*
Alessi, S.M., 53, 104, *139*
Alexander, P.A., 52, 106, 113, 114, 131, *139*, *147*
Allen, V.L., 79, *139*, *145*
Allington, R.L., 39, *139*
Alvermann, D.E., 49, 77, 78, 82, *139*
Anderson, J., 89, 91, *147*
Anderson, M.C., 5, 6, *140*
Anderson, R.C., 1, 4–9, 13, *139*, *140*, *153*, *156*
Anderson, R.I., 40, 47, *141*
Anderson, T.H., 19, 49, 53, 104, 116, *140*, *149*
Arbitman-Smith, R., 132, *142*
Archwamety, T., 2, *155*
Armbruster, B.B., 19, 49, 50, 54, 105, 106, 116, 124, 129, *140*, *142*, *143*, *148*, *149*
Asarnow, J., 109, 133, *151*
August, D.L., 48, 95–97, *140*, *146*
Ausubel, D.P., 7, *140*

B

Baker, L., 17, 19, 29, 31, 40, 45–47, 50, 54, 87, 88, 97–99, 100, 105, *140*, *141*, *142*
Ballstaedt, S., 74, *141*
Bandura, A., 125, *141*
Bartlett, F.C., 6, *141*
Baumann, J.F., 78, 134, *141*
Beal, C.R., 91, 94, 95, *141*
Beaugrande, R. de, 1, *141*
Beebe, M.J., 101, *141*
Belcher, V., 81, 111, *147*
Bell, J.A., 108, *150*
Belmont, J.M., 107, 108, 122, *141*

Bereiter, C., 38, 74, 128, 129, 132, 135, 136, *141*, *155*
Bigi, L., 34, 35, 37, 67, *151*
Bird, J.E., 66, 67, *158*
Bisanz, G.L., 118, *157*
Bisanz, J., 49, 62, 69, 82, 118, *149*
Blanchowicz, C.L.Z., 118, *141*
Blank, M., 66, *141*
Bluth, G.J., 12, *151*
Bohn, L., 86, 102, *144*
Bonitatibus, G.J., 44, 91, *142*
Book, C., 109, *145*
Boothby, P.R., 49, *139*
Borchardt, K.M., 106, 111–113, *148*
Borko, H., 39, *142*
Borkowski, J.G., 26, 64, 65, 68, 108, *144*, *149*, *150*, *153*
Bower, G.H., 65, *142*
Bracewell, R.J., 79, *142*
Brandt, D.M., 12, *151*
Bransford, J.D., 4, 16, 17, 51, 58, 108, 118, 132, 134, *142*, *143*, *152*
Braverman, M.T., 81, *153*
Brennan, S., 12, *149*
Bronfenbrenner, U., 93, 122, *142*
Brown, A.L., 16, 17, 19, 22, 23, 26–29, 31, 33, 38, 50, 54, 56–58, 67, 92, 105, 106, 108, 111, 124, 128, 131, 134, *141*–*144*, *152*
Bruner, J.S., 28, *143*
Burland, S., 35, 65, 68, *151*
Budwig, N.A., 123, *158*
Buss, R., 81, *153*
Butterfield, E.C., 107, 108, 122, *141*

C

Calfee, R., 22, 138, *143*
Cameron, R., 35, 65, 68, *151*
Campione, J.C., 16, 17, 23, 29, 50, 58, 106,

108, 134, *143*
Capelli, C.A., 43, 87, 100, *143*
Carey, N.B., 137, *155*
Carnine, D., 116, 117, 125, *139*
Carr, T.H., 31, 50, *144*
Carter, D.B., 90, *153*
Case, R., 29, 107, 133, *144*
Cassidy, D.J., 28, *144*
Cavanaugh, J.C., 17, 24, 26, 35, 62, 64–66,
    68, 79, 108, *144*, *149*, *150*
Chi, M.T.H., 26, 27, *144*
Chiesi, H.L., 6, *156*
Christie, J.M., 55, *144*
Clift, R., 48, *140*
Cole, M., 92, *148*
Collins, J., 17, *157*
Collins, K.W., 105, *144*
Corno, L., 125, *144*
Cosgrove, J.M., 94, 95, *152*
Covington, M.V., 125, *144*
Cross, D., 78, 119–122, 129, 131, 136, 137,
    152
Cubberly, W.E., 117, *157*

D
Dahl, P., 2, *155*
Danks, J.H., 44, 86, 102, *144*
Danner, F.W., 12, 102, *144*
Dansereau, D.F., 105, *144*
Day, J.D., 23, 57, 58, 106, 108, 111, 113, *143*,
    144
DeBritto, A.M., 119, 121, *152*
deCani, J.S., 129, *158*
DeLoache, J.S., 28, 92, *143*, *144*
Devin-Sheehan, L., 79, *145*
Diekhoff, G., 105, *144*
DiVesta, F.J., 52, *144*
Doyle, W., 109, *145*
Duffy, G.G., 39, 109, 122, 134, 137, *145*
Durkin, D., 39, 110, 136, *145*

E
Ellis, S., 124, *145*, *154*
End, L.J., 44, *144*
Englert, C.S., 12, *149*
Epstein, W., 48, *147*
Ericsson, K.A., 26, 34, 62, 63, 65, 67, 75, *145*
Evans, S.H., 104, *144*

F
Fears, R., 86, 102, *144*
Feldman, R.S., 79, *139*, *145*

Ferrara, R.A., 16, 17, 58, 134, *143*
Ferretti, R.P., 108, *141*
Feshbach, N.D., 79, *145*
Fillmore, C.J., 86, *145*
Fischer, P.M., 25, *145*
Flammer, A., 5, *155*
Flavell, J.H., 15–21, 24, 26, 32–34, 44, 48,
    50–52, 56, 64, 80, 86, 91, 94–97, 135,
    140–142, *145*, *146*, *150*
Floden, R.E., 1, 21, *146*
Flower, L.S., 69–71, 74, *148*, *149*
Forrest, D.L., 36, 37, 38, *146*
Forrest-Pressley, D.L., 56, 64, *146*
Fredericksen, N., 22, 106, *146*
Freebody, P., 7, *140*
French, L.A., 124, *143*
Frese, M., 108, *146*
Frick, T., 35, *146*
Friedrichs, A.G., 26, *146*

G
Gage, N.L., 30, *146*
Gallagher, M.C., 109, *153*
Ganger, S., 12, *158*
Garland, J., 105, *144*
Garner, R., 25, 26, 29, 37, 38, 44–46, 49, 50,
    52–55, 59, 63, 65, 76, 78–81, 87, 89, 91,
    97–99, 104–106, 111, 113, 114, 131,
    139, *146*, *147*
Gardner, W., 124, *154*
Gelman, R., 26, *147*
Gersten, R., 116, 117, 125, *139*
Ghatala, E.S., 108, 126, *150*, *154*
Gibson, E.J., 3, *147*
Gillies, L.A., 56, *146*
Glaser, R., 27, *144*
Glenberg, A.M., 48, *147*
Glenn, C.G., 9, *156*
Glieberman, J., 17, *157*
Glover, J.A., 64, *153*
Goelman, H., 52, *147*
Goetz, E.T., 7, 8, 53, 104, 110, 122, 129, *139*,
    140, *148*
Gold, C., 2, *157*
Golinkoff, R.M., 50, *148*
Goodman, K.S., 2, 101, 102, *148*
Goodman, Y.M., 101, 102, *148*
Gordon, C.J., 8, 119, *148*, *153*
Gorin, L., 43, 97, *150*
Gough, P.B., 136, *148*
Grabe, M. 88, *148*
Graves, M.F., 12, *156*

Green, F.L., 95–97, *146*
Griffin, P., 92, *148*
Gruson, L., 35, 65, 68, *151*

H

Hansen, J., 8, 118, 119, *148, 153*
Hare, V.C., 52, 76–78, 82, 106, 109, 111–114, 131, 132, *139, 147, 148, 158*
Harris, K.R., 109, *148*
Harris, P.L., 46, 47, *148*
Hayes, J.R., 69–71, 74 *148, 149*
Hayes-Roth, B., 70–73, *149*
Hayes-Roth, F., 70–73, *149*
Haynes, J., 52, 106, 113, 114, *147*
Hayward, K.G., 52, *144*
Heldmeyer, K., 108, *142*
Hiebert, E.H., 12, 39, 67, 102, *144, 149, 158*
Hildyard, A., 86, *149*
Holley, C.D., 105, *144*
Hoyt, J.D., 26, *146*

J

Jacobs, J., 119, 121, *152*
Joag-dev, C., 7, *156*
Johnson, M.K., 4, 118, *142*
Johnson, N.S., 9, *150*
Johnson, R.E., 13, 56, *149*
Johnston, P., 47, 69, 89, *139, 158*
Jones, R.S., 58, 111, *143*
Just, M.A., 55, *144*

K

Kail, R.V., 49, 62, 69, 82, 105, *149*
Kamil, M.L., 3, *155*
Kantor, R.N., 49, *149*
Karabenick, J.D., 92–94, *154*
Kellogg, R.T., 62, *149*
Kendall, C.R., 108, *149*
Kieras, D.E., 10–12, *149*
Kintsch, W., 2, 3, 10, 11, 57, 118, 131, 136, *149, 150, 157*
Kister, M.C., 90, *153*
Kitchener, K.S., 27, *150*
Kleiman, G.M., 44, *150*
Kolers, P.A., 2, *150*
Kotsonis, M.E., 90, *153*
Kraus, C., 37, 38, *147*
Kreutzer, M.A., 32–34, 64, 80, *150*
Kruithof, A., 46, 47, *148*
Kurtz, B.E., 68, *150*

L

Larkin, J., 22, *150*
LaZansky, J., 86, *156*
Ledger, G.W., 29, *155*
Leonard, C., 32–34, 64, 80, *150*
Lesgold, A.M., 3, 136, *150, 153*
Levin, H., 3, *147*
Levin, J.R., 108, 126, *150, 154*
Light, R.J., 128, *150*
Lindauer, B.K., 52, 94, 119, *152*
Lipson, M.Y., 20, 50, 78, 119, 121, 131, 137, *152*
Litrownik, J., 119, *154*
Lodico, M.G., 108, *150*
Loman, N.L., 49, *150*

M

Maccoby, E.E., 123, *150*
Macready, G.B., 25, 29, 55, 78, 79, 105, *147*
Mandinach, E.B., 125, *144*
Mandl, H., 25, 74, *141, 145*
Mandler, J.M., 9, *150*
Mann, S., 88, *148*
Markman, E.M., 19, 42, 43, 46, 86, 88, 93, 97, 100, *143, 150*
Masur, E.F., 50, 51, 56, *150*
Mathews, S.R., 67, *158*
Mayer, R.E., 21, 49, 116, *150, 151, 157*
McCagg, P.B., 118, *151*
McCaleb, J.L., 111, *147*
McCombs, B.L., 126, *151*
McDermott, J., 22, *150*
McDonald, B.A., 105, *144*
McIntyre, C.W., 50, 51, 56, *150*
McLane, J.B., 123, *158*
McNamee, G.D., 123, *158*
McNeil, J.D., 4, *151*
Meichenbaum, D., 35, 65, 68, 74, 109, 133, *151*
Meyer, B.J.F., 10, 12, *151*
Miller, P.H., 21, 34, 35, 37, 67, *151*
Milligan, B., 78, 132, *148*
Miyake, N., 66, *151*
Morris, C.D., 51, 56, *152*
Mosenthal, P., 39, *151*
Murphy, M.D., 108, *143*
Myers, M., 34, 36–38, 87, *151, 152*

N

Neisser, U., 7, 52, *151*
Nesdale, A.R., 99, *157*
Newman, D., 92, *148*

Nezworski, T., 9, *156*
Nisbett, R.E., 26, 62, 65, *151*
Norman, D.A., 66, *151*

O
O'Brien, C., 90, *153*
O'Brien, R.G., 94, 95, *152*
Oka, E.R., 119, 121, *151, 152*
Olshavsky, J.E., 75, 76, *151*
Olson, D.R., 86, *149, 151*
Omanson, R.C., 13, *152*
Orlando, V.P., 52, *144*
O'Sullivan, J.T., 108, *153*
Owings, R.A., 51, 56, *152*

P
Pace, A.J., 97, *152*
Palincsar, A.S., 56, 108, 124, *143, 152*
Paris, S.G., 20, 34, 36–38, 50, 52, 78, 87, 94,
    119, 121, 122, 125, 129, 131, 136, 137,
    151, 152
Patterson, C.J., 90, 94, 95, *152, 153*
Pearson, P.D., 4, 8, 109, 110, 113, 118, 119,
    126, 136, *140, 148, 153, 154*
Perfetti, C.A., 3, 136, *150, 153*
Perlmutter, M., 17, 24, 35, 62, 68, 79, *144*
Peterson, G.A., 51, 56, 81, 126, *152*
Peterson, P.L., 81, 126, *153*
Phifer, S.J., 64, *153*
Piché, G.L., 12, 13, *153, 156*
Pichert, J.W., 7, 9, *140, 153*
Pillemer, D.B., 128, *150*
Pratt, C., 99, *157*
Pressley, M., 106, 108, 126, *150, 153, 154*

R
Raphael, T.E., 113, *154*
Reid, M.K., 68, *150*
Reif, F., 106, *154*
Reis, R., 44, 53, 54, 113, 131, *147*
Resnick, L.B., 2, 8, 119, 127, *154*
Revelle, G.L., 92, 93, 94, *154*
Reynolds, R.E., 7, 8, *140*
Rice, E., 10, *151*
Rigney, J.W., 113, *154*
Robinson, E.J., 43, *154*
Roehler, L.R., 109, 134, *145*
Rogoff, B., 124, *145, 154*
Rohwer, W.D., 116, 119, *154*
Rosenshine, B., 109, *154*
Ross, K.A., 126, *154*
Rothkopf, E.Z., 12, 20, *154*

Rubin, A., 44, *154*
Rumelhart, D.E., 3, 7, 9, 10, *155*
Ryan, E.B., 29, 64, 108, 109, *155*

S
Saarnio, D., 119, 121, *152*
Samuels, S.J., 2, 3, 12, 136, *155, 156*
Scardamalia, M., 38, 74, 128, 129, 132, *155*
Schallert, D.L., 7, 8, *140*
Schoenfeld, A.H., 75, *155*
Schumacher, G.M., 26, *158*
Schwarz, M.N.K., 5, *155*
Semmel, M.I., 35, *146*
Serra, J.K., 134, *141*
Shavelson, R.J., 39, *142*
Shirey, L.L., 9, *140*
Short, E.J.., 29, 108, *155*
Shulman, L.S., 92, 137, *155*
Simon, D.P., 22, *150*
Simon, H.A., 21, 22, 26, 34, 62, 63, 65, 67,
    75, 108, *145, 150, 155, 156*
Slater, W.H., 12, 13, 131, *147, 153, 156*
Smiley, S.S., 56, 59, *143*
Smith, D.C., 76, 77, 82, *148*
Smith, F., 2, *156*
Smith, T., 26, 29, 52, 54, 78, 81, 104, 111, 113,
    131, *147*
Speer, J.R., 95–97, *146*
Spilich, G.J., 6, *156*
Spiro, R.J., 5, 6, 7, *140, 156*
Stanovich, K.E., 2, 3, *156*
Steffensen, M.S., 7, *156*
Stein, B.S., 51, 56, 132, *142, 152*
Stein, N.L., 9, *156*
Stern, P., 39, *142*
Sternberg, R.J., 22, 23, 24, *156, 157*
Stevens, R., 109, *154*
Stewart, J., 108, *146*
Stone, C.A., 28, 123, 124, *158*
Swing, S.R., 81, 126, *153*

T
Taylor, B.M., 8, 12, *156*
Taylor, M.B., 129, *158*
Terwogt, M.M., 46, 47, *148*
Thorndyke, P.W., 9, *156*
Tierney, R.J., 86, *153, 156*
Tirre, W.C., 7, *156*
Tobias, S., 103, 104, 107, *156*
Torrance, N., 86, *151*
Trabasso, T., 118, *157*
Tulving, E., 2, *157*

Tunmer, W.E., 99, *157*
Tyler, S.W., 118, *157*

U
Underwood, V.L., 105, 117, *157*

V
van Dijk, T.A., 2, 3, 10, 11, 57, 131, 136, *149, 157*
Venezky, R.L., 118, *157*
Vesonder, G.T., 6, *156*
Visser, T., 46, 47, *148*
Voss, J.F., 6, 118, *156, 157*
Vye, N.J., 132, *142*
Vygotsky, L.S., 28, 107, 123, *157*

W
Wagner, R.K., 22, 24, *157*
Wagoner, S., 19, 25, 26, 29, 43, 52, 54, 55, 78, 79, 104, 105, 113, 147, *157*
Waller, T.G., 36, 37, 38, 64, *146*

Weed, K.A., 29, *155*
Weinstein, C.E., 105, 116, 117, *157*
Wellman, H.M., 16–19, 24, 92–94, *146, 154, 157*
Wertsch, J.V., 28, 123, 124, *157, 158*
Wesselman, R., 109, 134, *145*
White, P., 63, 64, *158*
Wicker, F.W., 117, *157*
Wilkinson, A.C., 44, 48, *147, 158*
Williams, J.P., 11, 12, 129, *158*
Wilson, T.D., 26, 62, 65, *151*
Winfield, E., 81, 111, *147*
Winograd, P.N., 29, 47, 52, 59, 89, 102, 106, 109, 111, 113, 114, *144, 147, 158*
Wittrock, M.C., 1, 25, *158*
Wixson, K.K., 20, 50, 120, *152*

Y
Yarbrough, J.C., 11, *150*
Young, D.R., 26, *158*
Young, S.R., 11, *150*
Yussen, S.R., 66, 67, *158*

Subject Index

Cognitive-behavioral modification, 109
Cognitive monitoring, *see also* Metacognitive
    experiences
  and listening, 40–44
  and reading, 44–49
Comprehension monitoring, *see*
    Metacognitive experiences
Computer records of reading processes,
    103–104

Error detection, *see also* Metacognitive
    experiences
  conditions affecting results, 85
    explicit directions to locate errors, 86–88
    inclusion of blatant errors, 89–91
    provision of standards for the error-
      detection task, 97–100
    use of nonverbal measures of detection,
      94–97
    use of relatively naturalistic research
      settings, 92–94
  criticisms of, 40, 47, 85
  future of, 100–104
  methodological alternatives to, 101–104
  as paradigm in recent research, 39–40
Executive control, 21–26
  boundaries with metacognition, 23–26
  and debugging, 22
  processes, 23
  teachability, 23

Information processing, 1–2, 15, 21–22, 24

Main ideas, 11–12
Metacognitive experiences, *see also* Error

detection
  age-related and reading achievement-
    related differences in, 29, 40–49
  development of, 27–28, 31
  differences in reading and listening tasks,
    44
  and flawed texts, 49
  for listening tasks, 40–44
  for reading tasks, 18–19, 44–49
  relation to metacognitive knowledge and
    strategy use, 20–21
  when cognitions fail, 19
Metacognitive interviews, *see also*
    Metacognitive knowledge
  concerns about, 61
    accessibility of cognitive processes, 62
    general cognitive events, 67
    hypothetical events, 67
    inadvertent cuing, 65
    knowledge versus use, 64–65
    memory falure for cognitive processes,
      63–64
    verbal facility in young children, 66–67
    young children as subjects, 66–67
  methodological alternatives to, 78–83
  as paradigm in recent research, 31
  suggestions for collecting and
    interpreting data, 67–69, 82
Metacognitive knowledge, *see also*
    Metacognitive interviews
  age-related differences in, 32–36
  of attention, 34–35
  development of, 27–28, 31
  instruction, impact of, 38–39
  interactive nature of knowledge